THE SUBSTANCE
OF ECONOMICS

THE SUBSTANCE
OF ECONOMICS

FOR THE STUDENT
AND THE GENERAL READER

BY

H. A. SILVERMAN, B.A.

AUTHOR OF "ECONOMICS OF THE INDUSTRIAL SYSTEM," "ECONOMICS OF SOCIAL
PROBLEMS," "TAXATION: ITS INCIDENCE AND EFFECTS," ETC.

TENTH EDITION

LONDON
SIR ISAAC PITMAN & SONS, LTD.
1937

SIR ISAAC PITMAN & SONS, Ltd.
PITMAN HOUSE, PARKER STREET KINGSWAY, LONDON, W.C.2
THE PITMAN PRESS, BATH
PITMAN HOUSE, LITTLE COLLINS STREET, MELBOURNE

ASSOCIATED COMPANIES
PITMAN PUBLISHING CORPORATION
2 WEST 45TH STREET, NEW YORK
205 WEST MONROE STREET, CHICAGO

SIR ISAAC PITMAN & SONS (CANADA), Ltd.
(INCORPORATING THE COMMERCIAL TEXT BOOK COMPANY)
PITMAN HOUSE, 381–383 CHURCH STREET, TORONTO

MADE IN GREAT BRITAIN AT THE PITMAN PRESS, BATH
C7—(B.1881)

PREFACE
TO TENTH EDITION

The Substance of Economics was conceived and published for the benefit of students and others who, it was thought, were in need of a book which combined a descriptive survey of the economic system with an elementary account of the governing principles, and which, furthermore, was presented in as concise a manner as was compatible with clear understanding. The continued and growing demand for the book indicated that such a need existed and that it was to some extent being met.

The events of recent years have inspired a greater interest in economic matters than ever before, while no little change has come about in the doctrines themselves. As one edition has succeeded another the writer has become more and more conscious of the inadequacy of the numerous alterations and additions that have had to be fitted into a prescribed space, and of the necessity sooner or later of a complete overhaul.

In this, the tenth, edition the opportunity has been taken to re-write whole parts of the book in the light of changing conditions and modifications in theory. The general plan, however, and the form of presentation remain little altered. To a large extent the exposition takes the form of notes and summaries, with a loss only of words. But where the subject requires fuller consideration the statement is more reasoned and detailed, though still in succinct form.

The usefulness of the present book will be increased

if it is read in conjunction with the companion work, *The Economics of the Industrial System*, which presents a deeper course of study and amplifies points and arguments to which only brief reference can be made in this volume. Particulars of larger and more specialized works will be found in the bibliography.

H. A. S.

September, 1937.

CONTENTS

Chapter II
Labour and Population

Chapter III
Land and Capital

Chapter IV
Organization and Enterprise
Section 1. *The Division of Labour*

Section 2. *Economic Organization*

Chapter V
Competition and Monopoly

Section 1. *Perfect and Imperfect Competition*

Section 2. *Monopoly Organization*

PART II
VALUE

Chapter VI

The Theory of Value

Section 1. *The Labour and Cost of Production Theories*

Section 2. *The Marginal Theory of Value*

CHAPTER VII
SUPPLY AND DEMAND
Section 1. Competitive Price

Section 2. Monopoly Price

PART III
DISTRIBUTION OF THE SOCIAL PRODUCT
CHAPTER VIII
THE NATIONAL INCOME

Chapter IX
Wages
Section 1. *The Payment of Wages*

Section 2. *Theories of Wages*

Section 3. *Labour and Wages Problems*

Chapter X
Interest and Profits
Section 1. *Interest*

CHAPTER XVII

TRADE FLUCTUATIONS AND DEPRESSIONS

Section 1. Trade and Credit Cycles

Section 2. "The Great Depression"

PART V

PUBLIC POLICY AND FINANCE

CHAPTER XVIII

PUBLIC SERVICES AND EXPENDITURE

Section 1. Public Intervention and Services

Section 2. The Cost of the Public Services

CHAPTER XIX

PUBLIC REVENUE

Section 1. The Canons of Taxation

CHAPTER XX
TAXES AND RATES
Section 1. Direct and Indirect Taxes

Section 2. Local Taxation

CHAPTER XXI
PUBLIC DEBTS

APPENDIX
THE DEVELOPMENT OF ECONOMIC THOUGHT

THE SUBSTANCE OF ECONOMICS

INTRODUCTION

SECTION I

THE NATURE OF ECONOMICS

Nature and Definition of Economics

PEOPLE have wants and have to work in order to satisfy them. As time goes on their requirements grow in number and variety, while the methods and organization of supply become increasingly complex. In the following pages a study will be made of these wants, and the efforts that are exerted to produce those commodities and services for their satisfaction.

The older economists, applying the term "wealth" to all those things that are necessary to gratify one's needs, used to say that Economics was a subject concerned with the principles of wealth-getting and wealth-using. This definition, however, did not satisfy economists who viewed the science as essentially a study of man. Marshall, for example, re-defined the science in the following terms, which acquired a wide acceptance—

"Political Economy or Economics is a study of man's actions in the ordinary business of life; it inquires how he gets his income and how he uses it. . . . Thus it is on the one hand a study of wealth, and on the other, and more important side, a part of the study of man."

On the other hand, some recent authorities take a more restricted, yet it is claimed more scientific, view of the scope of Economics. They begin with the fact that the means of satisfying wants are limited, and define Economics as being concerned primarily with the study of human behaviour in relation to ends and means that are relatively scarce.

Fundamentally there is little difference between these views. Indeed there is much to be said for reverting to the old use of the term "Political Economy." *Polis* meant the city-state, which was the territorial and political unit of Greek civilization. *Oikonomia* signified household management. The laws governing the management of the household were applied to the miniature state. In the same way as the housewife was expected to conserve and make full use of the household revenue, so the statesman was to strive at getting the maximum benefit for the community from the available income. Economic science, as we now understand it, has come to have a much wider scope, but it is still largely concerned with deriving the maximum advantage from available resources.

Economics in Relation to Other Social Sciences

Economics is but one of several social sciences, each of which deals with a special form of human activity. It may be regarded, for ordinary purposes, as an offshoot of the parent science of Sociology, which studies the general principles of all social relations. Other connected sciences are Ethics, Politics, Jurisprudence, Psychology, etc., each of which deals with different, but related, aspects of man's behaviour. The distinction between these sciences is largely one of convenience, and is more feasible in theory than in action. Especially in the working out of practical problems is it very difficult for the economist to remain uninfluenced by ethical and political considerations. This becomes inevitable as he goes beyond a mere study of wealth, and concerns himself with the *welfare* of a community. Recent economic writings, while showing an increasing degree of specialization, recognize the intimate connection between the several social sciences, with man as the common centre, and are not so exclusive, or self-contained, as the works of previous generations.

Methods of Study

In a scientific treatment of any subject, facts are observed, collected, and classified; hypotheses and inferences are provisionally formulated; while the validity of such laws as emerge is constantly being tested by reference to facts already known, and others as they present themselves.

The modern economist combines the inductive and the deductive methods.

The **Deductive** method involves the reasoning from a few fundamental propositions, the truth of which is assumed, to further propositions and conclusions. The "Classical" economists [1] of a century ago used this method, and tried to make all economic phenomena come within the framework of some half-dozen laws. These economists were followed by the "Historical" school, who preferred the **Inductive** method, whereby a number of undisputed facts were collected, generalizations made about them, and these, in turn, tested by reference to further facts. In the last few decades there has been an increasing amount of scientific inquiry into economic and social conditions, and many valuable statistics and data have been obtained.

Some branches of economics lend themselves better to one method than the other. The deductive method is suitable, for example, in dealing with the problem of valuation. The inductive method, on the other hand, is more appropriate in studying systems of production and

[1] See Appendix on "The Development of Economic Thought."

distribution. It is not always possible, however, to adopt one method to the entire exclusion of the other, and the best results are often obtained when the two are combined.

Economic Laws

The "laws" of economic science cannot be expected to be so "exact" or be formulated in the same precise terms as the laws of the physical sciences. Even as statements of bare tendency, which is all that the so-called laws commonly are, they are liable to be offset by external and changing circumstances. But the fact that the operation of an economic law may be counteracted or concealed does not disprove its validity. Conditions may require that the normal operation of an economic law should be prevented or mitigated, as for example price-fixing in time of war or other emergency. Such action, however, is more likely to be effective if it is based on an adequate knowledge of economic principles.

General Survey of Subjects to be Studied

In the definition given above, it was stated that wealth is an important, though by no means the only, subject in economic science. One may, therefore, begin the study of the subject with an inquiry into the nature of wealth and into the factors that go to produce it. These factors and the principles governing their application are examined in the economics of PRODUCTION.

It is a truism that man's desires impel him to productive effort. His wants decide what and how much will be produced. These wants are studied under the head of CONSUMPTION, but the subject is so complex and so bound up with other social sciences, notably psychology, that in a book of this order only the simpler aspects of the problem can be presented.

In developed communities there are very few people

who produce for themselves everything they require. Modern conditions and requirements make it practically impossible for a man to be economically self-dependent, even if he desired to be so. Most people specialize in supplying a particular kind (or part) of a commodity or service, taking it for granted that other members of society are producing the rest of the things required. This assumption rests upon an effective system of evaluation and exchange of goods. Hence the importance of the economics of VALUE and the MECHANISM OF EXCHANGE.

Having examined the principles of production and value, one proceeds to study the way in which the social product is shared out among the various factors of production, corresponding more or less to the different classes of the community. The question of how much goes to labour, capital, and other agents, is discussed in the economics of DISTRIBUTION.

Finally, the position of the State in relation to industry and trade has to be considered. In this connection attention is given to national and local taxation, public borrowings, and the bearing on the economic welfare of the nation as a whole. These and allied subjects are considered under the head of PUBLIC FINANCE.

Equilibrium and Variation

The interdependence of economic problems has led to a greater unity in presenting the science, and many economists re-arrange the divisions and study the subject under two main heads, the theory of equilibrium and the theory of variation. A danger in the traditional exposition of economics is that too much emphasis is placed on the social product and the distribution of this among the several claimants. In the alternative approach the economic system is considered as a series of relationships between men and economic goods, and inquiry is made into the circumstances (*a*) in which these relationships are constant (analysis of equilibrium) and (*b*) in which they change (analysis of variation). Thus, for example, production is dealt with as an integral part of the theory of equilibrium. The several agents of production are shown to be brought together by the mechanism of value and exchange, while the proportions employed are determined by the amounts of the rewards.

The beginner, however, may find difficulty in embarking straightaway on an analysis of equilibrium, and there is some advantage in following the conventional course, provided that the sections into which the subject is divided are not taken to imply a separation in reality, but are recognized to be purely for the purpose of facilitating the task of the student. Production, consumption, valuation, and distribution are all inextricably bound together and no part of the economic mechanism can be properly understood without a knowledge of the system as a whole. In the following chapters, while the customary division will be largely adhered to, the interdependence of all forms of economic activity will be kept constantly in mind.

Economic Evolution

IN order to understand the present-day economic organization of society it is helpful to have some knowledge of the factors that brought it about. A study of economic history is, indeed, the necessary complement to that of economic science, but it is possible here to make only bare mention of the principal stages in the evolution of industry.

Economic evolution may be regarded from several standpoints. One may look at it from the viewpoint of production, or from that of exchange and the market, or from that of the social and economic unit.

In early times, man's material wants were few and simple, and could be satisfied by his own direct efforts. Hunting and fishing were the principal means of living. As there was little specialization of functions, little exchange, no complex system of distribution, economic problems as we know them to-day did not exist. As time went on, man learned to tame and domesticate animals. This led to the **pastoral stage**, in which existence was made more secure and wealth was increased. What little exchange took place was effected by barter.

So far, man lived a more or less nomadic life. The third stage, **agriculture**, was reached when he learned how to cultivate the soil. The land, which at first was held in common, added to the material comforts and supported a larger population, which became less migratory and more fixed.

In primitive times, man had to be content with what he could *find*; subsequently his wants became more numerous and he began to *make* what he desired. Alongside agriculture developed **handicrafts**, which gradually assumed an increasing share of man's activities. By now money was in regular use, and industry came to be regulated by the gilds. Effort for the satisfaction of wants was by this time very indirect, and the specialization of functions was becoming more intense. Eventually, the **factory era** was reached. Machine production supplanted handicraft to an ever-increasing extent, while, with the growth of a complex system of banking and credit, commerce as well as manufacture underwent a considerable change.

Growth of Social Unit

While this evolution was proceeding, the unit of social life was growing in size. Beginning with the **family** in a tribal relationship, it developed into the manorial organization prevalent in the Middle Ages. The **manor** was a small community, economically self-sufficing. Agriculture was the principal occupation of the people, who held and cultivated the land in common. Almost everybody had a share of land, however small, the tenure being bound up with feudal dues and obligations. Common pasture and cultivation practically disappeared as the manor decayed, though traces of the old system are still to be found in a few parts of England.

The unit of communal life grew in size as the **town** evolved. Early town life was by no means inconsistent with agriculture, which was often carried on within the town walls. Indeed, the holding of land used to be a necessary qualification for a burgess.

The town economy eventually developed into a **national** economy when the country as a whole became the economic unit, and this in turn is being replaced by an **international** economy.

Development of Industrial Organization

Industrial organization has passed through the following stages—

(i) The Family System—Preceding and also contemporary with the medieval manor.

(ii) The Gild System—A town economy, from the Middle Ages to about the sixteenth century.

(iii) The Domestic System—Coinciding with a national economy, roughly between the sixteenth and eighteenth centuries.

(iv) The Factory System—An international economy, typical of the nineteenth and twentieth centuries.

(i) **The Family System.** The household was the centre of economic life. Wants were very few and were usually satisfied by the family's own direct efforts, with comparatively little specialization. Agriculture was the main occupation, and wage-earners in the modern sense of the word did not exist. Organization accordingly was very primitive.

(ii) **The Gild System.** The gilds were of first importance in the growth of the town, which gradually supplanted the manor as the social unit. Hence there was greater scope for economic enterprise, both in the size of the market and in the nature and variety of the products. In many towns there was a gild for each of the principal trades, and membership was strictly limited. The gildsman, as a rule, was a small master, according to present-day standards, working alongside a few apprentices and journeymen, and the body to which he belonged exercised a powerful control over the production, quality, and sale of the goods.

(iii) **The Domestic System.** As the gild system decayed, a new type of organization evolved in the form of the "domestic" system. People still worked in their homes, but—different from the "family" system—not for themselves, but for a merchant-employer. The *middleman* became prominent in industrial organization. Division of labour was extended, the organization being largely in the hands of the merchant, who was comparable to the modern employer. Relics of this system are still to be found among the hand chain-makers in the Black Country and the home-weavers in the Hebrides.

(iv) **The Factory System.** In the last two centuries, the economic system has become very complex. Production is now for a world market, specialization of functions has become advanced and minute, the unit of business organization has enormously increased, while the mechanism of exchange has adapted itself to meet the new conditions.

The Industrial Revolution

The changes in our industrial methods and structure that came about during the eighteenth and nineteenth centuries are commonly described as the "Industrial Revolution." Hitherto, production had been relatively simple and on a small scale, carried on mainly by hand power, often in people's own homes. Agriculture had been the principal occupation, and England, until the end of the eighteenth century, exported food. The governments of the sixteenth and seventeenth centuries, influenced by the prevailing Mercantilist views, had played a prominent part in the regulation of economic conditions. Thus, they had stimulated certain vital industries, had taken an interest in trading companies, had passed a series of Navigation Acts, and had imposed apprenticeship and wages regulations. The industrial changes at the end of the eighteenth century were accompanied by a reaction against the restrictive Mercantilism, whose place was taken by a policy of non-interference or *laissez-faire*. The new attitude was soon reflected in the legislation of the period, while it also facilitated the application of the new industrial methods.

The economic changes were of several kinds. First, there were the discoveries of new *resources*, such as wheat fields abroad and ore supplies at home, and of new foods such as sago and tapioca. Secondly, there were the inventions of new *processes*, so characteristic of the period. Thus, in mining and engineering, there were the inventions of the steam-engine, Cort's rolling and puddling processes, the mild steel processes, the Davy lamp, etc.; in textiles, the flying shuttle, the spinning frame, the power loom, etc.; in agriculture the introduction of scientific fertilization, the rotation of crops, etc. Thirdly, there was great progress in *transport*, without which the mechanical inventions could not have been so fully extended. The roads were developed, canals were constructed in the new industrial districts, while the application of steam-power led to the steamboat and the locomotive. Fourthly, important changes occurred in the country's *economic structure*. Thus, large-scale production with its attendant economies became the rule, joint-stock companies were promoted in every direction, while the banking and credit system received a great impetus.[1]

The general results of the Industrial Revolution may be shortly noted. Manufacture took the place of agriculture as the principal occupation. The centre of industry moved from the fields and the villages to the factories and the towns. Hand- and water-power were largely supplanted by steam-power, helped on by abundant coal and iron supplies. Population became concentrated in the industrial districts of the Midlands and the North (though in recent years there has been a tendency for industry and population to move southward again).[2]

---

[1] The changes under the third and fourth heads were so important in themselves that they are sometimes referred to as the Commercial Revolution.

[2] See below, p. 40.

The new large-scale enterprise, for a world instead of a national market, had important social as well as purely economic consequences. The absence of adequate control over the new methods of production was responsible for many evils and abuses, which went unchecked during the early part of the nineteenth century, when Factory and similar Acts were either non-existent or ineffective, and the workers practically unorganized. Though the national income was considerably increased, and all classes came eventually to benefit from the great economies, the changes were not effected without great hardship.

Economic Evolution

The above stages in industrial and social evolution may be presented in tabular form—

Industrial Development	Social Unit	Exchange	Market	Central Government
Hunting and Fishing Pastoral (Family)	} Family	Barter	Little or none	Little
Agriculture Handicraft (Gild)	Manor Town	} Metallic Money	Local	} Mercantilism
Domestic	National		National	
		} Credit		*Laissez-faire*
Factory	Empire and Commonwealth		International	Regulation

These classifications are, of course, very rough, and overlapping naturally occurs. For instance, under the head of Exchange, there is evidence of metallic money having been used in very early days, while on the other hand our present-day monetary system is by no means as dependent on credit instruments as the table might suggest. Similarly, it should not be inferred from the table that in the period of *laissez-faire* public regulation was unknown, or that nowadays individualism in economic affairs is unimportant. The summary is intended not so much to depict the conditions at a particular time as to give an idea of the main lines of evolution throughout the centuries.

PART I

PRODUCTION AND CONSUMPTION OF WEALTH

CHAPTER I

PRODUCTION AND CONSUMPTION

The Meaning of Wealth

WEALTH is sometimes taken to mean "anything that can satisfy a want," but this definition is not precise or limited enough to be of much service to the economist. There are some kinds of goods that involve no effort and are so abundant in supply that they do not give rise to economic considerations, e.g. air and sunlight. These *free goods*, as they are known, may be indispensable to life, but are not customarily regarded as economic wealth. On the other hand, should they become scarce or entail some effort or sacrifice in their supply, they become *economic goods* or *wealth*—e.g. fresh air pumped into a crowded cinema.

Economic Wealth may be defined as that which—

(i) Possesses utility, or the power to satisfy a want;

(ii) Is limited in quantity; and

(iii) Is transferable in its use (not necessarily transportable). Economic conditions are ordinarily based upon exchange, and if the use or service of a thing is not transferable, no economic transaction can normally take place. While a singer's voice, for instance, cannot itself be transferred, the pleasure provided by it can have an economic value.

Wealth can be classified according to whether it is—

(i) *Personal*, e.g. skill of surgeon or artisan; or
Material, e.g. instruments or tools.

(ii) *External*, e.g. furniture, goodwill of a business; or *Internal*, e.g. singer's vocal ability.

(iii) *Private*, e.g. jewellery, clothes; or *Social*, e.g. roads, public offices.

These divisions should not be regarded as rigid or mutually exclusive. For example, goodwill or skill, while respectively external and internal, are both personal. Indeed it is often an arbitrary matter whether a particular form of goods is regarded as wealth or not. Thus ample water supplies, navigable rivers, and so on might be excluded by the formal definition, yet obviously they count for much in promoting the wealth of the country that enjoys them. Paradoxically, if their supply were restricted, or they came under private control, they might acquire a commercial value, and the aggregate wealth might appear on that account to be increased, whereas in reality the actual wealth would be no greater and might, under a restrictive policy, be considerably less.

Wants

The following characteristics of wants may be noted—

(i) *Wants are Unlimited*. A person's desire for one commodity or another may temporarily reach satiety, but in the aggregate and over a period wants grow and new wants are conceived.

(ii) *Wants are Competitive*. In consequence of the limitation of resources, people's wants compete for them. In another sense of the term, too, a want for one article may compete with a want for another.

(iii) *Wants are Complementary*. One want goes with another so intimately in fact that complete satisfaction is impossible without them both— e.g. a toothbrush and toothpaste.

(iv) *Wants are Recurrent.* Some commodities appear continuously in daily consumption for obviously physical reasons. Others, though perhaps not physically essential, come to have a permanent place because of habit and custom.

Nature of Utility

The utility of a thing is its power to satisfy a want, and should be distinguished from "usefulness" in the moral or social sense. It is not the purpose of the economist to determine whether a want is good or bad (this belongs to ethics), or whether the State should allow or prohibit its satisfaction (this belongs to politics). If a thing is capable of satisfying some want it possesses utility, though public policy may decide to limit or disallow its use.

Two men may put a different utility on the same thing (e.g. an economics textbook or hair-restorer), and one man may derive from the same thing different utilities at different times. Apart from purely personal preferences,
Utilities may be classified—

   (i) *Elemental Utility*, e.g. coal still in the seams or unhewn timber.

  (ii) *Form Utility*, e.g. coal at the pit-head or hewn timber.

 (iii) *Place Utility*—compare the utility of coal in an agricultural and an industrial district, or that of fish at a port and an inland town respectively.

 (iv) *Time Utility*—compare the utility of coal in summer and winter, or that of a cup of coffee before and after dinner.

The subject of utility is of first importance in economic theory, and will be considered at greater length in subsequent chapters.

Production and Producers

Production is the creation of utilities. When a chair is produced, the joiner takes so much wood, screws, etc., which have in themselves relatively little utility, and fashions them into something of greater utility. Similarly, the men who transport the chair from factory to home add a utility of place; the wholesalers, retailers, typists, etc., all have their part in the general process of production, and are entitled to rank as producers.

Instances occur, of course, in which there are too many intermediaries, causing a certain amount of waste. As the organization of industry improves, however, there tends to be less overlapping of effort, and the resultant economy proves advantageous to producers and consumers alike.

Production does not cease, therefore, when the commodity leaves the premises of the actual makers; the process is not complete until the article is in the hands of the consumer.

"Over-production" of a commodity, from the producer's point of view, takes place when the supply is greater than the effective demand and the article can be disposed of only at a loss. It may be caused by faulty organization, or by too optimistic anticipation of the market, or by unavoidable external factors. The notion has been criticized, especially as, from the consumer's point of view, over-production is inconceivable so long as any wants remain unsatisfied. This criticism, however, springs from the failure to distinguish between desire and effective demand. Here particularly, the problem of production cannot be studied apart from that of consumption.

Consumption

Consumption is the obverse of production, in that it involves the *destruction* (as opposed to the *creation*) of utilities. The act of consumption may occupy a second or two, or be spread over centuries (*cf.* the consumption of a sweet and of a picture), and applies both to material commodities and to services.

Production and consumption are, in a measure, relative terms, and the one often involves the other. What is the finished article to one group of men may be the material for others; e.g. iron used for making steel, steel for making pen-nibs, nibs "consumed" by the author in producing manuscripts, and so on.

Some writers have distinguished between the processes of consumption according to whether the wealth is used in advancing production by another stage (as just exemplified), or whether it is used for direct and personal satisfaction (as in the case of a hat or visit to a theatre). They term these respectively "productive" and "unproductive" consumption. This terminology, however, is apt to be misleading, for it might give the impression that the "productive" is superior to the so-called "unproductive" consumption. Actually the expenditure on the essentials of life would come within the latter category, as would also the large outlay on the comparative comforts and luxuries that modern conditions make possible.

Production and Consumption Goods

Goods that satisfy "final" wants are sometimes known as *consumption goods*, or goods of the first order. Included in this category are not only articles such as clothing, food, flowers, etc., but personal services directly rendered by professional and manual workers, such as doctors or gardeners.

Goods that are used up to advance production a further stage are known as *production goods*, or goods of the second order. Thus the wool or cotton used in making garments, and the machine or the metal in it, come within this category.

The distinction between the two types of goods is of considerable importance, particularly in the analysis of incomes, saving and spending.[1]

The Factors or Agents of Production

In earliest times only two factors were necessary for the production of any commodity, LABOUR and LAND or NATURAL RESOURCES. Production was very simple, no machinery or tools were used, and no long period of waiting elapsed between the first and last stages. As

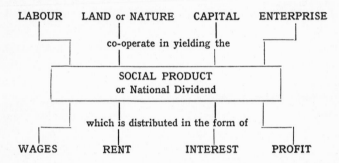

LABOUR   LAND or NATURE   CAPITAL   ENTERPRISE

co-operate in yielding the

SOCIAL PRODUCT
or National Dividend

which is distributed in the form of

WAGES   RENT   INTEREST   PROFIT

society evolved, man's needs grew more complex and his methods of production became less simple. He began to employ tools, and to set aside some of his product as a reserve or for use, either by himself or, later, by somebody else, in the production of further wealth. Thus, there developed the employment of CAPITAL as the third factor of production. In the course of time it was realized that a given amount of labour, land, and capital might have their collective yield increased if they were co-ordinated and directed under skilled guidance. This function, while having much in common with labour, of which it might be considered to be a higher form, became intimately bound up with ENTERPRISE or RISK-TAKING, which

[1] See below pp. 254–5

it became popular to regard as a fourth factor of production. There is no hard and fast difference between enterprise and labour, though the distinction is found useful in the comparison and analysis of profits and wages.

Labour and Enterprise may be regarded as the *active personal services*, while from Land and Capital are derived the *passive services of property*.

CHAPTER II

The Malthusian Theory of Population

THE supply of labour in general depends, in the first place, on the growth of population, about which there has been much controversy. Over a century ago Thomas Malthus formulated a doctrine which had considerable vogue for a time and in a modified form still has a certain currency. As first stated, his theory was that population tends to increase in a *geometric ratio* and to double itself every twenty-five years; e.g. in every successive period population would grow thus: 2, 4, 8, 16, 32, etc. On the other hand, natural supplies of food and other necessaries tend to increase only in an *arithmetic ratio*, e.g. 2, 4, 6, 8, 10, etc. According to this view, if everybody, to start with, has ample supplies and some to spare, the time must come, sooner or later, when the population outgrows the means of subsistence. When, in compliance with this alleged inexorable law of nature, such a stage is reached, population must necessarily be restricted. This is effected by the application of checks by nature, or by man himself, or by both. The *positive* checks of nature are famine, disease, etc., operating through a high death rate. The *preventive* checks applied by man are late marriages and moral restraint, resulting in a low birth rate. Since nature is apt to be ruthless and indiscriminating in cutting down the population, it behoves man in his own interests to apply his check consciously and deliberately.

This doctrine, when first enunciated, naturally aroused much criticism, and in the later editions of his work

Malthus modified somewhat the dogmatic statement of his theory and practically abandoned the use of mathematical terms. The substance of his main argument, however, underwent little change.

The Malthusian doctrine influenced economic thought for nearly a century, and did much to earn for economics the name of "the dismal science." Arising out of it, for example, was the "iron law of wages," which stated that any increase in the income of the workers leads to a growth in population, and eventually to keener competition for employment, which in turn must result ultimately in a reduction of the wages to the subsistence level. This and other equally pessimistic conclusions persisted through a large part of the nineteenth century, and, as will be shown later, were reflected in legislation and practical affairs.

Malthus's theory of population, however true it appeared at the time when he wrote, has lost much of its force, and is not borne out by the facts. First, population does not grow as quickly as he suggested. The birth rate has consistently fallen in recent times, but so also has the death rate. The official vital statistics show that the birth rate has diminished from 35 to 18 per thousand during the past half-century, and the death rate from 21 to 12. The *survival rate*, i.e. the excess of the birth over the death rate, has thus dropped in rate of increase from 14 to 6 per thousand. From the table on p. 23 it will be seen that the decennial increase in population during the last hundred years has fallen from 15 per cent to 5 per cent.

In the second place, the supplies of food and other necessaries have increased much more quickly than the pessimists thought possible. The standard of living of all classes is distinctly higher than it was a century ago. Malthus and his followers made insufficient allowance for the self-restraint of man in his desire to maintain and enhance his standard of life, and for his inventiveness in discovering and applying new resources.

Thirdly, reference must be made to the marked improvement in the *quality* of the race. One is apt to be pessimistic over the slowing-up in the rate of quantitative increase, and to overlook the enormous progress in the health and physique of the people as a whole.

POPULATION OF GREAT BRITAIN
1801–1931

Year	Population (millions)	Decennial Increase %
1801	10	—
1811	12	14
1821	14	18
1831	16	15
1841	19	14
1851	21	12
1861	23	11
1871	26	13
1881	30	14
1891	33	11
1901	37	12
1911	41	10
1921	43	5
1931	45	5

The Optimum Population Theory

The modern theory of population is less concerned with absolute numbers and more with the relation between the size of the population and the productive efficiency of the community. Whereas Malthus thought in terms of a maximum population present-day economists look to a maximization of satisfaction per head. The *optimum population* is said to be reached when, with the available amounts of the other factors (which themselves are of course subject to variation as well), the maximum product per head is attained. Any variation from this population, under the prevailing conditions and technical knowledge, tends to reduce the product and satisfaction per head. "Over-population" thus comes to have a different meaning from that relating to numbers and subsistence alone.

As already implied, the optimum is by no means a fixed quantity, but may change with variations in the other factors, such as increases in capital supplies, improvements in technique, etc. Thus a country may be over-populated at one stage, and under-populated at another, without there necessarily being a corresponding shrinkage in the number of the people.

Furthermore, the population of one country may be above the optimum at the same time as that of another is below the optimum. In these days of economic nationalism, the strengthening of political boundaries, and the decline in migration of peoples, the existence of such disparities is especially noticeable.

The Efficiency of Labour

Labour denotes all economic effort, mental and manual, that is devoted to the production of wealth, i.e. to the creation of utilities of one kind or another. Effort expended purely for the sake of pleasure, such as activity in games, is excluded from the definition, for it is conditioned by no direct economic motive.

The efficiency of labour depends on the following factors—

(i) Peculiarities of stock and breeding; e.g. the superiority of a white over a Lascar crew. These peculiarities are due partly to—

(ii) Climate and environment.

(iii) The standard of comfort, including quality and quantity of food and clothing. This depends largely on (iv) and (v).

(iv) The wages received. Up to a point, an increase in spending power may be accompanied by an increase in efficiency, though (as will be shown subsequently) beyond this point there may be a decline.

(v) The manner in which the wage is spent.

(vi) Number of hours worked. Up to a point, a reduction in hours may bring about an increase in efficiency during the hours worked. (Here again there is an obvious limit.)

(vii) Factory and sanitary conditions.

(viii) The organization of the workshop and of the industry as a whole. Individual efficiency may be improved through skilful management and co-ordination and a judicious allocation of tasks.

(ix) Moral and social causes. Where a worker is dissatisfied, the work may suffer.

(x) General and technical education.

In short, the efficiency of the labourer depends not only on his own qualities, natural and acquired, but also on a number of external conditions over which, as an individual, he has little or no control.

Mobility and Immobility of Labour

The ease or difficulty with which labour can "flow" from one direction to another is of great practical importance. Labour is generally immobile rather than mobile, especially when compared with many forms of capital.

Immobility of labour may be classified as follows—

(i) **Economic Immobility**

   (a) *Horizontal*, as between one employment and another, but still performing the same task; e.g. a typist moving from a textile to a mining office.

   (b) *Vertical*, as between employments of different kinds; e.g. a typist becoming a milliner.

(ii) **Geographical Immobility**; i.e. from place to place.

Home ties, sentiment, ignorance of better conditions else-where, the cost of moving, may all be responsible for the comparative lack of "fluidity."

(iii) **Social Immobility.** Certain professions, e.g. law and medicine, are difficult to enter owing to social and wealth barriers, and in some industries trade union restrictions serve as a bar.

Mobility of labour is usually more difficult among adults than youths, for the latter are less settled and therefore more adaptable. On the whole, too, female labour is less mobile than male labour.

The comparative immobility of labour is very important in considering the problems of wages and unemployment. It is much simpler to bring about a "flow" in (ia) and (ii) than in the others. Employment exchanges can hope to tackle successfully only horizontal and geographical im-mobility. Vertical immobility is bound up with the sub-division of labour, and involves more fundamental action and remedy.

CHAPTER III

Land

"LAND" is the term used in economics to denote the materials and forces supplied by nature for use in production. It covers not only land in the ordinary sense, but such materials as minerals, timber, brine and gases, and natural forces like tides, winds and sunlight.

The productivity of agricultural land depends on—

(i) *Physical conditions*, such as fertility of soil, latitude, climate, mineral wealth, etc.

(ii) *Economic application*. The yield may be improved through artificial manures, or irrigation, or even modification of climatic conditions. Also improvements in transport and communication may bring a place nearer, as it were, to the market, and so increase the net return.

Methods of Land Tenure

(i) *Landlord and Tenant-farmer*—the system usually found in Great Britain. Land is let and sublet on long or short leases. The money rent is fixed for a period by agreement.

(ii) *Peasant Proprietorship and Cottier Tenure*—common in Belgium, France, and elsewhere. In France about 40 per cent of the people are directly dependent on the land, and most of these are peasant proprietors.

(iii) *Métayer System*—to be found in Southern Europe. Here the landlord lends some capital with the land, and receives a return proportionate to the produce, usually a half.

(iv) *Ryot Tenure*—as in India. In this system the

owner-cultivator pays a fixed proportion of the produce to the Government.

Methods of Land Cultivation. Farming is said to be *extensive* when the cultivator works over a large area of land, as in the new countries, finding it more profitable to cover a wide territory in a comparatively superficial way, than to try and get every possible pound of produce from a more limited area.

In thickly-populated countries, where land costs more, farming tends to become *intensive*. The limited tracts of land are usually worked more thoroughly and scientifically so as to obtain a higher yield per acre.

Extensive farming is not necessarily the same as large-scale farming, nor intensive necessarily the same as small-scale farming. More capital may be invested in the intensive cultivation of a small area than in the working of a large area of land.

The Nature of Capital

Capital is wealth set aside for the production of further wealth. It has been observed in a previous chapter that, in early times, when one lived from hand to mouth, capital was comparatively unimportant. Labour was direct and for the satisfaction usually of one's own needs. With the growing demand for, and variety of, goods, production became more indirect and drawn-out, and involved the ever-increasing use of capital in such forms as tools, machinery, and stocks.

While capital is necessarily wealth, wealth is not necessarily capital. Thus, a tennis racquet would be capital only if it were used by a professional player in earning an income; if used simply for the purpose of enjoying the game it would be a form of wealth, but not capital.

The Two Conceptions of Capital

Confusion arising from different interpretations of

"capital" and "capitalism" is avoided if from the outset a distinction is drawn between the two following conceptions—

(i) **Capital as an agent of production.** This may be called its *natural characteristic*. Capital in this primary sense is indispensable in any form of industrial organization, whether individualist or collectivist. Critics of the present order do not dispute its importance as a material requisite of production. Their objection is really to capitalism as implied in the second conception—

(ii) **Capital as a source of income without direct effort.** This may be termed its *acquired characteristic*. On this point there is a pronounced difference of opinion. Some contend that all capital is the result of past labour ("crystallized labour"), and that the extra product due to the use of capital should accrue to the whole community. They urge, therefore, not the destruction, but the social ownership and control, of capital. The supporters of the existing system claim, on the contrary, that unless capital were retained as private property, and the interest enjoyed by the investor and his successors, savings would decline and business enterprise would suffer.

Forms of Capital

The different ways of classifying capital are set out below. It should be borne in mind that the classes are not mutually exclusive of each other, and that a particular form of capital goods may belong to more than one category.

Social and Individual. Capital is regarded in its social aspect when it functions as an agent of production. It is viewed in its individual aspect when it functions as a source of income, irrespective of the use made of the wealth. A person may draw interest from the loan of his wealth, though the latter may not be employed in furthering production.

Fixed and Circulating. Fixed capital is that which exists in durable shape, and is used repeatedly; e.g. machinery, ships, office furniture.

Circulating capital is that which fulfils its function in one use; e.g. nails, seeds, writing paper.

Sunk and Floating. Capital is "sunk" when it is highly special-ized in form, and cannot be adapted to other use; e.g. power loom, pit-shaft.

Floating capital is that which is not specialized, and can be employed in different uses; e.g. money, coal.

Material and Personal. Material capital is that which has a concrete form, and of which the ownership is transferable; e.g. a singer's piano.

Personal capital, on the other hand, is the purely personal ability, in the training of which some wealth may have been invested; e.g. a singer's voice.

Remuneratory and Auxiliary. Remuneratory capital is that used for paying wages and salaries.

Auxiliary capital is that devoted to machinery, material, etc. Different occupations involve different proportions of each; *cf.* the capital costs of a solicitor and a boot manufacturer.

Capital and Savings

Land is a *natural* factor, while capital is a *produced* factor. The formation of capital depends on both the power and the will to save.

The *power to save* is governed largely by the capacity to produce wealth in excess of immediately necessary consumption; also by the efficiency of the joint-stock and banking systems for collecting relatively small amounts of wealth, and putting the total to more productive use.

The *will to save* is influenced by the amount of preference for future over present satisfactions, by the desire to provide for oneself and dependants, by the anticipated revenue from savings, and by the prevailing condition and security of the times.

Saving, as viewed by the individual, involves the abstention from consumption. From the standpoint of the community it usually means the transference from one person who could put the wealth to comparatively little, to another person who puts it to greater, economic use. The total volume of consumption may undergo little change in terms of quantity during a short period, though ultimately the alteration in the *character* of the consumption may have a considerable bearing on productive capacity.

Money deposited with the bank is ordinarily reinvested, but in times of difficulty the bank may have little outlet for safe investment, causing perhaps a certain congestion, and a lack of proportion between the amounts respectively saved and immediately spent. "Over-saving" is said to take place when too much of current income is devoted to, or is available for, the provision of capital or production goods, and too little is left in the pockets of "final" consumers, wherewith to purchase the products of these instruments. "Economy," if taken to mean not so much a wise management and utilization of available resources as a blind reduction of expenditure and accumulation of funds that remain unused, may prove to be the very reverse of economical to the community as a whole.

The Laws of Non-proportional Returns

At this stage some reference may be made to the laws of diminishing and increasing returns, which are of first importance in the economics of production.

Diminishing Returns. The Law of Diminishing Returns states that, after a certain point, an increase in the capital and labour applied in production causes a less than proportionate increase in the amount of the product.

It may be otherwise stated as the **Law of Increasing Costs** per unit produced.

Suppose that a farmer has applied £700 worth of capital and labour to his land, and finds that the 7th dose of £100 yields a smaller return than the 6th; say, a product of £130 as compared with £140. He is thus experiencing a diminishing return, but he will not necessarily cease investing as soon as the additional yield per dose begins to fall. He will stop applying capital and labour only when the return falls below the minimum which is considered worth while to produce.

It is essential to note that the doses of capital and labour which yield diminishing returns need not necessarily be *consecutive* in order of application. They may be applied *simultaneously*, and still show the same result.

Thus, 10s. worth of capital and labour applied to a field every day for a week may yield a smaller extra return for the sixth application than for the fourth. Similarly, £3 worth of capital and labour applied *at a time* may not yield six times as much as if only 10s. were applied. In the same way, a farmer taking on men may find that the extra product due to the tenth worker employed is less than that obtained from the addition of the ninth man, though the men are all working together and their efforts and abilities are of the same grade. Diminishing returns, therefore, are not necessarily a matter of time.

Increasing and Constant Returns. The Law of Increasing Returns (or Diminishing Costs) is said to operate where an increase in the capital and labour applied in production leads to a more than proportionate increase in the amount of the product.

When the opposing tendencies to diminishing and increasing returns balance each other, there are said to be constant returns.

The example taken above started with the farmer's sixth dose. He may have found on commencing to invest, however, that the first dose of £100 had to be spent on preliminaries with very little yield, say £25. The second £100 may have produced £75, the third £125, the fourth

£140, the fifth £140, and the sixth £140 (the stage reached above).

Under these conditions the farmer would have experienced increasing returns up to the fourth dose, constant returns from that stage to the sixth dose, and diminishing returns afterwards.

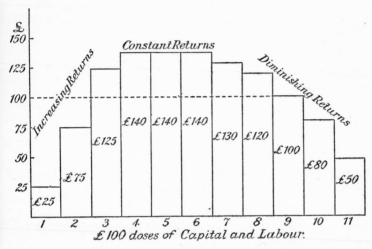

Each rectangle represents the produce from £100 application. For simplicity the produce is measured in terms of value. Doses 1 to 4 yield increasing returns; 5 and 6 a return constant with 4; 7, 8, 9, etc., diminishing returns. It is obvious that the farmer will stop applying capital and labour after the ninth dose, for his return will be less than the outlay. The "marginal" dose is that which just pays for itself, leaving no surplus.

It should be realized that *the laws of non-proportional returns refer to the quantity, and not necessarily to the value, of the product.* A farmer may experience a falling-off in the amount of his additional produce, but nevertheless, if the price is high, find it to his advantage to increase his outlay. On the other hand, a producer may find that the economies of producing on a larger scale are offset by the fall in price consequent upon an addition to the supplies on the market.

The Laws of Returns in Extractive and Constructive Industries

In agriculture, particularly, does the law of diminishing returns evidence itself, for the amount of land available is comparatively fixed. Although by modern methods of fertilization, scientific rotation, and improvements generally, the operation of the law is less in evidence than at the time when Malthus wrote, the existence of the tendency cannot be ignored.

In constructive industry, on the other hand, the producer has more scope. His resources are not so limited in supply and, by a proper arrangement of the labour and capital goods at his disposal, he more fully enjoys the benefits of increasing returns. To turn out but a few motor-cars, for example, would, in view of the heavy preliminary and overhead expenses, entail a high unit cost, but, as the number of cars in production increased, the cost of each would diminish.

The co-ordination and selection of the different factors of production, in such proportions as to get the maximum return, is in accordance with the principle of substitution,[1] which applies to all spheres of economic production and consumption.

It may be stated as a general rule that diminishing returns are more common in such "extractive" industries as agriculture, mining and fishing, and that increasing returns are characteristic of "constructive" manufacturing industries.[2] After a certain point, however, irrespective of the industry, the tendency to diminishing returns is liable to show itself, and man therefore has constantly to use his inventiveness and ingenuity to overcome it.

The significance of these laws may be illustrated by a couple of examples—

[1] See pp. 72–3 and 78–9.
[2] See p. 36.

If a man is producing under increasing returns, it may pay him to spend money on advertising and create an extra demand, thus enabling him to increase his supply at a diminishing cost per unit. The cost of advertising under such conditions need not entail an addition to the price, which might in fact show a reduction. On the other hand, excessive advertisement of something produced under diminishing returns might so raise costs as to inflict a loss on the seller and public alike.

The size of a business is largely influenced by the nature of the returns. Since the large farmer, in competition with the small farmer, reaches diminishing returns at an earlier stage than the large manufacturer in competition with the small manufacturer—in other words, as the manufacturer is better able to secure the economies of large-scale enterprise—it is more difficult to squeeze out the small farmer than the small manufacturer.

Thus the tendency is for large-scale production to be more usual in manufacture than in agriculture, and for the small producer to be more common in agriculture than in manufacture.

CHAPTER IV

Section 1. The Division of Labour

Occupational Groupings

ONE of the chief characteristics of modern economic organization is to be found in the division of labour. This involves the specialization of labour-power, both among groups and individuals, in such a way that the output is greater than would otherwise be possible. In primitive times there was little or no specialization, beyond the apportionment of heavy and light duties among men and women respectively. As communities developed, the division of functions among various groups evolved more or less spontaneously. Later there was division of labour within the group, and, with the evolution of the modern system, still further subdivision.

The occupational groupings may be roughly classified as follows:

(i) **Extractive**; i.e. extracting raw supplies from nature (e.g. farming, fishing, lumbering).

(ii) **Constructive**; i.e. manufacturing and making up into finished articles.

(iii) **Commercial**—

    (*a*) Distributive; e.g. shopkeepers, travellers;

    (*b*) Transport; e.g. railway services;

    (*c*) Banking, insurance, and other financial services.

(iv) **Direct and Public Services**; e.g. services of teacher, singer, judge.

Originally, even this elementary type of specialization was not much in evidence. Men were practically self-sufficing. When the division of labour developed among individuals, districts, and finally among nations, these groupings became more distinct. Little over a century ago, Great Britain, like other countries, was primarily extractive. To-day such interests are overshadowed by the constructive and the commercial. It is the "new" countries that are mainly extractive, providing the "old" countries largely with food and raw materials.

Forms of Division of Labour

Division of labour, in addition to the wider groupings indicated above, takes the following forms—

(i) **Division into whole industries and callings ;** e.g. wool manufacturing, mining, teaching. This is a form of division of labour so primary that it is often overlooked.

(ii) **Division of these occupations into groups of complete processes ;** e.g. the wool industry into sheep rearing, spinning, weaving, dyeing, merchanting.

(iii) **Division of these processes into part-processes.** There is now specialization, for example, within the wool-spinning industry, into the "woollen" or "worsted" sections. Within the factory, subdivision is growing more and more minute.

(iv) **Territorial division of labour.** The localization of industry is due to—

(*a*) Physical and climatic conditions — including mineral resources and natural means of transport.

(*b*) Arbitrary and semi-political reasons; e.g. the settlement of foreign refugee craftsmen under royal protection, such as the Flemings and Huguenots.

These are original causes of localization, which becomes more established as a result of—

(*c*) Adaptation of means of transport and communication.

(*d*) Specialization of labour and capital.

(*e*) Rise of subsidiary industries.

(*f*) "Industrial inertia." An industry may continue in a particular district long after the original cause has disappeared. The Potteries, for example, no longer depend mainly on local clay, nor the West Riding on local wool supplies. It is more economical to bring the materials to the areas where the structure of the industry is firmly established, than to start anew nearer to the source of supplies.

Advantages of Division of Labour

The advantages of the division of labour may be shortly summarized—

(i) **Accruing to industry generally**—

(*a*) Increased output.

(*b*) Superior quality of work, as a rule.

(*c*) Saving of time in workshops.

(*d*) Increased use of machinery.

(*e*) Economical use of machinery:

1. A complete set of tools is no longer necessary for each worker.

2. Delicate and expensive equipment is entrusted only to skilled men.

(*f*) Increased scope for inventions and new appliances (as distinct from greater inventiveness on the part of the worker himself, who may in fact have his senses dulled rather than sharpened by the mechanical routine).

(*g*) Local supply of specialized labour, accompanying the localization of industry.

(ii) **Accruing to the worker**—

(*a*) Increase of dexterity and skill through constant repetition.

(*b*) Saving of time in learning a trade.

(c) Diminution of physical strain (though this benefit may be lessened where the machine sets the pace).

(d) Opportunity for organizing ability.

Disadvantages and Limits

(i) **Disadvantages.** These fall mainly on the worker, but are liable indirectly to affect the whole of industry.

(a) Monotony and narrowing influence of the work.

(b) Immobility of labour; i.e. the difficulty of movement from one occupation to another.

In a few instances, the subdivided processes of one industry may resemble those of another (e.g. wool-spinning and cotton-spinning, or processes common to the making of clocks and typewriters), making possible a "flow" of labour from one group to another. But when industry as a whole is depressed, this possible mobility counts for little.

(c) Loss of sense of responsibility.

(d) Disadvantages attributable to machinery. (See below.)

(e) Drawbacks of factory-life and overcrowded towns.

(f) Where the enterprise is on a large scale, the loss of personal relationship between employer and employed.

(g) Where the industry is localized, the liability for a depression in trade to cause more intensive distress than where the industry is widespread.

(ii) Limits to Division of Labour

(a) If the article has a very limited demand, it may not be economical to carry specialization to an extensive degree.

(b) Where the market is such that an increase in supply causes a considerable fall in price, it may not pay to add to the output.

(c) Similarly where diminishing returns set in, it

may not be advantageous to carry the sub-division beyond a certain point.

(iii) De-localization of Industries

Of late there have been certain forces in operation that tend to restrain the movement to further localization, and in some cases have resulted in a degree of de-localization.

(*a*) The increased use of electrical power, and its economical transmission, compared with steam or other forms of power, over long distances. Parts of the Midlands and South, now that dependence on coal is not so great as formerly, have developed in recent years partly at the expense of the industrial North.

(*b*) More rapid and economical transport.

(*c*) Improved organization for collection and distribution of goods, and for the financial operations involved.

(*d*) The lower rent and rates in comparatively undeveloped areas away from thickly populated centres.

(*e*) The diminishing reliance on special skill ordinarily associated with particular localities, as the industry becomes more mechanized and the period of training is shortened.

De-localization, it may be noted, need not imply decentralization of control. An industry may become more unified as a whole, even though the establishments become more numerous and widespread.

The Benefits and Drawbacks of Machinery

The advantages and disadvantages of machinery are closely bound up with those of division of labour.

(i) Advantages

(*a*) Machinery relieves man of many heavy duties, some of which would be too burdensome for him working alone.

(*b*) It reduces the amount of drudgery by taking

over monotonous repetitive tasks (though monotony is created in other directions).

(*c*) Machinery works more quickly, and so yields a greater output.

(*d*) Machinery is more accurate and regular.

(*e*) "Standardization" is made possible.

(*f*) Goods are produced more cheaply.

(ii) **Disadvantages.** Certain of the following drawbacks are inevitable, but they can be alleviated to some extent by private and public regulation.

(*a*) Skilled craftsmen are frequently reduced to, or replaced by, semi-skilled machine operators. (Controlling certain types of machinery, however, calls for special skill of a high order.)

(*b*) Hand-work is said by some to be superior to, and more artistic than, machine-work. (This, however, is not always true, and where accuracy is called for the machine has the advantage.)

(*c*) Where a man has to keep pace with a machine, there is a certain amount of strain.

(*d*) The introduction of machinery is commonly stated to be a cause of unemployment. While this is certainly true in a short period, machinery in the long run may increase output, reduce prices, and stimulate further demand. The relationship between machinery and employment, on which there is a certain difference of opinion, is considered more fully later. [1]

Section 2. *Economic Organization*

Organization and the Entrepreneur

Organization of industry is not as determinate or definable as the agents of production previously discussed, and it is a matter of opinion whether it should be considered as a branch of labour rather than as a distinct

[1] See pp. 131-3.

factor in itself. But, however regarded, its importance in modern industry and commerce is so considerable as to demand separate treatment.

Enterprise may be regarded as apart from, or included in, organization. Most production is now carried on in anticipation of demand, and success or failure depends largely on the ability of the **Entrepreneur** (Fr. *entreprendre* = to undertake). He determines the nature and direction of the business, and arranges the resources available in such a way as to get the best return. The ideal entrepreneur is he who possesses foresight, the power of judgment, the knowledge when to take risks, and the ability to lead men and inspire confidence.

The theoretical difference in function between the entrepreneur and the capitalist should be noted. The former, in the strict sense, is concerned with the taking of risks, the latter with the investment of capital. In practice, however, it is difficult often to draw a clear distinction, for a capitalist necessarily undertakes a certain amount of risk, while the entrepreneur, as a rule, invests some capital. Also, under the modern system of capitalizing industry, the risks are commonly spread over a large number of persons. It is best, therefore, to regard this form of enterprise as a function in which many may participate rather than the exclusive contribution of a particular type of person.

Enterprise and speculation are naturally connected, though the latter term has come to have a narrower meaning in ordinary usage. Some economic aspects of speculation, in the market sense, are discussed in Chapter XIV, Sect. 3.

The Size of a Business

The scope and functions of the entrepreneur naturally vary from one type of industry to another, and he finds as a rule the greatest opportunities where organization can be conducted on a large scale. Though this type of organization is characteristic of modern production, the small-scale firm still survives and even flourishes in certain industries. It may be roughly generalized that the large firm tends to be the rule in the constructive industries, and that the small firm retains a hold in the extractive industries and in the retail trades. Important exceptions, however, are to be found. There are many prosperous small concerns in manufacture, while, especially in the "new" countries, farming and other extractive operations are conducted on a large scale. In the retail trades, too, the position of the small shopkeeper is being increasingly threatened by the large departmental store, with its mail-order service, and by the ubiquitous multiple store.

The size of a business is largely determined by—

(i) Nature of the industry. There is more scope for large-scale enterprise in constructive and commercial concerns than in extractive industries. In the latter, diminishing returns tend to appear at an earlier stage, thus limiting the economical extension of the business.

(ii) Nature of the market. If the demand is seasonal or spasmodic, or subject to serious fluctuation, there is little opportunity for successful expansion.

(iii) Ability and enterprise of the employer.

(iv) Amount of capital available for further development.

The Optimum Size of a Business. As a business increases in its scale of production, the unit costs of production tend up to a point to diminish. Beyond this stage there is a liability for the costs to increase. At the point where costs are at the minimum, a business is said to have reached its optimum (i.e. not necessarily largest) size.

Advantages and Disadvantages of Large- and Small-scale Production

The benefits and drawbacks of large- and small-scale production respectively may be briefly noted—

(i) **Advantages of Large-scale Production.**

(*a*) Economies of large purchases and sales.

(*b*) Advantages of efficient division of labour, previously enumerated.

(*c*) Economy of material and power.

(*d*) Utilization of by-products.

(*e*) Fixed expenses (e.g. rates, insurance) spread over large volume of business.

(*f*) Continuity of production without wasteful intervals.

(*g*) Power to spend money on advertising, experiment, and research.

(*h*) Greater ability to cope with trade fluctuations.

The above may be described as *internal economies*, for the reason that they are controlled and planned within the structure of the individual firms. The larger the firm the greater, as a rule, are the internal economies. *External economies*, on the other hand, are those which arise in the industry as a whole, not necessarily at the instigation or for the special benefit of any particular firm. Thus, research institutions, technical and transport facilities, etc., are at the service of all firms, large and small.

(ii) **Advantages of Small-scale Production.**

(*a*) Personal interest and supervision.

(*b*) Greater regard for detail.

(*c*) Knowledge of customers and ability to suit individual needs, especially where the market is small and specialized.

(*d*) Greater adaptability to changing conditions.

(*e*) Direct contact between employer and employed.

(iii) The **Drawbacks** of the one are, of course, implied by the advantages of the other, but the following special disadvantages of large-scale enterprise may be added—

(*a*) A highly specialized large concern finds more difficulty than a small firm in changing the nature of its structure, or the direction of its effort, to meet altered circumstances.

(*b*) The cost of breakdowns, where they occur, is relatively much greater in the case of large producing units.

(*c*) The failure of large businesses often involves many other firms and may cause widespread losses.

(*d*) There is a tendency to the formation of monopolies, which often, though not necessarily, pursue a policy that is contrary to the general interests.

Joint-stock Enterprise

The principle of joint-stock was understood and practised in the sixteenth century and even before, but it was not until the nineteenth century that company formation became widely established.

Before the Industrial Revolution there was comparatively little need for large amounts of capital; production was simple, and few long periods of waiting elapsed between the first stages of production and the sale of the commodity; while agriculture, which was then the main occupation of the people, required little financial outlay. What money was required could, as a rule, be supplied by one man or a small partnership.

After the Industrial Revolution large capital investment became indispensable, and it was found increasingly difficult to find small groups of men who were able or willing to lay down the necessary sums. Without the agency of the joint-stock company the construction of the canals and, later, the railways, would have been seriously impeded.

A drawback of early joint-stock organization was that the liability of the shareholder was unlimited, and there was the danger, about the middle of the nineteenth century, that the supply of capital would run short of the demand. The difficulty was overcome by legislation, which established the principle of limited liability, according to which the liability of an individual shareholder was limited to that part, if any, of his holding which was not paid up. This assurance to investors was followed by a considerable development in company formation, and ever since the number of corporations has steadily increased. At the present time there are well over 100,000 registered companies in Great Britain.

The general results of joint-stock organization may be briefly summarized—

(i) Increased ability of people with relatively small means to take part in production, their capital being, as a rule, used to greater advantage than if left in their hands.

(ii) Growth in the size and scope of business undertakings.

(iii) Division of functions of capital ownership and control, leading to a strong "impersonal" element in industrial organization.

(iv) Increased economic powers due to large capital control.

Co-operative Organization

An important feature in modern industrial and distributive organization is the co-operative society, which is to be found in practically all parts of this country.

Though the consumers' society is the best known, other forms of co-operative activity should be distinguished—

(i) **Producers' Societies.** In the earliest days of the movement, co-operation was chiefly confined to organizations of producers. Working men subscribed some capital between them, or obtained it from wealthier sympathizers, and combined to produce commodities, the profits from which were distributed in some agreed proportions among the members of the society. The ventures were self-governing, and were carried on alongside and in competition with ordinary capitalistic concerns. After the first enthusiasm, however, most of the societies of producers in this country disappeared. On the Continent they had greater success, but in Great Britain they failed to obtain a solid foothold. In certain industries, notably in the boot and shoe, textile and printing trades, there are still a few flourishing producers' societies, but, regarded in general, the experiment has not been successful.

(ii) **Agricultural Societies.** In some countries, for example Denmark and Ireland, co-operation has made some progress with agriculturists, particularly in the provision of credit, the use of appliances, and the marketing of produce. Up to a point such corporate activity might be regarded as a form of producers' co-operation. There are, however, important differences. In the first place, the co-operation frequently does not begin until comparatively late in the productive process, the farmers being left to cultivate their land or raise their stock in their own fashion and without restrictions. Secondly, and a more vital difference from the standpoint of *labour* organization, agricultural societies are ordinarily composed of farmer-employers whose motives for combined action, however meritorious in themselves, have little in common with those inspiring labour self-government, and, indeed, when the co-operation takes the form of fixing prices above the level possible under competition, the policy may be inimical to the interests of the workers in general.

(iii) **Co-operative Credit Societies.** Largely, but not exclusively, in connection with the agricultural societies, are co-operative organizations for the advancing of loans to members. The pooling of resources in this way is of considerable value to small producers especially.

Consumers' Societies

Following the several experiments in producers' co-operation in the early part of the nineteenth century, people turned to the less ambitious, but, as events proved, much more successful, method of corporate trading. Goods were bought collectively at wholesale prices, and the ordinary trading profits were thus retained by the members of the society. The new form of co-operation made a wide appeal, and societies sprang up all over the country, especially in the industrial areas.

The next step to cutting out the middleman between the wholesaler or the manufacturer and the co-operative member was to embark on production itself. Individual societies began to bake bread and supply some of the simpler necessaries, but a more important step was taken in the 'sixties, when the Co-operative Wholesale Societies were established for the purpose of producing and merchanting on a large scale and furnishing the co-operative stores with as large a proportion of their requirements as possible. The new venture was enormously successful, and the wholesale societies now supply from their own factories and fields three-quarters of the goods bought in the retail stores.

Though production is now conducted on a large scale, the system should be distinguished from that envisaged by the self-governing producers' societies. The employees in the C.W.S. factories are in some ways better off than in ordinary concerns, but essentially their position is the same. They are paid on a wage basis, and the control comes almost entirely from the consumers. The wholesale societies are in a similar relation to the retail societies as the latter are to the individual members. The profits of the C.W.S. are distributed among the local societies in proportion to purchases, and are in a like manner passed on to the members. The control is from the consuming, not the producing, end.

The consumers' movement in Great Britain is now very extensive, its membership amounting to about 5 millions. Since one member sometimes represents a whole family, the number of persons actually affected is considerably higher. It has been estimated that nearly one-half of the population are supplied with about one-half of their foodstuffs and one-tenth of their other household requirements through co-operative agency.

The Co-operative Society and the Joint-stock Firm

Despite certain similarities between the structure and methods of the co-operative society and the ordinary joint-stock company, there are several important, even fundamental, differences—

(i) No member of a retail co-operative society may, as a rule, hold more than £200 worth of shares.

(ii) The share capital receives a fixed rate of interest, and the profits in excess of this payment are distributed according to purchases made.

(iii) The capital can be withdrawn on short notice.

(iv) At shareholders' meetings voting is on an individual and not on a share basis.

(v) There is no limit to the number of shareholders who wish to join the society.

Advantages of the Co-operative Society

In competition with joint-stock companies and individual traders the co-operative society enjoys certain advantages:

(i) Regular and guaranteed market. The loyalty of co-operative members to their stores is an important feature in the movement, and makes for economy in the keeping of stocks.

(ii) Saving in advertisement and in distribution costs. For similar reasons the co-operative societies are not required to advertise so lavishly as their competitors, while it is not necessary to employ a large number of travellers and representatives to make the goods of the C.W.S. known among the retail societies.

(iii) Dissemination of knowledge of new methods throughout the societies.

(iv) Social benefits to members, such as thrift facilities, educational services, and experience in self-government.

Defects and Limitations of Co-operation

Co-operative ventures have up to now suffered from certain disadvantages, some of which arise from imperfect organization and are likely in time to disappear, though others are deeper-lying and are not so easy to rectify. While certain of the drawbacks are shared by joint-stock and private firms, perhaps to an even greater degree, others appear to be more common in co-operative undertakings.

Organizational Defects

(i) Overlapping of areas of retail societies, with consequent friction. This disadvantage, however, is even more prevalent among ordinary traders, both in competition with each other and with the co-operative stores.

(ii) Less efficient direction and management. The co-operative movement does not pay the same high salaries as are to be earned elsewhere, with the result that it does not always attract the best talent, while it is in danger of losing some of its most competent officers. It is a tribute, however, to the loyalty in the co-operative movement that there is less drifting away to better-paid appointments outside the society than might at first be supposed.

Such defects, however, are not fundamental and should not be very difficult to overcome. More serious are the following limitations to co-operative activity—

(i) **Limitations of Custom.** The co-operative society has not so far made a wide appeal to the very poor, who are able to pay only the lowest prices, and to whom the prospect of a deferred dividend on purchases makes little appeal. Also, the co-operative movement does not as yet include such a large proportion of clerical and professional workers as the leaders would like. The reason may be personal aloofness, or the wish to purchase from a wider selection of less standardized goods, or simply indifference. With the spread of the co-operative movement, however, the appeal among these different classes is, on the whole, becoming less limited.

(ii) **Limitations of Supply.** Though the co-operative movement, in its productive departments, has branched out in an unexpected number of directions, by no means confined to the primary necessaries of life, there would appear to be certain types of industrial activity which it is not yet in a position to undertake. Where, for instance, a heavy risk is to be incurred, it is doubtful whether it is a proper function of a co-operative society, to which are entrusted the savings of its working class members, to go far beyond the safety line. The guarantee of a fixed interest on shareholders' capital, and the liability, too, to have to repay capital at short notice, serves to restrain the local societies from becoming too venturesome. The wholesale societies, it is true, are in a better position to undertake risks, but even their powers in this respect are not so wide as those of the large capitalistic undertakings.

Finally, there are several long-established industries and services, which for one reason or another are likely to remain for a long time outside the scope of the co-operative movement. Some began too early to enable the co-operators now to gain a footing. Others are concerned with branches of production, such as iron and steel production and railway transport, which it is hardly feasible under existing conditions for co-operative societies to undertake. Certain of the expensive luxury trades, too, are beyond the range of co-operative activity. But, apart from obvious limitations such as these, the scale of co-operative enterprise is steadily growing, and, in view of the remarkable expansion in the past half-century it would be rash to lay down a too rigid definition of its area of useful and economic service.

CHAPTER V

Section 1. *Perfect and Imperfect Competition*

Conditions of Competition

IN analysing economic organization one may begin with the competitive system, even though, as will be shown later, the number and forms of intervention and control seem ever to be increasing. Competition manifests itself in a variety of ways, e.g. rivalry between producers to obtain supplies and to find markets for their goods; between workers for employment; between investors for the most remunerative use of their capital; between the suppliers of different materials (e.g. cotton and artificial silk); between the labour and capital factors of production; and so on.

Competition is said to be perfect—

(*a*) When buyers and sellers have complete information of market conditions;

(*b*) When perfect mobility exists in the disposition of labour, capital, and commodities—i.e. when there are no restrictions on the movement of factors in search of the maximum return;

(*c*) When consumers as well as producers are free from restraint in the allocation of their resources;

(*d*) When no single body, whether an individual or a corporation, has the power by its own policy and action to determine the price of an article bought or sold.

Imperfect Competition

Perfect competition between seller and seller on the one hand, and buyer and buyer on the other, is not usually realized in practice. The chief reasons for the absence of free competition are:

(i) *Ignorance of producers and consumers.* Producers are frequently unaware of the nature and extent of their rivals' activities. Similarly, consumers are often ignorant of the requirements of, and prices offered by, competing buyers.

(ii) *Custom and habit.* Custom may keep the market price above the normal price level, though it can rarely, in a business world, keep it below.

(iii) *Immobility of labour.* Personal inertia and immobility, which were noted in Chapter II, frequently prevent the complete operation of economic forces.

(iv) *Long-period production.* Production commonly begins a considerable time before marketing, rendering precise calculation difficult.

(v) *Large fixed capital.* Where a heavy capital expenditure is an essential preliminary to production, competition may be restricted. Here conditions are akin to monopoly.

(vi) *Monopoly.* Where there is a monopoly of producers, the price may be considerably above the cost of production; where there is a monopoly of buyers, the price may, for a short time, be below the cost of production.

Industrial Combination

One of the important factors limiting competition is industrial combination or integration. Combination need not lessen the force of competition, and indeed in some cases intensifies it. In so far, however, as it is a stage in the formation of monopoly it is a means of instituting the central control which is fatal to competition.

Combination is said to be *horizontal* when the firms concerned have been engaged in a similar type of business, making or selling similar things; e.g. combination of a number of iron smelters. They unite for the purpose of getting—

(i) Lower prices from the firms who supply their material.

(ii) Higher prices from their customers.

(iii) General economies resulting from a co-ordination of efforts, and elimination of overlapping activities and departments.

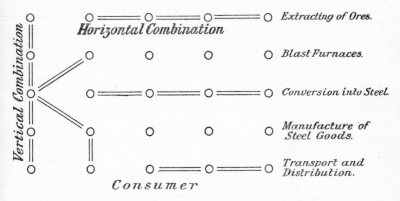

In this diagram, each circle represents a firm engaged at one stage or another in the chain of production. Horizontal and vertical combinations are indicated.

Obviously the most effective form of monopolist organization would be amalgamation of the two forms of combination.

Combination is said to be *vertical* when the firms have been engaged at different stages in the production of an article. Vertical combination in the iron and steel industry, for example, may allow of the metal going through several stages without cooling—literally of " striking while the iron is hot." The motive may be efficiency of production, or monopoly, or both. Vertical combination alone may merely be a stage in large-scale production; though it is not necessarily monopolistic, it may be a step in that direction.

Section 2. Monopoly Organization

The Tendency to Monopoly

The nineteenth century was a period of acute competition. Under the new industrial régime manufacturers tended to take full advantage of the increasing returns accruing to large-scale enterprise. As the costs of production per unit diminished, the prices to the public were cut and undercut, until, in certain industries, only the firms producing in great quantities could sell their products at a profit.

As the size of these businesses increased, the rivalry between them was emphasized. Firms were either crushed or absorbed by the new mammoth enterprises until comparatively few concerns were left in the field. Competition now became so intense that the alternative for many became still further combination or ruin. From this state of affairs emerged the Trust, which suppressed suicidal competition and controlled production and price.

The system of joint-stock and free-transferability of shares was of great assistance in the formation of these monopolies. A firm need only, as a rule, acquire a majority of the shares of a rival concern to obtain effective control of policy and output. Such a method was found cheaper than buying a business outright for its full cash value.[1]

Types of Monopoly

Monopolies may be classified as follows—

(i) *Natural monopolies*, arising from limitation of nature's supply.

(ii) *State-granted monopolies*. These may take the form of patent rights, copyright, trade-marks, etc.; or they may be due to the public recognition of (iii).

---

[1] The positions between perfect competition and perfect monopoly are sometimes known as *oligopoly*. The comparatively simple position of *duopoly* is said to exist when there are two sellers (or buyers) that are in a dominant position confronted by a large number of competing buyers (or sellers).

(iii) *Monopolies that are, in certain industries, a necessary condition of full economic efficiency.* It is wasteful to have competing enterprises in gas, electricity, and water supply, tramways, postal services, etc. In such instances, the State or municipality insists (or should insist) on single direction, either by taking over the service itself or granting sole privilege to a limited number of concerns, reserving the right of final control. Monopolies in this class are usually more permanent than those in (iv).

(iv) *Monopolies that are the result of industrial combination brought about to eliminate competition, but not necessarily for purposes of efficiency.* A trust is formed, as a rule, with the object of keeping competitors out of the field, though the incursion of the latter might be for the good of the community. It is this form of monopoly which meets with the severest criticism.

(v) *Temporary monopolies,* such as the "cornering" of supplies. This type, too, is generally condemned.

Forms of Monopolistic Structure

The principal forms of monopolistic structure are set out below. It should be observed, however, that a particular organization may partake of more than one type, or adopt more than one practice.

(i) Agreement to fix prices, which may or may not be accompanied by—

(ii) Division of market. It is a common practice for combinations to allocate fixed selling areas to the component firms.

(iii) The Pool. Under this arrangement the profits are pooled and divided among the firms in proportion to the respective volumes of business.

(iv) The Cartel, and

(v) The Trust. These two important forms of monopolistic structure, covering also to some extent (vi) and (vii), are dealt with more fully below.

(vi) The Holding Corporation. This is a nominally independent company, which holds a major proportion of shares in the other companies, thereby obtaining virtual control.

(vii) The Merger. This is but an advanced form of trust. The principal company buys in and cancels stock of other companies which thereby cease to exist.

Cartels and Trusts

Some forms of monopoly take the form of a selling agency, commonly described as a Cartel. The associated firms, which retain their identity and independence up to a point, form a central sales bureau through which all their output must be distributed. The cartel fixes the selling price and the quotas of the participating firms in such a way as to obtain the maximum total profit. Firms that exceed their quota are liable to be fined; those that produce less may receive some compensation.

The cartel is thus a federation rather than a physical amalgamation of firms, but the organization may become so closely-knit as to resemble an actual integration. It is more common in Germany and neighbouring countries than in Britain and the United States, though in recent years the type of structure usually described as the trust has considerably developed in Continental countries.

The Trust takes the form of an amalgamation rather than an association of firms, and is a more unified form of organization. The cartel ordinarily links up firms in a horizontal direction. The trust often, though not necessarily, entails a vertical integration as well.[1] It

[1] The distinction in structure between the trust and cartel is to a small extent due to the difference in the Common Law in the English-

derived its name from the "trustees" in whom originally the control of the combined firms was vested.

The cartel tends to enjoy a certain advantage over the trust in that the members have a greater freedom of action and opportunity for enterprise. The trust, on the other hand, benefits from a more centralized and co-ordinated system of production. It is better adapted to present-day conditions of mass production and of large, perhaps world-wide, markets, and from the nature of its structure is likely to be more permanent.

" Rationalization " of Industry

The "rationalization" of industry, about which there is little new except the name, does not always involve monopoly, though under certain conditions it doubtless tends in that direction. It is usually taken to mean the action by the majority of producers in an industry, if not by some central authority, to impose some co-ordination or control. Ordinarily it brings together units of a similar type, and resembles therefore horizontal rather than vertical combination.

The economic advantages of rationalization are indisputable. In addition to the general benefits of large-scale organization, which have been previously noted, the following call for special mention—

(i) *Concentration of production in the best equipped factories.* Though rationalization often entails the closing-

---

speaking countries and in Germany. A contract that would be "in restraint of trade" according to English legal principles is enforceable at law in Germany. There, two firms may contract to sell not more than so much produce, or at less than an agreed price, and if one party breaks its bond, the other can sue it for breach of contract and obtain damages. In the United States and Great Britain, on the contrary, the law is opposed to agreements in restraint of trade. A surer way of obtaining monopoly had, therefore, to be devised, and this was effected by bringing the firms into a single corporation, with central direction and control. In the United States the position has lately been modified by legislation, under the National Recovery Administration, which permits and even encourages a degree of combination for entire industries.

down of redundant establishments, it is usually the less
efficient units that are so affected.

(ii) *Regular instead of intermittent production.* If there
were too many factories prior to the association, regular
working of them all would have meant over-production.
It is more economical to have a comparatively small
number of works producing all the year round than a
large number working intermittently. This also leads to
regular and ready supply.

(iii) *Economy of freights.* Under competitive conditions,
factory A might send goods a long distance to a place
not far from factory B, which was producing the same
kind of commodity, while B might send to a place near
A. These "cross-freights" are very uneconomical, and are
eliminated under single control, each factory being required to supply the nearest market.

(iv) *Patent rights, special brands, and trade-marks* of
particular firms can be utilized by all the members of
the association.

(v) *Costs of advertising* are considerably reduced. The
money spent in advertising to capture a competitor's trade
thus tends to be saved. This is advantageous also from
the consumer's point of view.

(vi) *Reduction in number of salesmen and travellers.*
Though the dismissal of these men might mean hardship,
there is usually a net benefit to producers and consumers
regarded as a whole.

Objections to Monopolies

Against the benefits of rationalization have to be set
the disadvantages that might result if the organization
came under monopoly control—

(i) *Prices usually raised and output restricted.* When
competition is keen, prices are naturally low, but they
tend to be increased as soon as an amalgamation or some

form of association is reached. There is the danger, too, that the output may be unduly restricted. It is important to note, however, that a monopolist will not necessarily charge a high price if a reduction in demand is the result. Much depends upon the nature of the article, the elasticity of the demand, and the possibility of a substitute. It may yield a higher net profit to sell a large quantity at a low price than to sell a little at a high price.[1]

(ii) *Unfair methods of competition*. It is a common criticism of certain trusts that they have frequently eliminated competition by selling for a time under cost of production until the rival has been compelled to give way; by charging different prices for the same products according to the capacity of the consumers and the relative strength of competition in particular areas; by deferring discounts that are contingent upon the placing of further orders; by allowing secret rebates to influential customers; and by other questionable methods.

(iii) *Unemployment* caused through the discharge of factory hands, salesmen, travellers, etc. This need not be a disadvantage in the long run, if there have been too many firms producing. The unemployment may take the place of the under-employment, in the form of short time, from which the employees in the industry have probably suffered in the past.

(iv) *Speculation and over-capitalization* made possible on the formation of trusts. In floating the new company, stock is often issued to an amount that exaggerates the capitalized value of the additional profit-earning capacity.

(v) *Slackening of efficiency*. The elimination of competition between rival firms is liable to lessen the degree of enterprise, particularly if the size of the organization grows to an unwieldy extent. Also a combination

[1] See pp. 93–96 for the theory of monopoly prices.

may include a number of inefficient units that survive only because of a vested interest. On the other hand, the trust leaders may succeed in maintaining the spirit of emulation by competitive selection schemes for higher posts, bonuses to departments, and similar means.

The Control of Monopoly

Measures for restoring competition. Various attempts have been made in different countries to prevent or minimize the abuses of monopoly. In the United States, where the trust has most developed, much legislation has been passed to reduce the evil, but evasion so far has not been over-difficult. An attempt was made there to split the amalgamation into its component parts, but with the nominal breaking-up there emerged the "holding corporation," a super-company which held all, or a majority of, the shares of the subsidiary companies, thus exercising a control as strong as that of the original "trustees." Attempts to prevent the practice of discriminating prices were countered by special "fighting brands" which had only one price, but whose sale was restricted to areas where a rival was in the field. Other preventive schemes had equally limited success.

Measures for protecting the consumer. Recognizing the difficulty, even futility, of attempts to break up a monopoly into competitive units, more recent reformers have concentrated upon measures intended to protect the consumer against the rapacity of the monopolist. One policy is to impose a statutory maximum scale of charges. Though certain industries lend themselves to such regulation (e.g. railways) because of their standardized and easily graded products or services, others are not so suitable, particularly those in which a constancy of price need not imply a constancy of quality.

A second policy is to place a maximum on the profits rather than on the price. Such a practice has for long been employed in regard to gas and water supply companies and other public utility undertakings. But most monopolies are not so readily controlled, and would present considerable difficulty even if the desirability of limiting their profits were accepted in principle.

A third scheme, not so ambitious as the first two, is to secure publicity for all the dealings of the monopolist, in the hope that objectionable practices (such as secret rebates, or sales at nominal charges to subsidiary concerns) will thereby be discouraged. Measures of this kind might serve a salutary purpose, but obviously their real effectiveness must be limited.

In recent years, especially in the United States where anti-trust legislation is most common, the attitude to combination and monopoly has undergone an appreciable change. Association or integration, provided that it leads to a greater economy of production, is welcomed nowadays and even encouraged. The problem, however, which is not yet solved, is to attain the highest form of productive organization while safeguarding the interests of the consumers.[1]

[1] For a fuller account of industrial organization, of combination and monopoly, and of the attempts at public regulation, see the author's *Economics of the Industrial System*, from the same publishers.

PART II
VALUE

CHAPTER VI

THE THEORY OF VALUE

Section 1
The Labour and Cost of Production Theories

The Nature of Exchange and Value

IN the foregoing analysis it was pointed out that production is nothing more than the creation of utilities. Any man who adds a utility is a producer. Shopkeepers and bankers may add nothing tangible to the goods they help to distribute, but their services are indispensable. The utility they add is not one of form, but one of time or place.

It used to be contended that if one man benefited by exchange, another man must necessarily lose. This notion, however, is misleading. It is now held that if A exchanges, say, his watch for B's cycle, A values the cycle *at least* as much as the watch, while B values the watch *at least* as much as the cycle. Both parties may gain by the transaction, proving the adage that "exchange is no robbery." Similarly, in the employment of money, the utility of the thing bought is not less than that of the money given. In Jevons's words, exchange is generally accepted as being the "barter of the comparatively superfluous for the comparatively necessary."

The most fundamental problem in exchange, and, indeed, in the whole of economic science, is the consideration of the principles governing the exchange-power, or value, of a commodity or service.

In ordinary speech the word "value" is employed in several senses. We speak of the value of food, the value of a suit of clothes, the value of fresh air, the value of literature, and so on. In early economic writings the distinction was commonly drawn between "value in use" and "value in exchange," but modern economists denote these conceptions simply by "utility" and "value." By the former, they mean the capacity to satisfy a want; by the latter, the power of exchange that one commodity has for another.

Price indicates the value in exchange as measured in terms of money. The general theory of value must not be confused with the narrower theory of the purchasing-power of money, to which examination will be given at a later stage.

Value as Regulator

Value serves as a regulator of most forms of economic activity. It serves as a guide to *producers*, who tend to adjust the character and scale of their output according to the market valuation. A high value may be taken as a sign of scarcity and may stimulate producers to increase their supply. A low value may be interpreted as indicating a large supply, and producers may curtail their output in consequence.

Similarly, *consumers* regulate their purchases according to the respective values, and thereby, indirectly, to conditions of supply. A low value tends to encourage consumption; a high value to limit it. Thus, under conditions of plenty a low value enables stocks to be quickly consumed; under conditions of scarcity a high value serves to conserve the stocks and spread their consumption over a longer period.

Also, in *distribution* value serves, up to a point, to regulate the shares paid in the form of wages, profits, interest, and rent, and the individual amounts paid within each group. The factors of production compete in a sense for employment and the rewards are more or less commensurate with the values of their respective additions to the total. The relationship of value, however, to distribution is not so evident as it is to production and consumption, particularly as in the apportionment of the social income arbitrary forces and conditions count for so much.

Labour and Cost Theories of Value

It is helpful, before proceeding to the modern theory of value, to indicate the earlier attempts at explanation, for realization of their failings assists one in comprehending and appreciating the later doctrine.

The Labour Theory was expounded at different times and in different forms by Adam Smith, Ricardo, Rodbertus, and others; but it was left to Karl Marx to develop it most fully, and the theory is usually associated with his name.

Briefly, it states that the value of anything depends on the amount of labour embodied in it. Labour is considered to be the source and measure of all values. The exponents of this theory recognize the necessity of capital goods, but prefer to consider them as the products of past effort, regarding them, in effect, as "crystallized labour."

Marx and his followers used this doctrine as a weapon against the capitalist organization of society. Labour, they maintained, creates all value, but is paid only a bare subsistence wage. The difference between the real product of labour and the wages paid is the "surplus value" which goes in the form of interest, profits, and rent to the capitalist class.

While Marx did not overlook (as is sometimes asserted) the condition of utility, he could not accept it, owing to its variability, as a factor determining value. Adam

Smith had pointed out nearly a century before that things with the greatest use-value often had a low exchange-value (e.g. water), while things with an apparent low use-value had a high exchange-value (e.g. diamonds). This "paradox of value" only confirmed Marx in disregarding utility as a standard in the fixing of value.

The Cost of Production Theory, resting on a broader basis, states that the value of a commodity is governed by the cost of the various factors employed in its production. Like the labour theory, it argues from the side of supply; different from that theory it takes into account the agents of production besides labour. Under free competition the theory appears at first to be a sound statement, since high profits due to a large surplus of price over cost will attract competitors, who will add to the supply and reduce the price; while low profits or a loss will drive producers out of the market, causing a shortage in supply and a consequent rise in price. Eventually, it is maintained, the price must equal the cost of production.

These early cost theories of value are subject to similar general criticisms. They both approach the problem chiefly from the side of supply, giving insufficient consideration to utility and conditions of demand. They do not satisfactorily account for "scarcity value," or changes in value after production is completed, nor do they allow sufficiently for possible misdirection of labour and other resources.

Although in the older theories of value the necessary distinction between nominal cost (expressed in terms of money) and real cost was drawn, the latter still appeared as the sum of efforts and sacrifices that could be given a monetary measurement. In the modern theory real cost is expressed in terms of alternative use; it is maintained that the real cost of an article is not merely the summation of efforts and sacrifices, but is the amount of other things that could have been obtained for the same outlay.

Early Utility Theory

Following the economists who attempted to find the explanation of value in supply came those who sought for it in utility, the basis of demand. Jevons, for instance, stated dogmatically that "value depends entirely upon utility," though his reasoning showed that the relationship was such that it could not be expressed in a simple direct ratio.

It could readily be proved, however, that a theory based entirely on utility is no less one-sided and misleading than a theory based on labour or cost alone. Obviously, no explanation of value can be complete that does not take conditions of supply into account. The modern theory, as will be shown in Section 2, pays equal attention to both sets of conditions. Though the conclusions of Jevons[1] are no longer accepted in their entirety, his *method* of treatment, involving the conception of "marginal" increments, retains a place of first importance in the current exposition.

Section 2. The Marginal Theory of Value

In the following analysis value will be studied in turn from the sides of demand and supply. It will be shown that the marginal utility is the governing factor in demand, that the marginal cost of production is the principal factor in supply, and that value is determined at their point of coincidence.

The Law of Diminishing Utility or Satiable Wants

It is necessary at the outset to consider the Law of Diminishing Utility or Satiable Wants which states that

[1] The Austrian school of economists can claim equal credit for the development of the utility theory. See Appendix.

the additional satisfaction that a person receives from an increase in the supply of anything that he possesses, diminishes with every unit that is added to the stock. To put this another way, the total utility of a thing increases at a slower rate than an increase in the stock.

A person who is hungry obtains considerable satisfaction from his first slice of bread. Though his hunger is not satisfied, the edge has been taken off, and he will probably derive less utility from the second than from the first.[1] In the same way a person who is sight-seeing, finds that the pleasure derived from view after view gradually declines, even though the sights are of equal interest in themselves. This tendency to diminishing satisfaction is apparent in all forms of consumption, and rests upon man's physical and mental nature. It is conceivable that the stock of a commodity may so increase that the utility of additional amounts falls to nothing, or even below. If the stock increases to such an extent that the consumption of additional units gives discomfort rather than satisfaction, *disutility* may be said to have set in.

It is essential to realize that the amount and quality of the successive units do not vary. Each slice of bread in the above example is identical, yet the first gives more satisfaction than the fourth. The fact that these units are interchangeable as regards quantity and quality is of considerable importance in the statement of the marginal doctrine.

Diminishing Utility as Applied to Money

Diminishing utility occurs not only in the consumption of goods, but also in the use of money with which to

[1] It might appear that increasing utility exists in certain cases. Thus, if 3 yd. of cloth are necessary for a garment, a cut length of 2 yd. would have less than two-thirds the utility of 3 yd. An extra yard would thus afford increasing utility. Yet, it may properly be contended, diminishing utility really obtains, since 3 yd., and not 1 yd., constitutes the proper unit for comparison, and an extra length of 3 yd. would give a smaller satisfaction than the first length.

buy those goods. With the first part of his income a man purchases the absolute essentials of life and devotes the remainder to the purchase of goods in a diminishing order of necessity. A man with twice the income of another does not necessarily derive twice the satisfaction, so far as this can be measured, while the utility from the last pound of a very wealthy person's income may be fractional compared with that of the only pound of a poor man's income.

Applications of the Principle of Diminishing Utility

The law of diminishing utility has some considerable practical application. Reformers, who aim at a more equal distribution of the social income, deduce from this principle that a redistribution is by itself capable of increasing the total satisfaction in a country (provided, of course, that the redistribution is carried out in such a way that it does not impair the will and power to produce, and thus reduce the total income of the community). If a hundred pounds deducted from a rich man's income would mean only the deprival of comparatively little utility, while the addition of that amount to a poorer man's income would increase the latter's satisfaction by more than the rich man had lost, methods should be devised, they say, to redistribute the national income on a more equitable basis. In short, it is claimed to be possible to increase the aggregate satisfaction without *necessarily* increasing the total production, though the desirability of adding to the nation's gross income is not on that account denied.

Recognition of the principle of diminishing utility is, in effect, incorporated in the existing system of graduated taxation. Suppose A and B to have incomes of £2,000 and £500 respectively. If the income tax were *propor-*

tionate, say 10 per cent, A would pay four times as much as B, viz. £200 compared with £50. But, as a general rule, the loss of £200 to A would mean relatively less sacrifice than the loss of £50 to B. In the British income tax system the principle of *progressive* rates has been carried to an advanced stage, though urgency and expediency have probably been more responsible than the dictates of equity.

Marginal Utility

It has been seen that the utility of a thing diminishes with its supply. This does not imply, however, that a person will go on buying a commodity until the utility drops to zero; on the contrary, he will, consciously or unconsciously, be comparing with this utility the possible satisfaction to be derived from the consumption of *other* commodities. When a man is very hungry, the utility of 2d. worth of bread is greater than 2d. worth of pastry. But when he has somewhat allayed his hunger, he may find that the outlay of another 2d. would yield more satisfaction from pastry than from bread. The utility derived from that unit which the consumer is just persuaded to acquire is called its **marginal utility**.

The marginal utility need not be the smallest utility to be derived. It is simply the utility of that amount which, in the opinion of the consumer, is just worth purchasing at a given price. *The position of the margin is not permanently fixed*, even for the same person; it may move up or down according to different circumstances. Thus, a fall in the price of a commodity may induce a man to put it to some inferior use not considered worth the expense before. Or an increase in a man's income may have the same effect. In both cases, the marginal utility of the article will tend to fall. Conversely, a rise in the price or a fall in the income will tend to cause the margin to rise.

In perfectly competitive conditions there can be only one price for a commodity at a time. To differentiate in prices according to variation in utility would be practically impossible. At any given price there are some people who get the commodity for less than they are really prepared to give. On the other hand, there are some who do not purchase it, because they reckon the utility of the commodity as less than that of other things which they can buy at the same price. But there is the intermediate class of person who considers that, while he would not pay more, he is just prepared to purchase the commodity at the price charged. He is the **marginal purchaser.**

The Law of Substitution in Consumption

It follows that **a consumer tends to regulate his purchases of different articles in such a way that the marginal satisfactions derived from them are equal.** In other words, he gets most satisfaction out of his expenditure when he is getting equi-marginal returns from all the things consumed. This may be illustrated by a simple example. Suppose that a man, about to go on a long walk, is buying tobacco and chocolate, and wishes to spend 1s. on these to the best advantage. The table on the opposite page illustrates the degrees of utility to be derived from successive twopennyworths of tobacco and chocolate.

If he wishes to get the maximum satisfaction for his outlay, and assuming it is possible to make precise calculation, he will spend 8d. on tobacco and 4d. on chocolate, for at this point he derives 47 units of satisfaction, the highest in the scale. Another 2d. on chocolate would mean the loss of 1 unit; another 2d. on tobacco would mean the loss of 3 units.

Pence	Marginal Utility of Tobacco	Total Utility of Tobacco	Marginal Utility of Chocolate	Total Utility of Chocolate
2	10	10	8	8
4	9	19	7	15
6	7	26	5	20
8	6	32	4	24
10	4	36	3	27
12	3	39	2	29

1s. spent on tobacco yields 39 units of satisfaction.   Total, 39

10d.	,,	tobacco ,,	36	,,	,,	
2d.	,,	chocolate ,,	8	,,	,,	Total, 44
8d.	,,	tobacco ,,	32	,,	,,	
4d.	,,	chocolate ,,	15	,,	,,	*Total, 47* (maxsmum)
6d.	,,	tobacco ,,	26	,,	,,	
6d.	,,	chocolate ,,	20	,,	,,	Total, 46
4d.	,,	tobacco ,,	19	,,	,,	
8d.	,,	chocolate ,,	24	,,	,,	Total, 43
2d.	,,	tobacco ,,	10	,,	,,	
10d.	,,	chocolate ,,	27	,,	,,	Total, 37
1s.	,,	chocolate ,,	29	,,	,,	Total, 29

This tendency is differently expressed and is better known as **the law of substitution**. A consumer tends to substitute one commodity or unit of it for another, and obtains the greatest satisfaction for his expenditure when the respective marginal utilities are equal. The principle of substitution, which will be shown below to operate also in production, is of first importance in economic life.

Marginal Utility and Price

The relationship between marginal utility and price may be further illustrated. Suppose a woman to be buying butter, which may be used for more than one purpose in the household, and for which there are, of course, possible substitutes. It should be realized also that the woman is only one of thousands of purchasers, for whom, in a perfect market, there can be only one price at a time.

Her demand schedule at a certain moment may be imagined as follows—

2s. 6d. for the first pound
2s. 0d.   „   second „
1s. 9d.   „   third „
1s. 6d.   „   fourth „
1s. 3d.   „   fifth „

How many pounds of butter will she buy, and at what price? It is evident that if the price were 1s. 3d. per lb., she would buy 5 lb.; if the price were 1s. 6d. she would buy 4 lb.; if 1s. 9d., 3 lb.; and so on.

Assuming that the actual price is 1s. 6d. per lb., the marginal pound of butter will be the fourth. It is just worth buying 4 lb. of butter at that price; to buy 5 lb. would mean paying another 1s. 6d. for an extra 1s. 3d. worth of utility. *Since the pounds of butter are identical and interchangeable, the marginal utility of the fourth pound may be transposed to any other pound, and the price of the marginal pound of butter will be the price per pound of all the butter purchased.* Otherwise one would be paying different prices for the same thing according to the varying utilities derived from it. It follows that the price measures the marginal utility of the article purchased.

As the average purchaser aims at putting his money to the best use, and, consciously or otherwise, evaluates and compares the respective utilities of all the things he buys, it may be stated further that prices of all commodities and services tend to equal the respective marginal utilities as measured in terms of money, and relatively to the marginal utility of money.

Total Utility and Consumer's Surplus

The woman who bought 4 lb. of butter would derive 2s. 6d. worth of utility from the first lb., 2s. from the second, 1s. 9d. from the third, and 1s. 6d. from the fourth, a total utility of 7s. 9d. Presumably she would have been prepared to pay this sum rather than go without the 4 lb. But, as shown above, she would pay only 6s. for the 4 lb. (i.e. four times the utility of the marginal pound, measured in money). The difference between the price that one would be willing to pay, and that which

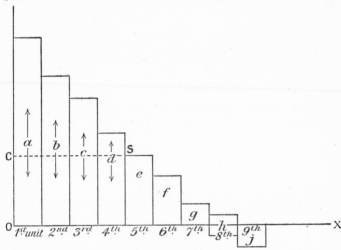

DIAGRAM ILLUSTRATING DIMINISHING UTILITY, TOTAL
AND MARGINAL UTILITY, AND CONSUMER'S SURPLUS

In this diagram rectangle *a* represents utility derived from the first unit of anything, *b* the utility from the second, and so on.

The utility is seen to diminish, until the eighth unit *h* is on the border between utility and disutility. A ninth unit *j* would yield complete disutility.

Suppose the fifth unit is the one which the consumer just finds it worth while to purchase at the price; *e* will represent the marginal utility. The total utility will be $a + b + c + d + e$. The consumer's surplus will be the inclusive area above line *CS* parallel with *OX*, and may be represented as total utility *minus* $5 \times e$.

is actually charged, is termed Consumer's Surplus, here equivalent in terms of money to 1s. 9d.

Determination of Margin for Consumers in General

Again reverting to the example above, it was shown that the woman would derive 7s. 9d. worth of utility from an outlay of 6s. It might be asked, why was she not charged (say) 1s. 11d. per lb., seeing that she would still

be getting 7s. 9d. worth of satisfaction for 7s. 8d.?
The answer has already been indicated, but may be repeated in brief form—

(i) If the price were 1s. 11d., the woman in question
would not buy the third and fourth pounds, which represent only 1s. 9d. and 1s. 6d. worth of utility respectively.

(ii) She is only one of thousands of purchasers, each
having varying preferences. Some would pay more, some
less, than the woman in our example. A different price
for every one would mean chaos.

(iii) The object of butter makers is not necessarily to
sell at the highest price (this may mean a small demand)
or to sell as much as possible (this may mean a serious
fall in price), but to sell at such a figure as will yield
the biggest profit. Selling large quantities of butter at
1s. 6d. per lb. might yield a greater profit than selling
smaller quantities at the higher price.

The Marginal Rate of Substitution

This theorizing about utility has been criticized on the
ground that satisfaction is a purely personal and subjective condition and that to give it a money evaluation
is to assume a bridge (*a*) between the evaluations of
different consumers, and (*b*) between utility and price,
that is of doubtful validity. Against this contention,
however, it is maintained that, even if individual satisfactions are incapable of measurement, people do nevertheless find means in practice of finding some common
denomination, or, as it has been expressed, some *quanti-
fication of utilities* is effected.

It has already been shown that consumers tend to
substitute alternative means of satisfaction for each
other until the point of maximum satisfaction is reached.
All exchange is based on this principle. One commodity
is not exchanged for another unless the marginal utility

to the seller is less than that to the buyer. The ratio of marginal utilities as between the parties to an exchange has been described as the marginal rate of substitution. Further, since the diminishing utility of successive units of one commodity leads to the substitution for units of another commodity, some economists prefer to describe diminishing utility as the increasing marginal rate of substitution. This new terminology has the merit, in that it is entirely quantitative, of avoiding the difficulties inherent in utility with its personal and subjective characteristics.

The Marginal Firm and Marginal Cost

Similar considerations arise on the side of supply. It is evident that, just as utility is the central factor in demand, cost of production[1] is the dominating force in supply. Utility varies from consumer to consumer; cost varies from producer to producer. At a single time there may be several firms producing an identical commodity at varying costs, according to the different standards of organization and efficiency. Which firm's cost is the determining factor? The answer is that of the **marginal firm**, i.e. the firm which just manages to pay its way. (There may, of course, be more than one such firm at the margin.) Its costs are higher than those of the supra-marginal firms producing at the same time, but, as the demand is sufficient to absorb the total output of all the existing firms at a

---

[1] The total cost of production is made up of *prime costs* and *supplementary costs*. By prime costs is meant the specific expenditure on the product on account of material, labour, etc., but excluding the general establishment costs of the factory. The prime costs stop when a factory stops. Supplementary costs, on the contrary, are regular establishment charges, like rental, taxes, interest, etc., which continue to be incurred whether the factory is running or not.

The importance of the distinction is seen in times of depression. A manufacturer with large supplementary costs is not so ready to stop producing as one with low supplementary charges, and may be willing for a while to produce for the price of labour and material only. It is usually less disadvantageous to adopt such a course than to close down entirely for a period, for on the return of good times the plant is in working condition for coping with the new orders while the difficulty of having to seek, and possibly train, new labour supplies is obviated.

price equivalent to the costs of the marginal firm (including the cost of selling and the minimum profit without which one would not normally carry on), these costs will tend to equal the supply price of all the firms. While some of the supra-marginal firms *could* sell for less if they wished (since their costs are lower than those of the marginal firm), they will not ordinarily do so because they are able to sell all their output at the higher price. Though a firm will not sell at a price below its cost of production, it will charge as much above as it can get.

In a similar fashion it can be shown that any individual firm tends to produce up to that point at which the selling price of the article just compensates for the cost of producing it. The firm may experience a diminishing return, i.e. an increasing unit cost, or, even if the physical volume of output is still showing a tendency to expand, the greater supplies placed on the market may cause the price to fall. Thus, not only is there a firm, or group of firms, that may be described as marginal, but there is also a stage of **marginal cost** up to which, but not beyond, it pays to carry production.

It follows from what has been said that there is a "producer's surplus" comparable to the "consumer's surplus," described above. In a group of firms turning out a given article, there are some producers who are making a profit over and above that with which they would be satisfied under less favourable conditions. Similarly, some of them are making an additional profit on that part of their output which is produced at less than the marginal cost. These surpluses will come up for further consideration at a later stage.

The Law of Substitution in Production

It was shown above that a consumer tends to lay out his expenditure in such a way that the marginal utilities of all the things purchased are equal. In the same way, a producer tends to employ the factors of production in such proportions that the marginal returns from each are equal. If a sum of money is about to be added to a business, and can be spent in the form of new plant or more labour, or both, the entrepreneur will try to apportion the expenditure in such a way as to get the maximum return, and this will be attained when the marginal returns are equal.

It may be asked why those supra-marginal firms mentioned above do not increase their output and make extra profits. The reason may be that they are already near the limit of economical production. A firm tends to produce up to the point at which the marginal costs equal price. Production after this point would mean adding more to the costs than to the receipts. Suppose, however, that the output of these firms is capable of profitable expansion, and the directors decide to increase their sales. In order to capture the market, they presumably reduce the price. The result may be that the firms which had been on the margin have to close down, for the price obtainable is less than their cost of production.

At any given time, therefore, there are a number of firms producing similar goods at varying costs, but all selling them at one price. This price tends to equal the costs of the marginal firm, or, simply, the marginal costs of production.

Marginal costs, it should be noted, are not permanently fixed any more than is the marginal utility to the consumer. The position of the margin in either case is determined by, as much as it determines, the level of the price.

Importance of the Time Element

Certain changes that occur over a long period of time render necessary a slight qualification of the theory of value as stated. In a short period, the technical equipment for production is usually limited, and producers can increase their output only by working their plant more intensively. Obviously there is a definite limit to the extra output that can thus be obtained. At any particular time the price tends to equal the highest cost of production. But, over a long period, conditions may undergo a considerable change. Producers may find it possible, if required, to extend their plant. Firms that were above the margin may increase their output in order to derive greater profits, and may desire, with the saving in unit production costs, to reduce the selling price. It is still true that, under the altered conditions, that price approximates to the greatest cost operating *at the time*, but the level of the margin is lower under the new than under the former conditions. Thus, although the price tends to approximate to the highest cost at any specified time, it tends to equal the lowest cost over a long period.

Further, the power of demand in determining value tends to be greater in the short than in the long period. In general, the supplies in a short period are relatively fixed, though they are alterable over a long period. The demand, however, may be variable, irrespective of the length of the period. Hence, in a short period, the buyers have a certain bargaining advantage over the sellers. Eventually, however, the producers are, as a rule, able to adjust their supplies to the requirements of the market, and thereby to improve their bargaining position.

It is possible, therefore, to generalize that the respective powers of demand and supply over price vary to some extent with the length of the period. *In a short period, demand tends to play a bigger part than supply in determining value. In a long period, supply tends to have a greater influence.*

Provisional Conclusions on the Marginal Theory

The labour and the cost of production theories were seen to be deficient mainly because they attempted to explain value from the side of supply alone. A theory which attempted to explain value from the demand side only would have to contend with at least as many difficulties. In the modern theory both supply and demand are considered. While due importance is attached to the cost of production, stress is also laid on the utility that the consumer derives.

It has been shown in the foregoing argument, first, that the principal factor in demand is utility, and that the exchange-power of a commodity tends to equal the marginal utility; secondly, that the chief factor in supply is the cost of production, and that the exchange-power of a commodity tends to equal the marginal cost.

Demand and supply tend to balance at a point at which the marginal utility is equal to the marginal cost of production, both as measured in terms of money. This point indicates the value. The shorter the period, the greater is the influence of conditions of demand; the longer the period, the greater is the influence of conditions of supply.

The marginal theory satisfactorily overcomes many of the difficulties that beset the earlier attempts to explain value, which were shown to attach too little importance to conditions of demand. Thus, the labour and the cost of production theories failed to account satisfactorily for the low value following a misdirection of resources, the true explanation resting mostly on the low utility afforded. They did not explain the high value attaching to commodities that were scarce, or the changes in value long after the time of production. Here, too, the reason is to be found mainly in the level of marginal utility. The marginal theory also disposes of the so-called "paradox of value," proving that there is really no paradox at all. The total utility of a commodity may be very high, but, if the supply is so abundant as to cause the utility of the marginal unit to be almost negligible, the value tends to be correspondingly low.

Limitations of the Marginal Theory

Though the marginal theory of value has proved more adequate than the preceding attempts at explanation, it has been subjected to criticism both on the score of incompleteness and on the ground of the method itself.

(i) There are certain factors helping to determine value that do not find a place in the theory as outlined so far.

(ii) To relate utility and cost, and to express them in common, usually monetary, terms over-simplifies the situation since utility is largely subjective in nature, while cost, as ordinarily stated, is largely objective.

(iii) Doubt is thrown on the capacity to analyse total utility and total costs into the very small units postulated by the theory and to measure and compare the respective marginal fractions.

(iv) Also the ease and rapidity are questioned with which consumers and producers are supposed to vary the quantities and substitute one unit for another.

In answer to such criticisms, however, it is pointed out that the marginal theory affords a *method of approach* rather than a complete statement of determining conditions. In the words of Marshall, who did more than anybody else to develop and apply the theory, it is at the margin that the forces governing value can best be studied. To state that the operation and interaction of forces can be most clearly observed at this point is not to imply that the marginal conditions are themselves the sole determinants of value. Regarded in this light the marginal theory commands wide, if not universal, acceptance.

CHAPTER VII

Section 1. *Competitive Price*

Markets

THE word "market" used to refer to a place or building where sellers and buyers congregated for the purpose of sale and purchase. The meaning, in principle, has remained the same, but has been extended to cover a set of conditions not necessarily confined to a particular place. The market for a commodity may be restricted in area or be world-wide; it may be of short duration or cover a long period.

Evolution of the Market. Four stages in the development of the market may be distinguished, and examples of each can still be found—

(i) *Localization of Markets*. Buyers and sellers would meet in an agreed place, where all the goods would be exhibited for sale.

(ii) *Dealing by Sample*. By this means the expense of transporting goods was reduced, the area of the market increased, and competition became more effective.

(iii) *Dealing by Grade*. This was a further development in the growth of the market. The different qualities were graded or standardized, with the result that a buyer need only quote the identifying mark of the grade required. Resort to samples became less necessary where grading was practicable.

(iv) *Specialization of Markets*. The modern market tends, for reasons of efficiency and convenience, to grow more specialized. While the old-type market sold almost everything, the market of to-day deals usually with one class of goods only.

Conditions of a Perfect Market

A perfect market requires the following conditions to be fulfilled—

(i) Wide and regular demand.

(ii) Easy and speedy means of communication between buyers and sellers throughout the market.

(iii) Free competition among sellers and among buyers.

(iv) Portability of article at low cost relative to bulk.

(v) Capacity of article to be uniformly described and graded.

Normal Price and Market Price

The **Normal Price** is the price that obtains through a long period, the pivot, as it were, about which the varying prices oscillate. Not necessarily the average of actual prices, it is the price which would result from the economic forces in a given period, if these forces were permitted to work out their full effects.

The **Market Price**, on the other hand, is the short-period price at which the amount offered for sale is equal to the amount demanded. Price variations are a common feature on the markets and, where the article is seasonal or perishable, the fluctuations are liable to be very pronounced.

If the market price is higher than the normal price, production tends to be increased until the price falls. If, on the contrary, the market price is below the normal price, production tends to be restricted until the price rises.

Normal price tends, under free competition, to equal the cost of production.[1] If the price is above the cost of

---

[1] See above, pp. 79–80, for the varying relationship between cost and price according to the length of the period.

production (including minimum profit) and competition is free, rivals will come into the market, increase the supply, and force the price down. Conversely, if the price falls below the cost of production, the supply will be restricted and the price will rise again.

Under perfectly competitive conditions there can be only one price for an article at a time. Although, as explained in the previous chapter, different units of a commodity may yield varying utilities or entail varying production costs, the fact that they are identical and interchangeable prevents any variation in their price so long as competition is effective. Ordinarily, as has been shown, competition is far from perfect, and normal price, therefore, fails to coincide with cost of production.

Nature of Demand and Supply

(i) **Distinguished from Desire and Stock.** "Demand" must be distinguished from "desire," which merely indicates a wish for something.

Economic demand postulates three conditions—

(*a*) Desire for a commodity;

(*b*) Means to purchase it; and

(*c*) Willingness to use those means.

Demand, therefore, may be described as *effective desire*.

In the same way, "supply" must be distinguished from "stock." Supply is the amount of the stock that is actually offered for sale. The more perishable a commodity, the closer is the identity between stock and supply.

Though desire and stock may be regarded without direct reference to price, *there is no such thing as demand and supply considered apart from the price prevailing at a particular time.*

(ii) **Elasticity of Demand and Supply.** The demand for anything is said to be *elastic* when a rise or fall in price causes an appreciable fall or rise in demand. It is said to be *inelastic* when movements in price have comparatively little effect on the demand. More precisely, elasticity of demand is less than unity when a change in price involves a less than proportionate change in demand, and more than unity when the change in demand is more than proportionate.

The elasticity of the **demand** for a commodity is influenced by—

(*a*) The degree of necessity. As a rule, the demand for necessaries of life is inelastic, and for luxuries elastic.

(*b*) The income of the consumer. A person with a small income naturally adjusts his purchases more closely to changes in prices than does a comparatively wealthy person.

(*c*) The proportion of a particular expenditure to income. Where the price of the article is small, a large increase may have less effect on the demand than where the price bears a considerable proportion to one's income.

(*d*) The presence of substitutes. The more readily a consumer can find alternative means of satisfying his wants, the more sensitive is his reaction to price changes.

(*e*) Influence of habit. A person is more likely to vary his orders for goods that have lately entered into his budget than for articles to which he has been for long accustomed.

(*f*) Durability of the commodity. Where an article is comparatively durable, an increase in price may induce a person to make longer use of it and so cut down his purchases.

Similarly, supply is said to be elastic when it varies appreciably with changes in price; inelastic when it is comparatively little affected.

As a general rule, an increase in the selling price of a commodity acts as a spur to producers to increase their output and for new producers to enter the field, while a fall in price exercises a restrictive effect. On the other hand, a fall in price is often accompanied by an increase in output, which may, in fact, be made possible only by the economies of providing for a wider market.

As it commonly takes some time for new stocks to be produced, the response of supply to price changes is not usually immediate, though over a long period it may be very elastic. Demand, on the contrary, may prove to be very elastic immediately following a change in the price.

Types and Combinations of Demand and Supply

(i) **Alternate Demand and Supply.** Demand is said to be alternate when a choice can be made between things that may substitute for each other. There is, for example, an alternate demand for butter and margarine, wool and cotton, electric and gas light, etc. A shortage in the one may cause a rise in price, but not so high as if there were no substitute. Thus, the price of the one will be influenced partly by the price of the other. The price of margarine may go up or down with the price of butter, independently of changes in its own cost of production.

Supply is said to be alternate when more than one class of goods can be produced in preference to each other from a single source. Thus, land can be used for growing either wheat or barley, whichever is the more profitable.

(ii) **Composite Demand and Supply.** Demand is said to be composite when a commodity is demanded for two or more different purposes (e.g. coal used in manufacture and the household).

Supply is said to be composite when a commodity can be produced from two or more quarters (e.g. different firms turning out boots; or a motor-car and a train supplying conveyance).

(iii) **Joint Demand and Supply.** The demands for two or more things used in conjunction with each other are said to be *joint* or *complementary*. Thus, there is a *joint demand* for pipes and tobacco. The ratio of one to the other may be variable, as in the above example, or fixed, as in steel knife-blades and ivory handles. Further, a thing may be demanded in more than one joint relation, and may also be required for its individual utility.

A demand for anything involves indirect demand for the factors that have gone to produce it. Thus, the demand for bread involves a *derived demand* for land, seed, labour, machinery, transport, etc.

Commodities are said to be in *joint supply* when they can be produced from a single source (e.g. mutton and wool; leather, beef, and milk). The ratio may be variable or fixed.

They are said to be in *multiple supply* when they come from a single firm, or alliance of firms, but have no common physical origin and can be produced in variable and independent quantities. Thus, a fountain-pen manufacturer may also be a purveyor of writing ink.

Influence on Price

These relationships are of great importance in the determination of prices. In the case of joint supply, for instance, while the price of the total product will obviously equal the sum of the prices of the constituent parts, the proportions of the latter to each other will depend partly on conditions of supply, and partly on those of demand. The producers of linseed and flax will aim at getting a gross return equal at least to the cost of the joint production. If the demand for one of the joint products is not sufficient to absorb the supply, the price may be lowered so as to increase the demand. Similarly, the price of the other product may be raised in order to restrict the demand. Where the goods are produced in a fixed ratio, it follows that their respective prices must be settled at that level at which they are demanded in the same proportion.

Market Price Determination

The interaction of demand and supply and the fixing of a market price at a point where there is equilibrium may be illustrated by simple schedules. Consider an article which might be priced at anything between 1s. and 5s. per lb., and assume a high elasticity of demand and supply.

Demand

If the price were 5s. per lb., 10 million lb. would be demanded

,,	,,	,,	4s.	,,	15	,,	,,	,,
,,	,,	,,	3s.	,,	20	,,	,,	,,
,,	,,	,,	2s.	,,	35	,,	,,	,,
,,	,,	,,	1s. 6d.	,,	50	,,	,,	,,
,,	,,	,,	1s.	,,	60	,,	,,	,,

The relationship between price and demand may be depicted graphically:

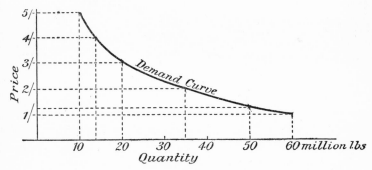

Regarding now the price from the producer's point of view, we see that the low price of 1s. per lb. would not result in much production. Only those firms whose

costs were very low could produce the article at that price
and make a profit.   If the price were raised, the supply
would be increased, partly because the first producers
would increase their output, and partly because the
number of producers would be increased.

Supply

If the price were 1s. per lb.,   5 million lb. would be supplied

  ,,   ,,   ,,   1s. 6d. ,,   20   ,,   ,,   ,,

  ,,   ,,   ,,   2s.   ,,   35   ,,   ,,   ,,

  ,,   ,,   ,,   3s.   ,,   45   ,,   ,,   ,,

  ,,   ,,   ,,   4s.   ,,   55   ,,   ,,   ,,

  ,,   ,,   ,,   5s.   ,,   65   ,,   ,,   ,,

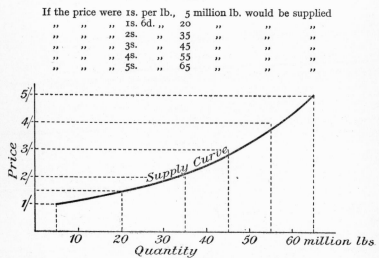

Balancing of Demand and Supply

Combining the tables of demand and supply, we have
the following schedule—

Demand.	Price.	Supply.
60 million lb.	1s.	5 million lb.
50 ,,	1s. 6d.	20 ,,
35 ,,	2s.	35 ,,
20 ,,	3s.	45 ,,
15 ,,	4s.	55 ,,
10 ,,	5s.	65 ,,

It is easy to see which will be the market price of the
article.   It cannot be 1s., for at that price there would be
60 million lb. demanded, but only 5 million lb. supplied.
Competition among buyers would force the price up.

On the other hand, it cannot be 5s., for at that price there would be 65 million lb. supplied, but only 10 million lb. demanded. Competition among sellers would force the price down. The price will approximate to that figure, viz. 2s., at which the demand and supply are of equal quantity.

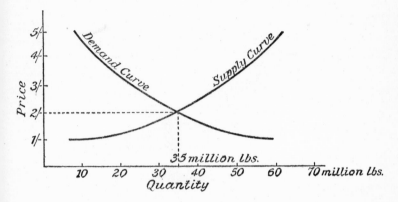

The Laws of Supply and Demand

We are now in a position to sum up the Laws of Supply and Demand.

(i) *If at a given price the demand for a commodity or service exceeds the supply, the price tends to rise. If the supply exceeds the demand, the price tends to fall.*

(ii) *A rise in price tends to restrict demand and increase supply. A fall in price tends to restrict supply and increase demand.*

(iii) *An increase in demand or restriction in supply tends to raise prices. A restriction in demand or increase in supply tends to reduce prices.* (See, however, qualification (*d*) below.)

(iv) *The price ultimately tends to the point at which supply and demand are balanced.*

To which should be added the general conclusion—

(v) *Demand and supply tend to balance at the point at which the marginal utility is equivalent to the marginal cost of production, both as measured in money.*

Qualifications of these Laws

(a) The above laws express tendencies only, and the implicit condition throughout is that all external conditions remain unchanged.

(b) The supply of some commodities is very inelastic or even fixed (e.g. land); in such circumstances, a rise in price cannot seriously affect the supply.

(c) The demand for some things is very inelastic and a rise in price may not have an appreciable effect on the demand. Indeed, in regard to bread, it has been found that a rise in price is often followed by an *increase* in the demand from poor families, who make up for the extra cost by economizing in other directions. They find that their reduced income will derive more utility from the purchase of more bread than of other things.

(d) With special reference to law (iii), the tendency there stated is true mainly for a short period. In the long period, everything depends on the nature of the returns. "The first effect of increased demand is to raise prices; the ultimate effect is to lower them." If the commodity is being produced under increasing returns (i.e. diminishing costs), an increase in demand will stimulate further production at a diminishing cost per unit, and thus bring about lower prices. A reduction in demand, however, will be followed by a smaller output at an increasing cost per unit, with a consequent rise in price. Where, on the other hand, the commodity is being produced under diminishing returns, extra production means increasing costs, with consequent higher prices, while less production results in smaller costs and lower prices.

Section 2. Monopoly Price

Theory of Monopoly Prices [1]

In a perfectly competitive market, price has been shown to be regulated by the marginal cost of production from the one side and by the marginal utility from the other. Undue profits made through selling considerably above cost of production would in the long run invite competitors to enter the field and bring the price down approximately to the cost of production.

Even where the seller enjoys monopoly powers, he cannot as a rule ignore the possibility of a revival of competition. He may owe his position to his efficient methods and low costs, with which no rivals can effectively compete. Or the goods that he sells may be subject to the potential competition of substitutes which are kept off the market only by the monopolist's low-price policy. Under such conditions he cannot raise his charges without incurring a grave risk of losing his hold over the market.

But if his monopoly is due to the exclusive ownership of natural supplies, or to some other conditions that make him fairly independent of competition, he is at liberty to charge any price above his cost of production that he chooses, leaving the amount demanded to be decided by the public. Or he can dispose of any reasonable supply that he wishes, leaving the price to be determined by the market. If he fixes the output, the price at which it sells will not be above the marginal demand price. If he fixes the price, the quantity of supply will be governed

---

[1] Monopoly prices are usually associated with monopolist producers, and are considered here in this sense. It is possible, however, to have a monopoly of buyers; e.g. people at an auction agreeing not to outbid each other, or a combination of producers acting in concert in obtaining raw materials which are required by no other manufacturers. But as the basic principles governing the determination of all monopoly prices are the same, it is not necessary here to enter specially into the subject of buyers' monopoly.

by the marginal purchaser. Thus, the power of the monopolist is further limited. *He may fix either price or output, but not both.*

The price (and also the profit) will be governed by the nature of the product and the demand, and, though to a smaller extent, by the nature of the returns in production.

(i) Where the article is a necessary and no efficient substitute is available, the demand will be relatively inelastic. This will enable the monopolist to raise the price appreciably without much falling-off in demand. Where, on the other hand, the article is not a necessary or can be replaced by a substitute, the demand will be fairly elastic. The monopolist may find that raising the price is accompanied by a serious fall in demand. He tends therefore to adjust it at such a level that the maximum net profit is obtained.

(ii) A reduction in price may increase demand and also net profit. But, apart from this possibility, a monopolist may find it profitable to reduce the price if he is producing under increasing returns (i.e. diminishing costs). Even if the demand were not stimulated in a corresponding degree, the loss from that quarter might be more than balanced by the economies of large production. If, on the contrary, the article is produced under diminishing returns (i.e. increasing costs), it will not pay a monopolist to reduce the price, unless the profit due to the additional turnover more than covers the extra unit costs of production.

Illustration of Monopoly Price Determination

An illustration of the way in which monopoly prices are determined is given in the table on page 95. It is assumed that the demand is elastic, and that the article is produced under increasing returns.

MONOPOLY PRICE DETERMINATION

Price	Number of Sales	Total Receipts	Cost per Unit	Total Cost	Receipts less Cost— Monopoly Profit
s.		£	s.	£	£
24	4,000	4,800	22	4,400	400
23	6,000	6,900	20	6,000	900
22	8,000	8,800	19	7,600	1,200
21	*10,000*	*10,500*	*17*	*8,500*	*2,000*
20	11,000	11,000	16½	9,075	1,925
19	12,000	11,400	16	9,600	1,800

The price of the article will tend to be 21s., for at that figure the largest profit (£2,000) is made.

Monopoly Price Discrimination

It is a common practice for monopolists to discriminate in their charges according to a variety of conditions—

(i) **According to area.** The monopolist may fix price zones within a country, especially where the transport costs are considerable. Or, while possessing a monopoly at home, he may have to face rivalry abroad, and thus charge lower prices to his foreign than to his own consumers. Or, even if he enjoys a monopoly abroad as well, he may find foreign customers less able or willing to pay the prices charged in the country of origin.

(ii) **According to time.** It is not uncommon for a monopolist to vary his charges from one time to another, according to changing circumstances. He may begin with low prices, and, having thereby assured himself of a market, raise them at a later date. Or he may start with a high price, and eventually diminish it in order fully to exploit the different markets at different prices.

(iii) **According to type of demand.** The monopolist may differentiate in his charges for the same commodity according to the nature of the demand or the capacity of the consumer. For example, an electricity concern or a railway company charges varying rates adjusted to "what the traffic will bear."

On the other hand, a monopolist may charge uniform rates for unequal services in a manner impracticable under competition. For example, the Post Office charges flat rates for carrying letters irrespective of distance. Similarly a local transport system may charge fixed amounts whether one travels a short or long distance.

PART III

DISTRIBUTION OF THE SOCIAL PRODUCT

CHAPTER VIII

THE NATIONAL INCOME

The Problem of Distribution

THE principles governing the distribution of the social product among the different classes of the community present some of the most controversial problems in economics.

In early times the problem of distribution was comparatively straightforward. When a commodity was produced with little or no resort to division of labour, a man could regard it as the specific result of his own efforts. Such raw materials and implements as were used might be his own, and therefore the question as to what were the respective shares going to land, capital, and labour did not arise to any serious extent.

When a small number of men assisted each other in building a hut and growing corn, the system of distribution of a collective product was emerging, but still in a relatively simple form. When, with the development of industrial organization, it took many men of different grades and a large quantity of capital and materials to produce a single commodity, the system became increasingly complex and controversial.

The study of distribution involves the consideration of many questions, of which the following three are the most important.

(i) How much is there to be distributed?

(ii) Among which people or factors is the income divided?

(iii) What decides the amount of the share to each group and to individuals within the group?

Value and Distribution

The last question touches the most fundamental problem of all. Stated another way, it asks what governs the value of each group's or individual's contribution to the social income. The theory of value, which was examined in the previous chapters, can be applied, with certain limitations, to the apportionment of income as well as to the pricing of goods.

The competition on the part of the different agents of production for use by the entrepreneur was noted in a previous chapter. It was seen that the factors tend to be employed in such proportions that the marginal returns from each are equal. Under perfect competition among these agents (though this is very seldom realized), a point is reached at which it becomes a matter of indifference whether "a little more or less" of one or other factor is employed. It will be shown in the following analysis of distribution that the product resulting from the various factors tends under free conditions to be distributed among them in a similar way, i.e. in proportion to their marginal contributions.

In the practice of distribution, however, certain factors may conspire to prevent the strict economic law from operating. In the determination of wages, for example, the rate may be influenced by custom, or by combination of workers or of employers; or its minimum may be fixed by some statutory body. Similarly, the fixing of the other forms of income is liable to be modified by "frictional" conditions. But, though the principles of value cannot be applied without qualification, a knowledge of them is an essential condition of a study of distribution as a whole.

" Functional " and " Personal " Distribution

A common method adopted in analysing the system of distribution is to take the factors of production in order, and observe the principles governing the share that goes to each. Land, labour, capital, and organization receive respectively rent, wages, interest, and profits. This method is a convenient one, and makes for simplicity. But it is not altogether satisfactory if over-simplified, since the danger then arises of paying too much attention to the *factors* and too little to the *persons* among whom the national product is distributed.

In this connection it may be observed that a person often receives an income from supplying more than one of the factors of production. A tradesman obtains a return from his labour and also from the capital invested in the various appliances that he possesses. If he owns the land on which his shop is built, he receives some return in the form of rent; while for his enterprise he gets a profit over and above the inclusive sum derived from the other three factors. In practice, he may not distinguish among the different sources of income, but if his business grows he may find it very necessary to do so.

Computation of the National Income

The National Income or Dividend was defined by Marshall as the "aggregate net product of, and the sole source of payment for, all the agents of production." Sir Josiah Stamp defines it as "the aggregate money expression of those goods produced and services performed by the inhabitants of the country in a year which are, as a fact, generally exchanged for money."[1]

The computation of the national income is beset with many difficulties. There is, to begin with, the danger of double counting. Some incomes, though they cannot be

[1] *Wealth and Taxable Capacity*, 1922.

overlooked in their individual aspect (e.g. for purposes of taxation), have also formed part of other incomes, and therefore should not be reckoned again. For example, if a man makes his widowed mother an allowance out of his earnings, it would be incorrect to include his gross income and that of his mother in the estimate of the total. But if the same man employs a domestic servant, both his income and that of the servant should be taken into account. In the first case there is merely a transference of income without any expansion in the national product. In the second case there is an addition to the total volume of production, and to ignore the value of the servant's work would give an understatement of the aggregate income.

Similarly, dividends from Government stocks should not be counted in the net national income unless they are drawn from foreign countries. These receipts are simply internal transferences from taxpayers in general to stockholders in particular. Of course, if the interest is the result of productive public undertakings, it should be included in the total estimate, in that it represents a net addition to the nation's income. Practically the whole of the dividends, however, paid on British Government stocks, comes not from productive investment of this kind, but from the taxpayer's pockets, and to include the amount in the total income would be to count the same sum twice over.

Such considerations help one to understand the manner in which statisticians arrive at their conclusions. Sir Josiah Stamp and Professor Bowley, for instance, calculated as follows.[1] They estimated the total income originating in the United Kingdom in 1924 to be £4,008 millions. They added to it £212 millions in respect of income from abroad, but deducted £56 millions representing

[1] *The National Income, 1924.*

home-produced income going abroad. The total gross income was stated, therefore, to be £4,164 millions. But the internal transferences on account of debt services alone came to £361 millions, and after deducting this amount from the aggregate, the figure of £3,803, representing the net social income, was obtained.

For the same year Mr. Colin Clark,[1] employing a similar definition of national income, computed the total to be £3,586 millions, or, on a wider definition, £3,977 millions. For subsequent years, on the latter basis, the same authority estimated the income as follows—

					£ millions
1927	.	.	.	.	. 4,287
1929	.	.	.	.	. 4,391
1931	.	.	.	.	. 3,890
1934	.	.	.	.	. 4,238
1935	.	.	.	.	. 4,530

Distribution of Income among Classes

Various estimates have been made at different times of the distribution of the total income among the different

THE NATIONAL INCOME

	1880			1913		
	Number of Incomes, 000's	Income		Number of Incomes, 000's	Income	
		Amount	% of Total		Amount	% of Total
		£ million			£ million	
Wages . . .	12,300	465	41½	15,200	770	35½
Intermediate income under £160[2] . . .	1,850	130	11½	4,310	365	17
Income assessed to tax over £160, excluding wage-earners . . .	620	530	47	1,190	1,030	47½
Totals . . .	14,770	1,125	100	20,700	2,165	100

[1] *National Income and Outlay*, 1937.

[2] I.e. the income tax exemption limit before the war. The "intermediate" class denotes non-wage-earners who were not liable to income tax. During the war the limit was lowered and about 4,000,000 wage-earners became liable to income tax.

classes. One of the best known is that of Prof. A. L. Bowley,[1] whose computation for the years 1880 and 1913 is summarized in the table on page 101.

His conclusions, briefly stated, were that—

"The proportion of the national income received as wages diminished [i.e. between 1880 and 1913] from about 41½ to 35½ per cent, but the receipts per wage-earner increased about 34 per cent.

"The proportion received by persons assessed to income tax increased slightly.

"The proportion received by the intermediate class increased at least . . . from 11½ per cent of the whole to 17 per cent in 1913.

"The average of all incomes was about £76 in 1880 and £104 in 1913, an increase of 37 per cent."[2]

Prof. Bowley also estimated that the distribution between property and labour was about the same in the two periods.

	1880	1913	Percentage in both instances
Incomes from property . .	£420 million	£810 million	37½%
Incomes from services of all kinds .	£705 ,,	£1,355 ,,	62½%
Total income .	£1,125 million	£2,165 million	100%

During and immediately following the war, the money income of the nation greatly increased (though it was, of course, offset by the enormous rise in prices). For 1918–19 Sir Josiah Stamp estimated the National Income to have been about £3,600 million to £3,700 million. For 1919-20, the same authority suggested £3,700 million to £4,100 million.

The ratio, however, in which the total income was apportioned among the different classes did not appear to have undergone any important change.

---

[1] *Change in Distribution of National Income, 1880–1913.*
[2] The purchasing powers of money in 1880 and 1913 respectively were near enough to afford a reasonable comparison.

"In 1914 some 8 per cent of the total income of the country belonged to a very small fraction, less than one-tenth of 1 per cent of the receivers of incomes. The next 22 per cent in amount went to 1 per cent of the number of incomes, and the next 15 per cent of amount of incomes to 4½ per cent of the people receiving incomes. This amounts to 45 per cent of the incomes going to about 5½ per cent of the people with separate incomes. Now the money levels of the incomes may alter, but these proportions have remained approximately constant."

In their later study (*The National Income, 1924*), Prof. Bowley and Sir Josiah Stamp submitted that, after the factor of taxation was allowed for, an appreciable addition had been made to the net share going to the wage-earners—

"The distribution of income between wage-earners, other earners and unearned income was changed slightly in favour of the earning classes. Manual workers on the average make slightly increased real earnings, and there have also been transfers for their benefit in insurance schemes and other public expenditure. In addition they have the advantage of a reduction of about one-tenth of the working-week. This change can be connected with the reduction in the real income derived from house property and investments bearing fixed rates of interest. The indications are that profits as a whole, reckoned before tax is paid, form nearly the same proportion to total income at the two dates. Within the wage-earning classes women and unskilled workers have received a substantial real advance in wages; the great majority of skilled workers made at least as much (after allowing for the rise of prices) in 1924 as in 1911. When the full effects of taxation are taken into account the real income available for saving or expenditure in the hands of the rich is definitely less than before the war."

Mr. Colin Clark draws a comparison between 1911 and 1929—

"For 1911 we have the numbers and incomes above £160, corresponding almost exactly, if the change in the cost of living is allowed for, to £250 at the present time; and the numbers and incomes of the then supertax limit of £5,000. . . . Since 1911 we have doubled the relative size of our middle class and have increased by half the number of our plutocrats. The shares of the national income which these two classes have taken have not increased. . . . Allowing for non-personal incomes, we can

say that both in 1911 and 1929 the same proportions prevailed—
that 10 per cent of the national income was taken by the very
rich, 35 per cent by the rich and middle classes, and 55 per cent
by the main mass of the population. Within the wealthier
classes the distribution of income has been somewhat more equal.
The working and lower-salaried classes do not enjoy a more
equal distribution in the sense of their having a greater share
of the national income. What they do now enjoy is a doubling
of their (still slender) chance of promotion to the ranks of the
middle classes: and the middle classes enjoy a greater chance of
promotion to all ranks of the very rich."

Inequalities of Incomes

The statistics of the distribution as a whole reveal
a considerable inequality. In 1929 (the year before the
great depression set in), those enjoying incomes of £1,000
or more a year amounted to $1\frac{1}{2}$ per cent of the income
receivers, taking over $22\frac{1}{2}$ per cent of the total income.
Those with incomes from £250 to £1,000 were less than
11 per cent, receiving nearly 20 per cent of the total.
The remainder of the population, $87\frac{1}{2}$ per cent, thus
received only $57\frac{1}{2}$ per cent of the national income. It
should be added, however, that these figures do not take
taxation and transfers by means of social services into
account.

Reasons for Inequality

The chief reason for the inequality of incomes in
general is the inequality in the ownership of capital and
land. This unequal division of property ownership tends
to perpetuate itself and become even more acute, in the
absence of corrective taxation, because of—

(a) the greater ease of saving out of large incomes,
and the consequent accumulation of greater amounts
of property;

(b) the system of inheritance, based on freedom of
bequest;

(c) the easier entry by the sons of the well-to-do into the higher-paid occupations and professions.

The reasons for inequality in the incomes from labour are indicated in the next chapter under the head of relative wages.

Redistribution and Welfare

It has often been stated that the present income of the country, however distributed, is insufficient for a general high standard of living, and that a pre-requisite condition of an improved standard for the people as a whole is an expansion of the total volume of production.

Without wishing to minimize the importance of an increased output, one may point out that the national welfare might be increased without *necessarily* adding to the volume of the national income. In the first place, in so far as redistribution meant the curtailment of very large incomes, there would be less money spent on luxuries and unproductive objects. Secondly, as was explained in Chapter VI, since a specific sum of money affords greater utility to a relatively poor man than it does to a rich man, the former would gain more satisfaction by the receipt of that sum than the latter would lose by its surrender. Thus, a more equitable distribution of the product would by itself increase the national welfare.

On the other hand, it may be contended that, while a redistribution might increase the total satisfaction at the time, the supply of capital might be curtailed in consequence of a diminished reward, while the quality of enterprise might be diminished. Hence, the total volume of production might suffer, and incomes of all kinds shrink in consequence.

The emphasis placed upon personal and voluntary saving, however, is not nowadays so great as it used to be. In this country a growing proportion of the supply of new capital comes from the reserves of the public companies. In Russia, where a different economic order obtains, much of the saving is effected by the State, which appropriates the sums required for capital purposes before individual distribution takes place.

Such circumstances have to be borne in mind in estimating the effects of income redistribution on economic welfare. The question will be considered more fully in the following chapters, and again in the section on taxation and public expenditure.

CHAPTER IX

Section 1. The Payment of Wages

THE problem of wages may be considered under the following heads—

(i) The share of the national dividend that goes to labour. This involves the study of *general wages*.

(ii) The variation in wages in different occupations, and also in different countries. This involves the study of *relative wages*.

(iii) The methods of remuneration.

(iv) Labour organizations and their effects on wages.

Nominal and Real Earnings

Nominal Income represents one's revenue in terms of money. But this, without reference to the level of prices, affords no criterion of the real worth of the income, whether in the form of wages or anything else.

Real Income is the purchasing-power of the money income. It is dependent on the prevailing level of prices, which may vary from time to time, or at the same time from place to place.

Real Earnings depend on—

(*a*) Variations in the level of prices.

(*b*) Payment in kind (e.g. the agricultural labourer's cottage and certain amount of food, the miner's cheap coal, the civil servant's pension, etc.).

(*c*) Length of working day and holidays.

(*d*) Extent of additional earnings in spare time.

(*e*) Additions to income by members of family.

(*f*) Character of work and effect on duration of working capacity (e.g. leadworking, metal-grinding, service in tropical countries, all of which, through periods of sickness or impossibility to continue after middle life, reduce the net earnings).

(*g*) Regularity of employment. Some trades are seasonal (e.g. agriculture, building, etc.) ; others are irregular (e.g. fishing, etc.). The real wage depends on the total earnings over a period.

(*h*) Scope for promotion. A man may be willing to work for a low wage for a time provided there is reasonable opportunity of advancement later.

(*i*) Pleasantness of and social prestige attached to the work. Some occupations carry a social position of which account is taken in reckoning the net gains of employment.

Nominal and Real Labour Cost

In the same way as the worker has to distinguish between his nominal and real income, so the employer, from his point of view, distinguishes between the *wages* and the *labour cost*. The two are by no means identical. The former indicates the sum paid out, the latter means the actual worth to the employer.

Wages may be high, yet the labour cost low. This is another way of expressing the view that "Low wages are dear wages." It has been proved abundantly that a wage which is below the "poverty line"[1] adversely affects the quality of the work done, and that the cost per unit is high in consequence. An increase in wages up to a point is accompanied by an added efficiency, perhaps

[1] Poverty has been defined as "primary" where the income is insufficient to provide the minimum necessaries of life; as "secondary" where the amount may be sufficient, but for various reasons is not spent to the best advantage—e.g. money spent on alcoholic drink at the expense of food and clothing.

more than sufficient to compensate for the increase in
the wage bill.

There is, however, an optimum point beyond which an
increase in wages does not add a commensurate amount
to the product, and may, in fact (if the worker decides
to "buy more leisure"), lead to a reduction in output.
In such circumstances the case for a further increase in
wages has to rest on different grounds.

Hours, Wages, and Machinery

The same principle applies to the number of hours that
a man works. If the working day is so long that the
efficiency of the man is impaired, it may be found that
a shorter working day is accompanied by such an increase
in his efficiency that as much work is done as hitherto,
if not more. The reduction in the working day, unaccompanied by a reduction in output, can take place, of course,
only up to a certain stage, beyond which the output
per man must necessarily decline, unless other improvements in organization and technique are adopted.

But there is another factor to be considered, namely,
the relationship to machinery. The introduction of new
machinery often means scrapping the old long before the
latter is worn out. To make full use of machinery an
extension of the shift system is commonly urged. Proposals for a seven- or six-hour day are not confined to
working-class advocates. Some employers contend that
if a system could be devised so that the machinery could
be used for (say) eighteen hours a day, entailing three
shifts of six hours each, the extra return from the fuller
use of the machinery, and the spreading of the standing
charges over a larger gross output, would be at least
sufficient to allow for the reduction in output (if any)
per man and pay the same wages for the shorter as for
the longer working day. Against such proposals, however,

is the greater expense, as a rule, of employing men at night (e.g. heavier lighting and heating bills), and the liability for the personal efficiency of the workers to be at a lower level.

Wages and the Proportion of Machinery to Labour. A further point must be noted in connection with machinery and wages. Where the capital expenditure on plant and tools is large compared with the sum spent on wages, an increase in the latter does not involve such a great addition to total costs as where the proportion of machinery to labour is small. Consequently, employers whose establishment charges are high feel an increase in the wage bill less severely than those whose establishment costs relative to the wage bill are low.[1]

Peculiarities of Labour Supply

Though labour is not a commodity, in the popular sense, it is virtually bought and sold in the market in the ordinary way. Certain peculiarities, however, have to be noted—

(i) A man's labour is part of himself, and therefore, different from material commodities, cannot be delivered except in person. The labourer, moreover, is concerned with the conditions in which his labour is utilized as well as with the actual price.

(ii) Labour withheld means, as a rule, so much labour power lost to the community. It cannot be kept back like goods to await a better market. Labour may thus be likened to a very perishable commodity.

(iii) In the absence of an effective trade union, a labourer is usually at a disadvantage in bargaining with an employer. His staying-power is comparatively weak, whereas the employer is equal in bargaining power to all the workers in his pay. One of the principal functions

[1] For the influence of machinery on employment, see pp. 131–3.

of trade unions is to substitute collective for individual bargaining and so remedy this disadvantage.

(iv) An increase in wages does not necessarily induce a worker to give more labour. Indeed it may induce him to work less hard than before.

(v) For reasons previously considered, the growth of new supplies of labour in general is very slow. Similarly, if supplies become redundant, they cannot be quickly reduced.

Methods of Remuneration : Time and Piece Earnings

Wages are paid in a variety of ways, but the principal methods are by Time or Piece, or a combination of both. In the calculation of one type of rate, however, it is essential to make reference to the other.

The following summary represents the main arguments adduced in favour of and against time and piece rates respectively. To a great extent, the advantages of the one correspond to the disadvantages of the other.

(i) Time Earnings

ADVANTAGES. Time earnings are said to be preferable—

(*a*) Where the work is not standardized and is difficult to measure (e.g. repair work).

(*b*) Where the work needs great care and minute attention.

(*c*) Where delicate and expensive machinery is used. In both (*b*) and (*c*) piece rates, if they led to "scamping" of the work, might cause serious loss.

(*d*) Where intervals of temporary idleness are inevitable (e.g. outdoor work dependent on weather conditions).

(*e*) In that the worker has a more regular income.

(*f*) In that, where the time rate takes the form of a salary, sickness does not necessarily mean loss of income.

DRAWBACKS. The critics of the system contend that—

(*a*) In the absence of safeguards, work may become slack.

(*b*) There is no inducement to full effort if the best and worst workers in one grade receive the same remuneration.

(*c*) It is difficult, therefore, to select the superior men for higher-class work.

(ii) Piece Earnings

ADVANTAGES. It is maintained by the supporters of this method that payment by results—

(*a*) Adds an incentive to work and therefore increases output.

(*b*) Remunerates the worker for extra effort.

(*c*) Distinguishes the superior workers.

DRAWBACKS. It is pointed out that—

(*a*) The worker who produces the largest quantity is not necessarily the most efficient. (See Advantages (*b*) and (*c*) of Time Earnings.)

(*b*) Piece rates cannot be satisfactorily applied to all kinds of work.

(*c*) Jealousy may be fostered between workpeople.

(*d*) Standard time rates are undermined.

(*e*) The worker's income is more irregular, which makes for instability of the family budget.

(*f*) Undue speeding-up and intensive labour adversely affect the worker's health.

On the whole, it may be concluded—

1. That where the product and methods are standardized, piece rates have certain advantages and do not as a rule encounter serious opposition from the side of labour.

2. That where the product and methods are not standardized, and a given effort cannot be depended upon to yield a given output, time rates are to be preferred, unless a system of payment by results is contrived, whereby the wage is assessed collectively for a large group of workers, and shared out in such a way that variations in the tasks are levelled out.

Other Methods of Remuneration

Several schemes have been devised to improve the system of remuneration, so as to combine the advantages of both time and piece rates and minimize their drawbacks. The following are the chief methods that have been put into operation, with varying success.

(i) **Premium Bonus Systems.** These are of several kinds, but the general principle is to fix upon an agreed standard output with a guaranteed minimum (subject to certain conditions), and to pay a premium, reckoned on a piece basis, for output over that amount. The bonus may be calculated individually or collectively.

(ii) **Efficiency Systems of Payment.** These are linked up with **Scientific Management,** which involves a detailed study of the work to be done, involving both *time-study* and *motion-study.* By the former method, a job that has to be priced is given to a "good average man, not a specially skilled workman, but one well above the ordinary run of the shop," or to a number of such men. The average time taken forms the basis of the *efficiency rate,* which, like the premium bonus systems, allows a percentage for all output over the agreed standard. The method of motion-study aims at regulating the motions and minute operations of the worker in such a way that the work is done in the minimum time and with the minimum number of motions.

Scientific management and its attendant systems of remuneration have encountered opposition from many workers. They object to the time-study method on the ground that the "good average man" may be well above the average, and that an unscrupulous employer or fore-man may thereby speed up the production beyond a reasonable degree. They object to the motion-study method in that it takes away a man's individuality and tends to reduce him to a mere automaton.

(iii) **Sliding Scales According to Price of Product.** The payment depends partly on the output and the price of the finished product, though usually (in present arrange-ments) there is a minimum below which the wage cannot fall. The system is not prevalent; it was formerly prac-tised in the coal industry, and still exists in some of the iron and steel trades. An inherent defect in such schemes is that the wage may fluctuate, though the efforts of the workers may not vary. High prices do not necessarily make for high profits and wages; and *vice versa*. Faults in management may to a certain extent be compensated by a reduced wage-bill. On the other hand, the worker stands to gain when the product fetches a good price. But uncertainty of income is disadvantageous at all times to the wage-earner, more so than to the employer and interest receiver, who are usually assured of the necessaries of life, whatever the fluctuations in their incomes.

(iv) **Sliding Scales According to Cost of Living.** The system of adjusting wages to variations in the official cost of living index number,[1] published by the Ministry of Labour (as distinct from the wholesale prices index num-

[1] See below, pp. 194-6, for the calculation of index numbers.

ber, issued by the Board of Trade), became very common during the war and post-war years. It had the advantage of affording a fairly definite basis, and of ensuring to the workers coming within the scheme a reasonably constant standard of living.

During the years when prices were very unstable and liable to fluctuate over a wide range, the system proved attractive, but latterly the defects have been becoming more apparent.

(a) Index numbers that are calculated by reference to so-called typical family budgets are unlikely to reflect with any accuracy changes in the cost of living of those families or individuals who depart from the average.

(b) The system is liable to be too rigid and to fix the wages of different grades of workers on too stereotyped lines. There is no satisfactory reason why the relative rates at the time when the system was introduced should continue indefinitely to fix the respective remunerations in different occupations. Adaptation to changing economic conditions and wage-paying capacities is in the long run inevitable, but the process of adjustment is not free from difficulty.

(v) **Profit-sharing and Co-partnership.** Profit-sharing and co-partnership schemes have been devised by certain employers for the purpose of improving the conditions and reward of employment, and thus of diminishing industrial discontent.

Profit-sharing takes the form of an arrangement between an employer and the workpeople under which the latter receive, in addition to their wages, a proportion *fixed in advance* of the profits of the undertaking. It thus excludes premium bonus arrangements, gratuities, and the like.

Co-partnership is an extension of profit-sharing schemes. As a rule, the worker is enabled to accumulate his bonuses and exchange them for shares in the employing company, though there are some systems which allow the workers to obtain shares without any preliminary distribution of a profit-sharing bonus. In a few instances, provision is made for representation of the workers on the board of directors, but the proportion so far has been only nominal.

Though a number of profit-sharing and co-partnership schemes have enjoyed a certain success, the majority have had to be abandoned. Profit-sharing and co-partnership schemes have not, as a rule, found favour with trade union leaders, who commonly aver that participation in the profits of a concern, even if it does not tend to reduce the wage bill and so nullify any financial advantage, may undermine the loyalty of the workers to their own organization, and in the end be against their true interests. This attitude of organized labour has doubtless been partly responsible for the very limited success of the systems so far put into operation.

Minimum Wage Legislation

In a number of industries trade unions have been either non-existent or too weak to negotiate satisfactory wages rates for their members. In consequence the State has intervened and passed protective legislation.

The Trade Boards Act, 1909, was the first legislation in this country for the establishment of a minimum wage. Trade Boards, equally representative of the workers and employers in a particular trade, together with a number of State nominees, were empowered to inquire into the conditions of remuneration and to fix minimum rates that would have the force of law. Boards were immediately set up for four "sweated" trades, viz., chainmaking, ready-made tailoring, paper-boxmaking, and lace-finishing, and in 1913, four other industries, viz., sugar confectionery and fruit preserving, shirt-making, hollow-ware making, linen and cotton embroidery, were brought within the terms of the Act.

The Trade Boards Act, 1918, which was wider in scope, was applied to several more trades, not as underpaid and unorganized as those first catered for. The new rates permitted a higher standard of life than provided for by the early Trade Boards. Within three years wages boards under the Act were set up in thirty-five trades, employing approximately 1,500,000 workers. Unfortunately, the period of falling prices and profits made it difficult in some cases to pay the stipulated minima, and led to an outcry from certain quarters for the abolition of the Trade Boards.

A Government Committee, appointed in 1921 to inquire into the subject, drew a clear line between the functions of Trade Boards in respect of (*a*) fixing minimum rates of wages; and (*b*) regulating wages in general. It virtually recommended that a return be made to the principle of the 1909 Act, i.e. to provide minimum rates for the "sweated" and unorganized trades only.

In a White Paper (July, 1922), the Minister of Labour stated that no Trade Boards would be set up in the future unless the Ministry were satisfied that the rate of wages prevailing in the trade was unduly low, and that no adequate machinery existed for the effective regulation of wages.

Events since then, however, have made it unlikely that any serious modification will be made in the Trade Board system, and in the last few years extensions of the system have, in fact, been made.

The Agricultural Wages Act, 1924, provided for the establishment of a National Agricultural Wages Board and for County Agricultural Wages Committees. The peculiar difficulties of the agricultural industry, however, have compelled the minimum rates to be much below those paid in the towns.

Section 2. *Theories of Wages*

The Subsistence Theory

It is helpful, before considering the modern theory of wages, to note in outline some of the earlier attempts at explanation. The Subsistence Theory, also known as the Iron Law of Wages, is usually associated with Lassalle, the German Socialist. But it had been formulated in slightly different form by the Physiocrats as early as the eighteenth century.[1]

In its earliest form, the theory stated that if the workers received more than a bare living, population would increase in consequence, competition for employment would become keener, and the wage would be dragged down again to the bare subsistence level. Alternatively, a fall below the subsistence level would cause a reduction in population and eventually lead to a rise in the wage. The theory appeared to fit in with the cost of production doctrine of value believed in by the Classical School of economists, subsistence being regarded in effect as the cost of producing labour.

Lassalle and his school, about the middle of the nineteenth century, adapted the subsistence theory, contending that, under a capitalist system, the employers and the landowners appropriated the whole of the social product in excess of the minimum amount necessary to keep the workers alive.

The appalling conditions in France and Britain during the eighteenth and early nineteenth centuries seemed to bear out the doctrine. Even to-day it would appear under some conditions to contain more than an element of truth. In some parts of the world (e.g. Egypt and India)

[1] See Appendix, pp. 316-7.

the position of the mass of the people has not been measurably improved despite the increase in the total wealth.

Criticism of Subsistence Theory

(i) The theory rests on the false premise that an increase in wages necessarily leads to an increase in the population; this is contrary to fact.

(ii) Real wages have generally advanced during the past hundred years or so, and the consumption of comparative comforts and luxuries by the manual working classes has steadily increased.

(iii) It does not explain the inequality of wages in different trades and countries.

(iv) It is disproved by the influence of trade unions.

(v) Like the cost of production theory of value it attempts an explanation mainly from the side of supply with insufficient reference to conditions of demand.

The Wages Fund Theory

The Wages Fund Theory succeeded the previous doctrine, and is usually associated with J. S. Mill, who stated:

(1) "That industry is limited by capital, but does not always come up to that limit, while the increase of capital gives increased employment to labour without assignable bounds." (*Principles of Political Economy*, Book I, Chap. V, Sects. 1, 2, 3.)

(2) "It is not, however, all capital, i.e. all wealth saved and appropriated to reproductive employment, which constitutes the wages fund of a country, but that part only which is circulating as distinct from fixed, i.e. that part only which is destined for the purchase of labour." (Book II, Chap. XI, Sect. 1.)

(3) This being so, "wages depend mainly upon the supply and demand of labour; or as it is often expressed, on the proportion between population and capital. With these limitations of the terms, wages not only depend on the relative amount of capital and labour, but cannot, under the rule of competition, be affected by anything else. Wages, meaning of course the general rate, cannot rise but by an increase of the aggregate funds employed in hiring labourers, or a diminution in the number of competitors for hire; nor fall, except either by a diminution of the funds

devoted to paying labour, or by an increase in the number of labourers to be paid." (Book II, Chap. XI, Sect. 1.)

In short, it was contended that at any time there is a fixed amount of capital to be devoted to labour; this is the Wages Fund, and represents the *demand*. There is also at any time a fixed number of labourers who must work whatever the rate of wages; this is the *supply* of labour. The fund is distributed among the labourers under the rule of competition. As in the subsistence theory, it was held that any rise in general wages would increase the population, leading ultimately to a fall in wages.

According to this theory, wages in one industry can rise only, in the main, at the expense of wages in another industry. Should wages in one trade be unusually high, there would be an inflow of labour from other trades, resulting in a contraction of the rates. Should *all* wages rise for a time, the gain would be at the expense of profits, capital would be driven out, the demand for labour would therefore be reduced, and wages would inevitably fall again.

The wages fund doctrine was widely held in the middle of the nineteenth century, and was frequently employed as an argument against trade unionists and others who were pressing for improvements in the remuneration of labour, whether of particular sections or as a whole.

Mill later qualified his theory, and eventually had to renounce it.

Criticism of Wages Fund Theory

(i) Wages may be increased sometimes without a reduction in profits. The theory confuses the nominal and the real cost of labour, and does not consider the possibility of increased efficiency resulting from higher remuneration, and therefore of an increase in the social dividend.

(ii) A fall in profits does not immediately drive capital out of an industry. Capital is not so sensitive and profits are by no means inelastic.

(iii) Wages may be high in one trade and low in another, yet the immobility of labour be strong enough to prevent a flow from the better to the worse paid trade. The theory credits the workers with greater adaptability and fuller knowledge of the labour market than they possess.

(iv) It does not explain inequality of wages in different trades.

(v) It is disproved by facts. Wages are often high in new countries where the amount of capital is small and population is increasing. In times of good trade, wages and profits both increase—obviously the result of a greater productivity, for which no allowance was made in the wages fund theory.

Productivity Theories

According to the Productivity Theories, wages are paid not out of a fixed fund, but rather from a "continuous stream," the volume of which is variable within wide limits. Stress is laid on increased efficiency and output, the wage being proportionate to the worker's productivity. These theories are therefore not so pessimistic as those which held that a rise in one man's wage must ultimately be at the expense of another worker.

An early stage in the development of the productivity doctrine was the Residual Claimant Theory, according to which the worker was regarded as the final claimant on the net product. To quote Jevons, "The wages of a working man are ultimately coincident with what he produces, after the deductions of rent, taxes, and the interest on capital." If this were true, extra efficiency on the part of the workers would result in their getting a greater share of the total product, which, however, is not in accord with experience. Also, the other forms of income are by no means so fixed or pre-determined as the theory suggested. As the same notion of a residual claim has been applied, too, to the other agents of production, the explanation cannot be considered satisfactory.

Higher and Lower Limits to Wages

The supply of labour is practically fixed within a short period, and, as "labour will not keep," it must be offered for sale. The *minimum* price for labour that can be accepted, however, is the cost of subsistence. In this case, therefore, the theory of value as applied to wages must be qualified. When the supply of water is practically unlimited, the price falls almost to nil; but if the potential supply of labour were unlimited, it would be clearly impossible to pay wages over a period below the subsistence level.

From the point of view of the demand for labour, it is obvious that the *maximum* that will be paid in wages is determined by the worker's contribution to the product. It is maintained in the productivity theories that there is a *specific product* attributable to labour, capital and land, and that each tends, under free competition, to receive a reward corresponding to its own addition to the product.

The *Principle of Substitution* is very important in this connection. The entrepreneur aims at employing the various factors in just those proportions that will render the maximum productivity. If the wage demanded is higher than the value of the specific product of labour, the result must be either dismissal of some workers or (unless effective substitution of machinery or improvement in organization is possible) stoppage of production.

Wage rates nowadays are settled in an increasing number of industries by negotiations between trade unions and employers' associations, and are fixed over a large field as well by Trade Boards and other statutory authorities. Thus the free competition postulated by the theory in its crude form does not exist (if ever it did in labour remuneration) to any material extent.

For the present, it may be stated that **wages may vary between the minimum set by the cost of subsistence and the maximum set by the productivity of the worker, according to the bargaining strength of the workers and employers respectively.**

The Marginal Productivity Theory of Wages

The Marginal Productivity Theory is an application of the general marginal theory of value previously outlined. A similar line of argument is followed. Suppose an employer to be taking on men for a particular grade of work. After a certain point, owing to diminishing returns or to a fall in the selling price of the product consequent on an increased supply, or to both, a stage is reached when the last man taken on yields no more than the wage paid; i.e. it will not pay the employer to take on any more men. But, as the men are by hypothesis identical and could be interchanged without any variation in the quantity or quality of the product, the employer will not pay a rate of wages higher than that measured by the output of the marginal man, or rather (for reasons explained in the discussion on value) by the value of the marginal product.

Where machinery or other capital instruments can be employed, with some alteration in the number of workers, the employer is constantly comparing the specific productivity of units of labour and capital. He tries to estimate the quantity of additional product due to taking on an extra man or utilizing an extra unit of capital. If competition is effective, the marginal productivities of both agents will tend to equality.

The marginal supply price of labour is not so easy to define, because of the peculiarities, already noted, governing the supply of labour. Earnings cannot over a period fall below subsistence level, and if an employer, or an industry as a whole, cannot afford to pay wages even at this low level, production, in the absence of any subsidy, must stop. Also the supply of labour does not, like that of ordinary commodities, vary appreciably with the price obtained. If wages fall, the supply of labour does not necessarily diminish. If they rise, the supply cannot be quickly increased. Indeed, as we have already observed, an increase in wages may lead to a reduction in hours or intensity of effort, and thus bring about a fall rather than a rise in labour supply.

Subject to such qualifications, it may be stated that, in accordance with the general theory, the wage tends to be determined at the point at which the marginal conditions of demand and supply are in equilibrium.

" Wages are the Discounted Marginal Product of Labour." A refinement of the marginal productivity theory is the application of the conception of a discount. Production takes time, and workmen have not the means to wait until their product is marketed and paid for. Employers advance these means during the period of production, but naturally have to take the loss of interest into account in computing their wage-paying capacity. Hence the actual wage is said to be equal to the value of the marginal product *less* the interest on the wage from the time it is paid to the time when the employer receives payment for the goods produced.

Limitations of the Marginal Theory of Wages

While the marginal productivity theory approximates to the truth more closely than the earlier theories, certain qualifications have to be made—

(i) The theory assumes a system of free competition and mobility not to be found in everyday life. It is not the case that if an employer can pay more, he will always

be driven by competition to do so. Similarly, a worker
may be receiving more than he would be prepared to
accept under less favourable conditions. "Economic friction" may be too strong to permit of an immediate adjustment, though in the long run the tendency is more evident.

(ii) "Productivity" is liable to be used in a double
sense. An addition to the quantity of goods produced
may entail a reduction in their value. Workers are, of
course, remunerated out of the proceeds of production
as determined by market conditions, and an increase,
therefore, in their efficiency and output need not denote
a proportionate increase in the wage-paying ability of
employers. Also, there is apt to be a certain confusion
between productivity and service to the community. As
Professor Henry Clay has remarked—

"This distinction is often forgotten, and the productivity theory
of distribution comes to be used (unconsciously perhaps) as a
justification of the present unequal distribution of the national
income. Each, it seems to show, gets what he produces; what
could be fairer? It is forgotten that the market value by which
this productivity is measured bears no constant relation to social
service. The theory is true (if at all) only if we give 'productivity' its second meaning, 'productivity of value'; the theory
justifies the present distribution (if at all) only if it has the first
meaning, 'output.' In the only sense of the word 'productivity' in which the productivity theory of distribution is true,
the man who receives £3 per week for looking after Pekingese
puppies for an American countess is four times as productive
as the Oxfordshire farm-labourer receiving 15s. a week; the services of the two to society do not bear the same relation."[1]

The exponents of the marginal productivity theory
of wages, however, do not claim that it offers a complete
explanation of wages determination. In Marshall's
words, "the doctrine that the earnings of a worker tend
to be equal to the net product has by itself no real meaning, since, in order to estimate net product, we have to
take for granted all the expenses of production of the

[1] *Economics for the General Reader*, pp. 319–320.

commodity on which he works, other than his own wages."
But the same authority emphasizes that "one has to
go to the margin to study the action of those forces which
govern the value of the whole"; and that the marginal
productivity theory "throws into clear light the action
of one of the causes that govern wages."

Though the doctrine is thus incomplete, it affords useful
indications of the influences on wages. A rise in efficiency
means an increase in the marginal worth and therefore
makes possible a rise in the wage. One industry pays a
higher wage than another because the marginal productivity is higher (i.e. in terms of market value). For the
same reason, one country may pay a higher *real* wage
than another. Further, an increase in wages may result
from improvements in the organizing ability of the
entrepreneur, and also from inventions and discoveries
of new resources.

Relative Wages

Variations in wages from one trade to another are only
partially explained by the general theory. The workers
in different trades may form *non-competing groups*,
between which there is imperfect mobility, and in consequence there may be a wide disparity in earnings.

In so far as wages vary from person to person because
of differences in personal skill, or from group to group
because of differences in productivity, there is no need
to modify the application of the general theory. There
are, however, several particular causes of variations.

(i) *Conditions of supply*. Where labour supplies are
comparatively plentiful (e.g. in the semi-skilled trades),
wages tend to be low.

(ii) *Ignorance and inertia*. For either of these reasons
labour may fail to move from badly to better-paid
employment.

(iii) *Cost of learning a trade.* The initial costs of training serve to limit entrance to certain occupations, and to keep wages in them disproportionately high.

(iv) *Attractiveness of occupation.* Trades that involve disagreeable or dangerous work frequently pay higher wages as a kind of compensation, though this is far from being a general rule. Frequently the pleasantest occupations are the best paid.

(v) *Bargaining strength.* In those trades in which trade unionism is efficient the rate of payment is usually higher than in those occupations in which the workers' bargaining power is not so good.

(vi) *Protection from foreign competition.* Workers in "sheltered" industries, such as the transport and public services, are not so subject to foreign competition as workers in such industries as mining and engineering, and wages in them are sometimes higher in consequence. But depression in one group of industries is almost bound to react ultimately on conditions of wages and employment in another, for most trades are inter-related and rest on a common basis.

(vii) *Custom and tradition.* The remuneration in certain occupations is determined partly by customary conditions, though with the spread of knowledge, the greater mobility of labour, and the growth of trade unionism, these factors are less powerful than formerly.

Net Advantages

It should be evident from these considerations that, even if competition were free and mobility perfect, money wages, though they would draw nearer to equality, would not reach a uniform level. The equalizing tendency of competition would be in the direction not of money wages but of *net advantages*.

Women's Wages

The question of women's wages as compared with men's is really part of the larger problem of relative wages, but, in view of some special problems involved, it may be separately examined.

The principal reasons for the relatively low wages of women workers in many (though by no means all) industries are the following—

(i) *Smaller physical needs*. The actual requirements in the way of foodstuffs may be less on the average for women than for men, but the cost of subsistence ought not to be expressed entirely in terms of food. On clothing the expenditure of women workers tends to be larger.

(ii) *Fewer dependants*. Men workers, in general, have more dependants to support, and therefore tend to conceive of a higher minimum than women workers. But, as previously stated, it is productivity rather than needs, whether of oneself or of one's dependants, to which wages in the existing economic system tend to conform.

(iii) *Inferior bargaining strength*. Women are, as a rule, more difficult to organize in trade unions than men are, and their bargaining power is thus on the average much weaker. Where the women are well organized, such as in the textile trades, the disparity between men's wages and theirs is not so pronounced, particularly where the men's unions take the view that low rates for women workers are liable to exercise a depressing influence on men's wages.

(iv) *"Meantime" character of occupation*. The reason for the weaker organization of women workers lies partly in the short view that they take of their industrial employment. Marriage ordinarily means the cessation of such employment for women, whereas for men it results, if anything, in greater application to work.

(v) *Inferior training*. The "meantime" nature of most

women's employment naturally affects the extent to which, either of their own volition or through the action of their parents, they enter upon a course of industrial training, and thus qualify for the better-paid work.

(vi) *Greater immobility.* Women are, on the average, less easily induced than men to move to another part of the country or, where opportunity offers, to change their employment. Hence, women's wage rates may show a wide disparity from one locality or trade to another without causing a flow of labour to the better-paid employment.

(vii) *Subsidy to earnings.* Many women in industry are subsidized from home in one form or another, and their insistence on the best possible rates is accordingly weakened. While the influence of the "pocket-money" worker is apt to be exaggerated, its presence in certain "light" occupations cannot be ignored.

(viii) *Weaker physical strength.* This factor, too, tends to be magnified, especially in recent times during which there has been a marked improvement in women's physique. Some of the more arduous occupations, however, are still closed to women, and this, together with other restrictions, tends to limit the field of women's employment. Large numbers thus tend to be concentrated in few occupations, and the competition for work helps to bring the wages rates down.

(ix) *Greater expenses of employment.* Partly because of the greater liability of women to sickness, and partly because of the heavier expense in which he is involved in complying with factory and other regulations concerning women workers, the employer is reluctant to pay them at the same rate as he pays the men. On the other hand, expenditure on "welfare" facilities commonly adds to the efficiency of the workers, and the fact that many employers incur expenditure of this kind far in excess of the legal requirements points to the limitations of the above argument.

(x) *Lower productivity and smaller demand.* Taking all these factors into account, it may be concluded that the net worth of women workers to the employer tends as a rule to be less than that of men workers, and the demand for women is smaller in consequence. There are admittedly certain trades in which women are no less efficient, and may in fact be more efficient, than men, but, over industry as a whole, the demand for women workers is definitely smaller, and their remuneration is lower in consequence.

Section 3. *Labour and Wages Problems*

Unemployment : General Causes

The unemployment problem can be dealt with here only in its purely industrial aspects. Unemployment, which affects resources as well, is wider than a labour problem only, being dependent on the functioning, or rather ill-functioning, of the entire economic system. With this proviso in mind, the economic causes of unemployment may be classified according to whether they affect (*a*) industry in general, or (*b*) certain industries in particular. The general causes may be considered first—

(i) **Imperfect Co-operation of Producers.** When production was simple and division of labour comparatively undeveloped, the amount of unemployment was inconsiderable. Even when the scale of production increased, there was, to begin with, a known market, and the risks both to the employers and to the workers were relatively small. In the course of time, however, not only did production become more and more extensive, but it came to be undertaken in anticipation of demand rather than for a known and certain market.

Against the economies resulting from large-scale and

continuous production has to be set the possibility, under competitive conditions, of an inadequate co-ordination among the different firms which, in their efforts to expand their own trade, may find that collectively they turn out a greater volume of goods than can profitably be disposed of. "Over-production" is followed by a period of restriction, which causes unemployment not only in the industries originally concerned and their ancillary trades, but indirectly in many other directions through the falling-off in purchasing power of the workers and others affected.

(ii) **The Trade Cycle.** The subject of cyclical fluctuations in industry, together with related conditions affecting employment, will be considered at a later stage.[1] To some extent the cyclical conditions are themselves the result of the lack of co-ordination indicated above, and of financial causes still to be examined.

(iii) **The Labour Reserve.** A "pool" of labour in excess at most times of the actual demand is to be found in many industries, though it is especially noticeable in certain occupations, such as at the docks and in the transport and building trades. These conditions lead to more or less chronic under-employment.

(iv) **Machinery.** Though machinery may be considered to be a general cause of unemployment, its effects in particular industries are especially acute. There are some authorities who see in the introduction of labour-saving machinery a major cause of unemployment. Against their contentions, however, the following arguments are commonly adduced—

(*a*) The introduction of machinery is usually followed by a reduction in the price of the product. Unless the demand for the commodity is very inelastic, the increased output called for by the new conditions may

[1] See pp. 252–5.

enable some, if not the whole, of the displaced workers to be re-employed.

(*b*) New employment is created in the making of the machinery and in the subsidiary industries that arise.

(*c*) Further, even if the public do not demand sufficient of the new machine-made goods to retain the original number of men in employment, the cheapening in price may release demands for *other* goods, entailing an increased demand for labour in those directions.

(*d*) It might be maintained that when everybody has all that is required, and no reduction in price induces further purchases, the problem of unemployment would be insoluble. On the contrary, it is pointed out that under such conditions people would work fewer hours, and that the supply of redundant labour would be reduced in consequence.

(*e*) Finally, it is urged that a long period often elapses between the invention and the actual introduction of a machine, especially where a large capital outlay has been made on the earlier equipment. The " time lag " acts as a brake on too speedy displacement, though it must be admitted that, under the stress of modern competition, the period between the invention and the utilization of the machine shows a tendency to diminish.

In qualification of these arguments, however, it may be observed that in several industries the demand for the products has not proved sufficiently elastic, nor are new demands growing at a sufficient rate to absorb all, or even a large proportion of, the men displaced. In agriculture, for example, following the introduction of machinery, there has been a net reduction in recent years in the number of men employed. The demand for corn is comparatively insensitive to price changes, and further, as the standard of living increases, expenditure on bread tends to decline rather than increase. In the British cotton textile industry, too, the introduction of machinery on a large scale appears to have resulted in a decline in employment in certain branches, notwithstanding the fall in prices and the large increase in consumption, and independently of the acute foreign competition to which the industry is subject.

(v) **Rationalization.** The reasoning with regard to rationalization and unemployment is fairly similar. The object of such schemes is usually to reduce costs and increase sales, and, though there is liable to be dislocation and unemployment during the period of transition, it is hoped that there will be more stability and possibly, though this is not so certain, greater employment under the new régime.

That the introduction of new processes, and of new methods of organization, should cause unemployment is no adequate reason why it should be opposed, for it is in the general interests that arduous labour should be lightened and eliminated wherever possible. The fault lies not in the labour-saving devices themselves, but in our at present inadequate organization, which so far has not succeeded in spreading the benefits of such improvements over the people as a whole, but tends instead to distribute the gains and losses very unevenly.

Causes of Unemployment in Particular Trades

The incidence of these general causes is by no means uniform, some industries being severely affected while others emerge almost unscathed. In addition to this unequal effect may be noted those factors that make especially for unemployment in certain trades.

(i) **Seasonal Demand.** Several industries are liable to seasonal but regular fluctuations in demand. The coal industry, for instance, is busier in winter than in summer; agriculture gives more employment in summer than in winter. Periodical unemployment due to seasonal causes takes place even when industry as a whole is prospering.

(ii) **Irregular Demand.** Some trades, such as dockside occupations, are subject to an irregular demand, and, except at the busiest times, unemployment or under-employment is common.

(iii) **Industrial Rearrangements.** The bearing of inventions and rationalization on unemployment has been considered under the general head, but, as there stated, the incidence may be especially severe in particular trades. Though improvements in technical processes and in administration add to the economy of industry in general, certain trades may be called upon to bear the brunt of the changes, and unemployment in these trades may be seriously increased.

Unemployment and Wages

In times of depression trade union leaders have often found themselves in the difficult position of having to decide between a policy of striving to maintain wages at the original level, with the possibility of workers at the margin being thrown out of employment, and a policy of accepting reductions, in the hope that the men will retain their employment. The former course has been usually preferred—

(*a*) Because of the unwillingness of the workers to renounce improvements in their wages for which they have fought hard in the past, and of their apprehension of the outcome of a renewed struggle on the return of better times with no certainty that the old rates will be restored.

(*b*) Because of the possible effects on wages in other industries, and the liability to general reductions which will outlast the depression.

(c) Because of the absence of any guarantee that a reduction in wages will have the beneficial effects on employment that are claimed, and the liability that a general fall in wages and, consequently, in the workers' demand, will tend to increase rather than diminish unemployment.

The unwillingness to reduce wages and, therefore, workers' purchasing power is shared by certain employers, who support the principle of high wages not only on the grounds of high efficiency and output, but on the grounds also that they permit of a larger market for the goods produced. This argument, however, for maintaining purchasing power should be treated with caution :

(a) An advance in, or the maintenance of, wages rates does not necessarily increase the *quantity* of purchasing power regarded as a whole. The result may simply be to transfer income from one section to another, without any direct bearing on the aggregate amount. On the other hand, there is likely to be a considerable change in the *nature* of the expenditure. There may be an increase in the purchases of necessaries of life and a decline in the more expensive luxuries. More important, perhaps, is the possibility that, with the decline in the incomes of the well-to-do, who ordinarily provide the bulk of the national savings, less will be devoted to capital goods and more to consumption goods, thus helping to remedy the alleged defect in the system of distribution and production to which reference is made elsewhere.[1]

(b) The argument of employers who see in high wages a large potential demand for their own products is obviously of limited application. For the argument to have real force, it is necessary that the policy of high wages should not be confined to a few firms, however

[1] See pp. 254–5.

large, the employees of which could consume only a small proportion of the products, but that it should be practised throughout the whole of industry. Even then there would only be a transference of spending power from one section to another, and the view that in the long run there would be a net addition to the aggregate demand, and therefore employment, would have to be supported on other grounds.

Trade Unionism

The trade union movement is mainly the product of the Industrial Revolution and of the factory system. Though workmen's combinations were by no means unknown, even as far back as the sixteenth century, it was not until workers became congregated in large numbers in factories and towns that organizations with the expressed object of safeguarding and advancing the workers' interests seriously developed.

A trade union has been defined as "a continuous association of wage-earners for the purpose of maintaining and improving the conditions of their working lives" (Webb). The element of continuity is important, as early labour organizations were usually called into existence only in times of dispute, and dissolved when they were no longer of urgent need. Continuity of association was soon found to be essential, not only for efficiency of organization and for preparedness in the event of dispute, but also as a means of holding in check those employers who, in the absence of a permanent organization of labour, might take undue advantage of their position.

Early trade unions were confined to male skilled workers, but following the "New Unionism" movement towards the end of last century, women and unskilled workers were admitted to membership. This change in policy was largely due to the recognition by the skilled "aristocracy of labour" that they were really acting against their own interests in excluding the less skilled workers. It was found that under the new industrial conditions, a person with comparatively little training could often, with the aid of semi-automatic machinery, effectively compete with the skilled craftsman. The former divisions between the grades of labour grew less distinct, and it was deemed necessary therefore to extend the benefits of organization to the less skilled workers if only to prevent their undermining the standards of the more skilled.

Trade Union Structure

The different forms of trade unionism do not lend themselves easily to classification, for each union has developed on more or less independent lines to cope with the peculiar conditions of the individual industry or occupation concerned. A rough division is as follows—

(i) **Union by Craft.** The early organizations of skilled workers consisted mainly of men engaged in performing similar operations, irrespective perhaps of the main industry in which they were employed. Even now, engineers in the railway, motor, iron, and steel industries, may belong to a single union, or group of unions, that cut sectionally across the ordinary industrial boundaries. Or, as in the case of the cotton weavers, the craft union may be confined to a single industry, but the organization be still "horizontal" in character in that it does not include operatives in other branches of the cotton industry.

There are some unions that are organized on the basis of the material used—such as the Woodworkers' Union, which comprises joiners, carpenters, and cabinet-makers —but for practical purposes they may be grouped along with the craft unions.

(ii) **Union by Industry.** Trade unionism in the nineteenth century was almost entirely on a craft basis, but during the past few decades the structure has largely altered in favour of the "industrial" basis. The new type of union aimed at bringing together the whole of the workers within an industry irrespective of their skill or grading. It was considered that this "vertical" form of organization would be more effective than the sectionalized craft union in negotiating with and wresting concessions from the employers. Thus, for example, it was the intention that the National Union of Railwaymen should incorporate all railway workers of every class, though so far the locomotive engineers and the railway clerks have retained their own unions. Similar attempts have been made in the mining and building trades, which are organized largely on an industrial but not as yet on a national basis. Even though the "industrial unionism" movement has not had all the success that its advocates predicted, and the craft union is still strongly entrenched in many trades where it is admittedly carrying out its functions with success, it is significant that the number of trade unions has shown a marked shrinkage in recent years, not because of a fall in membership (apart from some natural shrinkage in times of depression), but because of the spread of amalgamation. Owing to this concentration, about nine-tenths of the total membership of the movement are found to be in about one-sixteenth of the number of unions.

(iii) **Union of General Labour.** Unions of this kind have grown up in recent years without regard to skill or industrial attachment. Originally planned to combine the semi-skilled and unskilled workers of all industries, the General Workers' Union now includes skilled workers as well, drawn to some extent from extensive trades such as confectionery and food manufacturing, in which previously there was no effective organization.

Trade Union Functions

The form of structure of a trade union has naturally much to do with the functions it wishes to perform. Though all trade unions exercise the common duty of negotiating with employers, the extent to which they participate in the other activities varies from one organization to another.

(i) **Collective Bargaining.** Negotiation with employers, through appointed representatives, is recognized to be the most important and prevalent function of trade unions. It is only in recent times that employers in general have been induced to recognize the unions as the accredited agencies of negotiation, and now in most of the important industries collective bargaining machinery exists for regulating wages rates and working conditions. Thus, where the several unions in a particular industry have not amalgamated, some form of federation or understanding is an essential condition to negotiation on a large scale.

The machinery commonly takes the form of permanent Conciliation Boards, equally representative of both parties, which deal with problems as they arise and prevent many disputes from developing. These Boards have, on the whole, been very successful, and have secured concessions for the workers with less resort to the strike weapon than in industries where the collective bargaining machinery is not so advanced. Even so, the publicity given to strikes and lock-outs is apt to give a false impression of their prevalence. In average years 95 or more per cent of changes in wages rates are effected by peaceful negotiations.

The structure of a trade union is apt to be defective, and the fulfilment of its main function of collective bargaining incomplete, if it is unable to include such a large proportion of the workers as to exercise a virtual monopoly over labour supply. There are some functions that can be carried out if only a proportion of the workers are covered by the union, but for effective bargaining with the employers the trade union must be in a position to depend on the preponderance of workers in a trade.

(ii) **Mutual Insurance and Aid.** From the funds raised by members' subscriptions, various benefits are provided:

(*a*) Dispute benefit. This service is closely bound up with the primary function of collective bargaining, and might be equally included under that head;

(*b*) Trade benefits, such as unemployment pay;

(*c*) Friendly benefits, such as funeral, sick, and super-annuation pay.

The provision of friendly benefits has been opposed by one school of trade unionists, who contend that this is not the function of a union, which, in so far as it is a friendly society, tends to become conservative and over-cautious. Furthermore, it is held that the social insurance services of the State render this function of trade unions out of date and unnecessary. On the other hand, it must be admitted that the friendly benefits attract a certain number of workers who otherwise might not become members. Also a strong case can be made out for a system of insurance benefits supplementary to those pro-vided by the State, the amounts of which are usually inadequate to the maintenance of a reasonable standard of living.

(iii) **Legal Enactment and Political Action.** Long before the trade unions participated in party politics, they had played a part, though indirect, in influencing legislation relative to the conditions of the working classes. In the nineteenth century there were many instances of organized labour using its then limited powers to promote or to oppose parliamentary bills. In the present century political action has been more direct, and with the rapid rise of the

Labour Party the representation of trade union interests has been very much to the front. The importance attached to political as distinct from industrial action varies, however, with different unions, and the proper place of parliamentary activities among trade union functions in general is still a matter for discussion.

Industrial Disputes

The problem of industrial disputes, both as regards their causes and the machinery for settlement, is closely bound up with trade unionism. The general causes may be mentioned first—

(i) Nearly three-quarters of industrial disputes are put down to differences over wages. In times of rising prices and improving trade, the initiative comes from the workers who claim to participate in the greater profits. In times of falling prices and declining trade, the first move is usually with the employers.

(ii) Second only to wages as a cause of dispute is the length of the working day and, related to this, the conditions of employment. After a certain standard of income has been reached, workers are apt to lay less stress on further wage advances until some improvement in their hours and working conditions has been attained. To a large extent, of course, wages and hours considerations are bound together, for a reduction in the latter, provided that the daily or weekly income remains the same, involves in effect an advance in the rate of the former.

(iii) The question of the worker's status is coming to the fore as a factor in labour disputes. Though the official cause is usually attributed to other factors, these may be but the outward manifestation of the workers' desire to improve their position in the industrial system, and possibly to obtain some measure of control.

(iv) The right to negotiate through trade unions has

been a common cause of dispute in the past, but, now that employers in most industries recognize the right of their workers to join and bargain through their own organization, this cause has diminished in importance.

Settlement of Disputes

The methods of dealing with labour disputes vary considerably, each industry often having its own peculiar conditions and problems. The railway industry, for example, has its own tribunal which has had a considerable measure of success. It is possible here only to indicate in outline the principal means that are employed over industry in general.

(i) **Conciliation Boards.** These Boards, which may be permanent or temporary in nature, consist of representatives of employers and employed, and possibly of outside members in addition. Disputes are referred to the Boards and, in the event of no agreement being reached, there may be arrangements for appointing one or more arbitrators to give their award. As, however, the system works on a voluntary basis, the parties are not bound to accept such a decision.

(ii) **Arbitration.**

(*a*) *Voluntary*. The Conciliation Act of 1896 gave the Government the power to intervene in a dispute, to bring the parties together, and, if invited, to appoint arbitrators. But a decision given by an arbitrator can never be as satisfactory as one arrived at by mutual discussion, concession, and final agreement. It is difficult to find an arbitrator who is perfectly impartial, especially if he is connected with the particular trade. And if he is an "outsider" much time may be lost in the explanation of technical points.

(*b*) *Compulsory*. This mode of settling a dispute has never been popular in the United Kingdom, though it has been practised in New Zealand, Australia, and elsewhere. The Munitions of War Acts, 1915-17, introduced compulsory arbitration as an emergency measure, but ceased to operate in 1919.

An intermediate form of machinery is employed under the Canadian Industrial Disputes Act, 1907, whereby strikes and lock-outs in essential industries are prohibited pending public investigation. The Industrial Courts Act, 1919, mentioned below, provided for public inquiry, under the Ministry of Labour, but did not follow the Canadian example of forbidding strikes and lock-outs in the meantime.

(iii) **The Industrial Council.** In 1911 a Council was established, composed of twenty-six members, equally representative of employers and labour, and a chairman. It was to consider and inquire into trade disputes, and be regarded as supplementary to the machinery of the Conciliation Act of 1896. Provision was made for investigation, conciliation, or arbitration, as the occasion required. The Industrial Council could only make recommendations; it had no compulsory powers. The Council did not have a marked measure of success and was, in effect, superseded by subsequent schemes.

(iv) **Whitley Councils.** A Government Committee, which was appointed in 1916, recommended "the establishment for each industry of an organization representative of employers and workpeople to have as its object the regular consideration of matters affecting the progress and well-being of the trade from the point of view of all those engaged in it, so far as it is consistent with the general interest of the community."

For each industry there were to be permanent national, district, and workshop councils, all meeting regularly. These councils were to be concerned not only with wages and hours, but also with working conditions throughout all branches of the industry. Again the basis was voluntary.

The Whitley Councils were set up in over sixty industries and in the Civil Service, affecting more than three million workers. The high hopes that were held out, however, were not fulfilled, and in a short time most of the councils ceased to function with any effect. A number of Whitley Councils are still in existence and perform a useful though limited service in dealing with internal affairs, but the more ambitious expectations have not been borne out.

(v) **The Industrial Courts Act, 1919.** Under Part I of this Act, a standing Industrial Court was appointed by the Ministry of Labour, consisting of representatives of employers and workers, together with a number of independent persons. With the consent of both parties, any trade dispute may be referred to this Court, which makes full inquiry, and may take evidence. The chairman, who is chosen from the independent members, serves as umpire, but his decision cannot be legally enforced.

Under Part II of the Act, the Ministry of Labour was authorized to set up a Court of Inquiry for any industrial dispute and to make public the evidence and findings. The publicity given to the factors in dispute has been the means of expediting a number of settlements.

CHAPTER X

Section I. *Interest*

Analysis of Gross Interest

THE price paid for the use of capital is known as the rate of interest. This rate is of first importance in the present economic system for the reason that it largely determines the amount of capital employed in production, and also the direction of investment. Thus indirectly it affects the volume of employment of labour and the welfare of the community as a whole.

Interest should not be identified with profits, which in theory at any rate represent the return to the entrepreneur for his services as distinct from the payment for the use of capital alone. In practice, however, there is often a large element of profits in interest as popularly understood. Accordingly it is necessary to make a distinction between *Net* and *Gross Interest*.

Net Interest is the payment made for the use of capital, without any allowance for risk or any other factor. It is almost impossible to find actual instances of this pure return; but, for practical purposes, the interest on British Government stocks and similar gilt-edged securities may be taken as a near approximation.

Gross Interest is the inclusive return to an investment of capital, and may be analysed thus—

(*a*) Net interest.

(*b*) Reward for risk.

(*c*) Payment for possible inconvenience incurred in the outlay, book-keeping, etc.[1]

If there are several rates of interest being quoted at

---

[1] There may be, in addition, an element of "quasi-rent "; see pp. 170-1.

one time, the explanation lies in the different degrees of risk, etc. The lowest rate is that charged for loans involving the minimum risk and it approximates most closely to net interest.

The Nature of Interest

Interest was regarded as unjustifiable by early writers. From Aristotle down to the Middle Ages, philosophers contended that money was "barren;" that it could not breed money. Following the ban of the Church, usury came to be prohibited by law. In the course of time, however, the legislation proved irksome, and many subterfuges were adopted to overcome the restrictions. People were continually requiring money and offering a payment for its use. With the Industrial Revolution the need for capital was intensified, and Parliament, realizing that the usury laws were an anachronism, formally repealed them in 1854.

The objection to interest in the past can readily be understood. Capital was not used in the same way and to the same extent as now. Money borrowed was dissipated as often as not. There was little to be seen as a result of the consumption, and therefore nothing apparently to justify the payment of interest.

The Productivity Theory

It used to be contended by early economists that, in the same way as land produces crops, so capital produces interest. The early form of the theory attributed to capital a productive capacity *per se*. Where a loan took the form of live stock, there was an obvious specific productivity. But with the modern form of capital, the supposed power of specific production was not so easy to prove. A man working by hand turns out so many units; with the aid of a tool he doubles his output. Is the extra output the return to the tool or to the labour? It is not due to the tool alone, which is useless without labour, or to the particular man's labour alone, but to the combination of the forces as a whole. But whoever gets the fruit of the employment of capital, there is no question that by its use production is increased.

The productivity theory contains much truth, but it does not account for the payment of interest on that capital which, for different reasons, has not yielded any product at all. It tries to explain interest from the side of demand only. Other deficiencies can be ascertained by comparing this theory with other one-sided attempts to explain value in general.

The Abstinence Theory

According to this theory interest is said to be the reward of abstaining from the immediate consumption of wealth. As the word "abstinence" might be taken to imply some sacrifice, or even pain, which wealthy lenders can be hardly said to suffer, the term "waiting" is sometimes preferred. Applying the marginal method to this theory, some recent economists attempt to show by steps similar to those adopted before, that, on the supply side, the estimate of the marginal investor (or that placed on the marginal investment) tends to equal the amount of interest paid.

This view of interest is true up to a point, but it cannot be considered complete. Though productivity is not the only, it is an important, factor in the explanation of interest, and the abstinence theory gives to it insufficient attention.

The "Agio" Theory

In the "agio"[1] theory an attempt is made to explain what determines the rate which is just sufficient to induce

[1] Originally denoting a percentage paid on the exchange of currencies, "agio" came to mean the premium or discount on bills of exchange.

the supply of the marginal investment. The theory is usually associated with Prof. von Böhm-Bawerk, who, together with other members of the Austrian school, made considerable use of psychology in explaining economic phenomena.

The fundamental reason for interest, it is maintained, lies in the fact that *a man prefers present to future satisfactions.* If he is offered the choice of £100 in a year's time or now, he will prefer it in the present, quite apart from any consideration of risk (which is rewarded by a return to enterprise as distinct from payment for capital). If he is offered the choice of £103 in a year and £100 now, he may still prefer the latter. But the offer of £104 in a year's time or £100 now may prove equally attractive. The sum of £4 may be said to represent the loss in satisfaction that he experiences by postponing the consumption of £100 worth of goods for one year. It is this surplus of present over future satisfactions that is said to explain the payment of interest. Hence the expression, "*Interest is the price of time.*"

The "agio" theory, while probably nearer the truth than the earlier explanations, tends to regard interest too much from the side of supply. Again, one must emphasize that no theory relying mainly on one set of factors, whether of supply or demand, can offer a complete explanation of any value.

The Determination of the Rate of Interest

The rate of interest is determined in the same way as other values, borrowers in this case furnishing the demand and lenders the supply. The demand comes mainly from those who wish to employ the capital for productive purposes, but even where it is not so used, the loan confers a service and has to be paid for.

Capital, however, like anything else, is subject to the

law of diminishing utility. A manufacturer may find, for example, that the tenth unit of £1,000 yields a smaller specific product than the fifth £1,000. The greater the supply of capital, the lower will the marginal productivity become. From the side of demand, the value of the use of capital (i.e. the interest) tends to equal the marginal utility as measured by the value of the product.

The supply of capital, as previously shown, depends upon the power and the will to save. The rate of interest has a great influence on the accumulation of capital, though a certain amount of wealth would be conserved in any case.[1] As a general rule, however, it may be stated that, from the side of supply, the rate of interest tends to equal the recompense to the marginal investor, or better, tends to equal the estimate placed upon the marginal investment, as determined by the relative valuation of present and future goods.

The rate of interest tends ultimately to the point at which the marginal productivity of the capital and the estimate upon the marginal investment, both as measured in money, are equal.

The Tendency of the Rate of Interest to Fall

There is a certain tendency, as society advances, for the rate of interest to decline. It is true that there is a continual demand for new capital for the expansion and maintenance of industrial equipment, and that in war time and other periods of disorder there is considerable destruction of capital supplies, as a result of which a shortage of capital and rise in the rate of interest are generally experienced. Actually, however, the supply over a period has more than kept pace with the demand,

---

[1] Up to a point a diminution in the rate of interest may have the effect of stimulating greater savings on the part of those people who are aiming at a fixed income from their accumulations, while, for the same reason, an increase in the rate of interest may cause these people to lessen their capital accumulations.

and though there have, of course, been periodic and sustained increases, the tendency on the whole for the rate to fall has been fairly pronounced.

The reasons, in brief, are—

(i) The considerable expansion in productive capacity, which, despite the growth of consumption, permits of a larger surplus for capital purposes.

(ii) The greater ability of the people in general to save. Once the elementary necessaries of life are provided for, an increase in income permits of a more than proportionate increase in the amount of possible saving.

(iii) The increase not only in the ability and the desire to save, but also in the opportunity and scope of investment.

(iv) The existence of a large number of people who save with little or no regard to the rate of interest. This supply of capital more or less independent of the price offered naturally serves to strengthen the position of the borrowers in relation to the lenders as a whole, and the rate tends to be lower than it would be if every lender were out to get the best terms.

Theoretically, it has been maintained that the rate of interest may continue to decline until it disappears, but such a situation is extremely unlikely ever to arise. The surplus of production over consumption can hardly, even to the most imaginative mind, become so large in relation to demand that the marginal productivity sinks to zero. Long before such a point was reached, people would begin to buy more consumption goods, thus involving the use of more capital goods, and thereby swelling the demand for the available fluid capital.

Section 2. *Profits*

Analysis of Gross Profits

In the early stages of economic analysis the entrepreneur and the capitalist were regarded as identical, and therefore no real distinction was drawn between interest and profits. Later it was recognized that, while one man might serve as both capitalist and entrepreneur, he was really performing a double function, namely, supplying the use of capital and providing organization and enterprise. Though it is seldom that a man acts as entrepreneur without supplying a certain amount of capital, and that a man invests capital without at the same time incurring some degree of risk, it helps towards a better understanding of the distribution of income if the two functions and their rewards are separately considered.

In an analysis of the ordinary profits of a business, returns to some or all of the following elements may be found:

(i) **Net Interest.** Gross profits frequently include some return on capital, though the more accurately a statement of profit is prepared, the less is the likelihood of confusion.[1] A small producer, working with his own capital, may not trouble to separate the different items in the gross return, but a large business finds it essential to make the distinctions, and compute its net returns accordingly. The ratio of pure interest in the dividends from investments varies considerably. The yield from debenture holdings contains a higher percentage of net interest than does the dividend paid on ordinary shares. The proportion of actual profit in the gross yield increases as one passes from bonds and debentures at the one extreme to deferred shares at the other.[2]

(ii) **Payment for Organization or Management.** This is a reward for the duties carried out by the entrepreneur. In a sense, it resembles the remuneration he would receive if he acted as a paid manager, and is thus akin to wages (though allowance must be made for the advantages of

---

[1] Confusion is also apt to arise from the fact that "gross profits" to the economist may mean the same as "net profit" to the accountant.

[2] See p. 222, note.

the employer's position compared with that of a paid manager). The earnings of the entrepreneur cannot permanently fall below the "wages of management." If they did, and if he could dispose of his stocks and plant without serious loss, he might find it preferable to seek salaried employment.

(iii) **Payment for Risk.** Since production has to be carried out usually in anticipation of demand, there is always a certain amount of risk involved. Long before the final product is paid for by the customer, money has been paid out for labour, materials, and borrowed capital. The most skilled of entrepreneurs may have their estimates of demand upset by factors that cannot be foreseen.

(iv) **Monopoly Gains.** A firm enjoying monopoly may derive a profit considerably in excess of that which would prevail under competitive conditions. Even if it does not possess a complete control over the supply of a commodity, it may possess certain advantages that result in a greater gain than that accruing to less fortunate rivals. Such advantages may be due to superior management, or better situation in regard to the market, or to several other circumstances not shared by the marginal firm, whose reward is only just sufficient to induce continuance in production.

(v) **Conjuncture or Chance Gains.** Instances are innumerable of persons or firms making a profit through the conjuncture of circumstances that cannot be predicted, and that take place independently of any effort or foresight of those benefiting. While the element of chance in large profits is liable to be exaggerated, its frequent presence cannot be denied. It may be urged, however, that the very possibility of such gains serves as a stimulus to people to enter the industry and to sustain them at a high pitch of efficiency so as not to miss an opportunity when it occurs. To that extent the "unearned" item in the total receipts might be discounted.

(vi) **Normal Profit.** The net return to the marginal firm may be regarded as the normal profit. Unless the firms at the margin receive something over and above the rewards in respect of (i), (ii), and (iii), they are not likely to remain long in business. The firms above the margin receive a differential profit which, as shown above, has a certain resemblance to a monopoly gain, even though competition is not absent.

The Marginal Theory of Profits

Thus, a number of firms may be engaged in producing a given type of article that sells for the same price in all markets irrespective of the source from which it comes. The price is fixed *for*, and not *by*, the individual firms, and just covers the costs of the marginal firm, in which the minimum reward for enterprise is allowed for. The supra-marginal firms enjoy lower costs, but as they can sell the whole of their output at the prevailing market price, they are enabled to make a larger profit commensurate with their differential advantage. In the long run, they may extend their scale of production and lower their prices in order to capture their rivals' share of the market, and the nearer they approach to a complete control of supply, the closer is the resemblance between a part of their earnings and a monopoly revenue. The differential gain, whether it reaches the degree of a monopoly profit or not, is in some ways similar to an economic rent, as will be shown in the succeeding chapter.

The basic element in profits seems, then, to be that normal rate which the firm on the margin must receive over a period or cease producing. It is difficult to estimate what this is to be, as it depends on so many varying factors. The nature of the industry is one, the age of the firm is another. It cannot be said that profits tend to an equality any more than wages, but there appears to be in every trade a certain minimum profit below which, taking everything into consideration, a firm will not carry on for long.

This minimum, however, cannot always be reduced to a single type of reward or expressed as a simple amount, for, even when the measurable items for net interest, wages of management, and reward for risk, have been deducted, there frequently remains a dual element which does not admit of simple analysis.

Other Theories of Profits

The above theory of profits is admittedly incomplete, and there is still considerable difference of opinion among economists as to the real nature of this form of income, if indeed it can be reduced to a single type of reward.

Profits the Result of Change

A more recent theory maintains that profits are the result of change, which is always going on in the prevailing system. If we lived in a stationary and perfectly competitive system, there would be no profits at all. Prices of all services would be fixed in advance by the value of their marginal products. The rewards of wages, interest and rent would be sufficient inducement to keep production going. In practice, of course, the system is far from being stationary—population is increasing, wants become more numerous and diverse, new technical processes are discovered, and so on. It is in the process of adjustment from one stage to another that profits emerge. They are the reward to the entrepreneur, maybe temporary only, for his services in bringing about a new equilibrium.

A modification of this theory is the distinction drawn

between foreseen and unforeseen change. Where changes are predictable, necessary measures can be taken and thus there can be no profits that depend essentially on uncertainty for their emergence. It is only where change is unforeseen, and where there is ignorance of the future that true profits arise. In short, to quote Professor Knight, profits come from "the divergence of actual conditions from those which have been expected and on the basis of which business arrangements have been made."

The Marxian Theory

Karl Marx and his present-day followers take an altogether different view of profits. The total income of a community is made up of two constituents only—wages and profits. In the capitalist system, however, labour does not get the whole reward measured by its productivity. It tends to receive only that amount which is necessary to induce a continuous supply of labour-power, but which is in reality much less than the value of labour's product. (The relationship of this doctrine to the classical cost of production theory will be observed.) The difference between the output and reward (i.e. "surplus product") forms the basis of the "surplus value" or profits taken by the capitalist employers. The final allocation of this surplus among capitalists is determined by their respective bargaining powers.

The Tendency of the Rate of Profits to Fall

The close relationship between interest and profits is illustrated by the apparent tendencies for their rates to decline over a lengthy period. The trend of the rate of interest has already been considered. That of the rate of profits is subject to similar conditions. As business men improve in knowledge, and can take increasing advantage of new methods, both technological and administrative, the chances of very large profits, though still appreciable under the prevailing system, are liable to be less pronounced.

This tendency, however, is by no means universal, for the rate of profit in certain industries shows no sign of declining and is even tending to increase. In the newer industries, especially, there are special opportunities for skilled entrepreneurs, and the average rate of gain is comparatively high. Also, in those industries where monopoly has replaced competition—and this movement is likely to increase rather than diminish—the rate of profit usually made is hardly in accord with the general tendency as stated.

Allowing, however, for such qualifications, an important difference is to be observed between the general trend of the rates of interest and profits on the one hand, and that of rent on the other. The former rates, viewed over a wide field, are tending to fall rather than to rise. As will be shown in the next chapter, the rate of rent, being the payment for a factor of which the supply is limited, but for which the demand is constantly growing, tends rather to increase.

CHAPTER XI

Section 1. *The Theory of Rent*

The Meaning of Economic Rent

RENT, in the economic sense, denotes the payment for the use of the natural factor of production.

As defined by Ricardo a century ago, rent was said to be "that portion of the produce of the earth which is paid to the landlord for the use of the original and indestructible powers of the soil." As later re-defined by Marshall, it was stated to be "the income derived from the ownership of land and other free gifts of nature."

Economic rent and ordinary rental should be carefully distinguished. The rental of buildings or agricultural land usually includes not only a certain amount of pure rent, but also items in respect of interest, profits, depreciation allowances, etc. True rent may prove to be only a small proportion of the total hire value. In the long run, however, capital improvements may become absorbed in the land, and the total charge, therefore, come to resemble a true rent.

Confusion is also liable to be caused by property owners who refer to their net income as "economic rent." Actually, of course, they expect not merely a pure rent but a full return to their capital and enterprise. For a house that cost £1,000 when the rate of interest was 4 per cent, the interest alone would be £40 per year. In the rental of such a house the amount of economic rent payable on the land itself might be an extremely small item.

Peculiarities of Land

Land is strictly limited in quantity. It is different from the other factors of production in that it is permanently in existence; that no change in demand can affect the amount of land in existence.

But, though the area of land is fixed, its services as a factor of production have been greatly increased. Fertilizers have added to the quality and quantity of output; improvements in transport have made available certain regions whose products were not formerly available.

Thus, land in the everyday sense of the term may be classified as follows—

(a) That which possesses only natural or original powers of production (e.g. virgin land in a "new" country, not requiring any preliminary clearing). In an "old" country very little of this land is to be found.

(b) That which possesses in addition the powers of production that have been added to the elementary qualities (e.g. by fertilizers, clearing of ground, improved transport, etc.).

(c) That which possesses also situational advantages. Pressure of a growing population gives a value to certain areas considerably in excess of its "fertility" value (e.g. sites in the centre of a city).

The Ricardian Theory of Rent

Ricardo, in common with other members of the Classical School, held that value was determined by cost of production, and attempted to apply this principle to the rewards of the various agents of production. The subsistence wage was held, in effect, to be the cost of production of labour; interest, being the inducement to people to abstain from present consumption, was regarded as the cost of production of capital. But when it was attempted to apply the notion to the return to land, many difficulties arose. Land is not produced: its amount is constant whatever price is offered. Ricardo, therefore, sought another explanation of the nature and determination of rent.

The earliest and crudest form of the theory may first be outlined. Imagine a limited area of virgin land to which come a number of settlers. Presumably the newcomers appropriate the most productive land, which yields, say, 100 bushels of wheat for a given amount of land and labour. Suppose all the best land has been appropriated, and some more settlers arrive. The latter are at liberty to take up the second-best land, which for the same area and labour yields 90 bushels of wheat. Alternatively, they may approach the first-comers and ask them on what terms the best land can be rented. If no capital has been invested in the superior land, the owners will tend to demand a rent equivalent to 10 bushels (i.e. the difference in the productivity of the two lands). At that figure it is a matter of indifference to the new settlers whether they cultivate the second-best land paying no rent, or take over the best land and pay a rent of 10 bushels. If the owners of the best land ask for a lower rent than this, competition among the new arrivals will force the price up; if a higher figure is named, it will be more advantageous for the newcomers to cultivate the inferior land rent-free.

Suppose all the first- and second-class land to be appropriated when further settlers arrive. These may take up rent-free the third-class land, which yields 80 bushels for the given area and labour, or pay the owners of the second-class land a rent of 10 bushels, or the owners of the first-class land a rent of 20 bushels. Thus, increasing pressure on the limited amount of land causes the rent to rise *without any effort on the part of the owner.*

Importance of Situation

This purely imaginary illustration is brought a little nearer to actual conditions if with the fertility of the land is included its situation, which Ricardo did not stress. In such an instance as the above, the settlers would probably appropriate the land nearest to hand. The reason might be ignorance of where the most fertile land was to be found. But even if this were known, it might not pay to cultivate it on account perhaps of the expense of transport. If the most fertile land bore an advantage of 10 bushels over the land immediately available, but necessitated an expenditure equivalent to 20 bushels in transporting the crop, the *net product* of the less fertile land would be higher than that of the more fertile land, and would yield consequently a higher rent.

In thickly populated districts, and especially in industrial and commercial centres, rent of situation is of primary importance, while rent of fertility is practically negligible.

Diminishing Returns and Rent

It was shown in a previous chapter that, in the cultivation of land, one tends after a point to experience a diminishing return in the amount (not necessarily in the value) of the product. The reason why a plot of land is not cultivated as intensively as possible may be that the additional return is less than the extra cost of getting it. Thus, equal applications to a plot of land may yield a varying return, the differences being comparable in a sense to the differential advantage of one piece of land over another.[1]

The Determination of Rent

Having discussed the nature of rent, one may next examine the way in which its amount is determined. It

---

[1] As was emphasized in the earlier discussion, the "doses" of capital and labour applied may be *successive* or *simultaneous*, and still be subject to diminishing returns.

is not sufficient merely to say that it is measured by the difference in productivity. Consider, first, lands of varying fertility. Land A may have an advantage of 10 bushels of corn for a given area over land B, which in turn has an advantage over land C of the same amount. The advantage of A over C is, therefore, 20 bushels. There may be several other qualities of land, D, E, F, etc., all of which are found profitable to cultivate. Which land serves as the basis for final comparison and measurement of rent? The answer is *the land on the margin of cultivation*, i.e. the land which, at the price of the product ruling at the time, is just worth while cultivating. To put it another way, the receipts from the product of the marginal land just cover the expenditure of the labour and capital applied; there is no surplus. As demonstrated in the chapters on value, it is the cost of the marginal product to which the price tends to approximate. Whether it is grown on the more productive or less productive land, the crop (assuming the quality is the same) is sold at the price which is necessary to cover the expenses of the marginal product. For lands of varying productivity there is said to be an *extensive margin*.

Secondly, with regard to different "doses" applied, the cultivator of one piece of land tends to invest capital and labour up to that point at which the return just covers the outlay. As stated in the general discussion on value, he tends to produce up to the point at which the marginal costs equal price. For doses of capital and labour of varying productivity there is said to be an *intensive margin*.

The extra productivity of the superior over the marginal unit, whether the units be different grades of land or different doses of capital and labour, determines the amount of the rent.

If the price of the product rises, it becomes profitable

to cultivate the land or employ the dose of capital and labour that previously yielded less than the outlay. The margin is thus lowered, and the differential advantage or rent of the superior unit is raised.

If the price falls, it is no longer profitable to cultivate the land, or apply the dose of capital and labour, that was formerly at the margin. The level of the margin is therefore raised, and the differential advantage or rent of the superior unit is reduced.

As a general rule, a rise in the price of the product contributes to an increase in the rent; a fall in the price tends to bring about a reduction in the rent.

In practice, the rent paid for land does not visibly rise or fall automatically with the price of the product, since rentals are usually fixed by contract for a definite period, and any advantage or loss within that period accrues to the tenant. But this does not disprove the increase or decrease in the true rent. If a long period is taken, to allow time for contracts to terminate, the net payment (deducting interest, etc.) will approximate to the pure economic rent.

Diagrammatic Illustrations of the Nature and Determination of Rent

The foregoing analysis may be illustrated in diagram form—

(i) Suppose that the rectangles (p. 163) represent the output from equal doses applied to *different* pieces of land. The most productive land yields an output measured by the whole of rectangle *a* (shaded as well as light portion). The second-best land yields a product measured by *b*, the third yields *c*, and so on. Remembering that the price of the product is fixed *for* the cultivator by the general conditions of supply and demand, suppose that the price of the product is just sufficient to induce the cultivation of that land which yields an output of *e* per given unit of capital and labour. Obviously it will not pay to cultivate the less productive land which yields only *f*. The land which just yields sufficient to cover the outlay is on the margin of cultivation. The difference between the productivity of the superior and the marginal land is the rent, marked by the shaded portion of the diagram.

(i) and (ii)

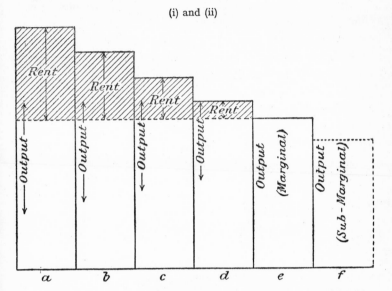

If the price of the product rises, then the sixth land may be brought into cultivation; *f* becomes the marginal output and the rents rise. If the price falls, the fourth land becomes marginal and the rents fall.

(ii) Referring to the same diagram, suppose that the rectangles represent the output from equal doses applied to the *same* piece of land. The illustration is now similar to that of diminishing returns. One unit of capital and labour yields a product measured by *a*. The second unit produces *b*. If two units are applied together, the yield is $(a + b)$, i.e. less than $2a$. The fifth unit yields *e*, the sale

of which just covers the cost. Assuming that the cultivator knows exactly where to stop (though often it is
impossible to know this precisely), no more than five units
will be invested. The "surplus" product of each of the
first four doses over the product of the fifth or marginal
dose is equivalent to a rent. As before, a rise or fall in
the price of the product will cause a rise or fall in the rent.

(iii) Still another way of demonstrating the nature of
rent is as follows—

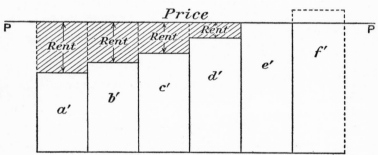

The law of diminishing returns may be otherwise expressed as that of increasing costs. In this diagram,
suppose a' (light portion only) to be the cost (including
minimum profit) of producing one unit; b' the cost of
producing a second unit; and so on. The price at which
all the units are sold is measured by the line PP. The
marginal cost is measured by e'. The shaded area between
a' and the price line is a rent, which also accrues in diminishing degree to b', c', and d'. The price just covers the
cost e', and in this case there is no rent. To produce
another unit would cost f', which is greater than the price
received.

"No-rent" Land

The Ricardian theory of rent leads to the conclusion
that land on the margin of cultivation pays no rent.

It is sometimes contended, however, that in developed countries like England no such land exists. This difficulty can be explained in more than one way—

(i) The marginal land which determines the rent payable in England need not be in this country: it may, for instance, be in America. Farmers here compete with American producers, and the price of corn is governed very largely by foreign competition. As the price rises or falls, rents at home vary accordingly; and if the worst land here is superior in productivity to the marginal land in America (allowing for the cost of transporting the American produce, which has to be deducted from the value of the gross output), it will yield a rent. Thus, in an old country all the land may bear a rent.

(ii) A tenant of a fairly large area cannot pick and choose, and pay rent only for the fertile tracts and at varying rates. Part of the land may be quite unproductive. An inclusive rent is calculated for the whole area, though actually it is paid only for the productive tracts. Thus the fact that no rent is paid for the non-productive land is concealed.

Rent and Price

The relationship between rent and price has been much discussed by economists. The notion that rent is not a price-determining, but a price-determined, quantity, was developed by Ricardo, who wrote—

> The value of corn is regulated by the quantity of labour bestowed on its production on that quality of land, or with that portion of capital, which pays no rent. Corn is not high because a rent is paid, but a rent is paid because corn is high; and it has been justly observed that no reduction would take place in the price of corn although landlords should forgo the whole of their rent. . . . Rent does not and cannot enter into the least degree as a component part of its price.

The same doctrine, with certain important reservations,

may be extended to the price of commodities other than agricultural produce.

Briefly the stages in the argument are as follows—

(*a*) Producers sell their goods for what they can get and not necessarily at as low a price as their expenses permit.

(*b*) The price tends to equal the costs of the marginal producer (or of the marginal product).

(*c*) The position of the price fixes that of the margin, at which no rent is paid.

(*d*) Producers above the margin receive a rent which increases or decreases with a rise or fall in the price.

(*e*) *Therefore, the rent is the result of the price, and not a cause of it.*

Applied to *urban rents*, the same conclusion is broadly true. (Again, one must bear in mind that the heavy interest and other charges on the enormous capital invested in buildings have to be deducted before the true rent is ascertained.) A shopkeeper in a fashionable thoroughfare does not charge high prices because his economic rent is high. *The economic rent is high because he is able to charge high prices.* If the payment of net rent were abolished, the shopkeeper could and probably would still keep the price up, and gain the advantage.

Even if the prices were no higher than elsewhere, there would still be a differential rent if the shopkeeper, owing to situational advantage, had a larger turnover and therefore a greater profit. A tobacconist in a main thoroughfare pays a larger rent, yet charges no higher prices than a rival in a side street. The heavier rent comes, not out of better prices, but out of the greater volume of business. The principle, however, that economic rent is not in itself a determining influence on price conditions remains unaffected.

Generally speaking, interest has to be paid to induce a supply of capital, and wages have to be paid to induce a supply of labour; but the supply of land cannot be increased or decreased by a higher or lower rent. Interest and wages have a direct influence on the price of the product ; rent has no such influence.

Qualifications of the Ricardian Rent Doctrine

Certain of the limitations of the Ricardian theory of rent, as originally formulated, have already been observed, and the necessary qualifications have been incorporated in the general exposition. Thus, rent of situation has been coupled with rent of fertility. Also, in the relationship to price, it has been shown that the real determining influence on rent is not so much the price of the product as the volume of turnover, which permits of a large gross profit and therefore of a high rent.

A further qualification is sometimes made in regard to *alternative uses* of land, each of which may have its own margin of cultivation. Thus, a plot may be used for growing wheat or barley; or it may serve for arable or pasture purposes; or it may be used for urban development; or it may be taken for pleasure parks or game preserves; or it may be acquired purely for the social position and prestige attaching to land-ownership. Judged from the standpoint of one of the more remunerative of these purposes, a piece of land might be marginal and bear no surplus for rent, but if employed in serving a minor object it might be found to yield a certain amount of rent. The charge thus incurred might influence the extent to which the land was used in serving a major purpose, and thus affect the position of the margin. In so far as the margin itself was affected by the rent payable for an alternative use of the land, the rent might be considered to be a price-influencing factor.

Historical Illustrations of Rents and Prices

The operation of the law of rent has been illustrated very clearly in the course of the nineteenth and twentieth centuries. During the Napoleonic Wars the shortage of corn supplies, combined with the high tariffs on imported corn, contributed to a considerable rise in prices. Land-owners and farmers made large incomes, and found it advantageous to cultivate the inferior land, hitherto below the margin. The rise in prices thus lowered the margin of cultivation and raised the rents of the superior lands. Many farmers, thinking the good times would continue, heavily committed themselves financially. When the war ended, prices gradually declined and, despite the protection afforded by the Corn Laws, several farmers were ruined. Rents fell with the prices.

In subsequent years, especially those during and following a war, whenever prices of corn rose or fell, rents almost invariably moved likewise. The Crimean War, the United States Civil War, the Franco-Prussian War, by cutting off foreign supplies and in other ways, all helped to raise the price of corn, and rents rose in consequence. When, in the 'seventies and onwards, foreign corn came into Britain in increasing quantities, prices fell continuously, and so did the rents.

During the Great War the same trend of prices and rent was experienced. The reduction of foreign supplies and increased demands on our own produce caused prices to rise. The productivity of the land resources at home was increased, for, apart from the fact that owners were compelled to put more land into cultivation, the high prices, with a guaranteed minimum, made it profitable to cultivate relatively inferior land and also to cultivate more intensively. The general result was a rise in the economic rent. State control of money, rents, and prices complicated matters, but did not hide the real tendency. Since the

War, much land has gone out of cultivation; the margin has therefore risen, with a consequent fall in the net rents.

Summary of Influences on Rent

The principal factors influencing rent may be shortly summarized.

A fall in rents may be due to—

(*a*) Improvements in methods of cultivation. There is less resort to inferior lands, the difference between the best and worst land under cultivation diminishes, and therefore rents tend to fall.

(*b*) Improvements in transport. These have the same effect. American corn is brought into this country and makes the use of much inferior land unnecessary. Similarly, railway and other travelling facilities may ease the pressure on congested urban areas, and so restrain the tendency for town rents to soar. On the other hand, suburban rents are likely to rise, but probably not to the same extent in the aggregate as the town rents would have risen.

(*c*) Growth of supply of substitutes. New foods serve to reduce the demand for corn crops, the fall in the price of which leads to a reduction in the rent of agricultural land.

A rise in rents may be due to—

(*a*) Growth of population and improved standard of life, entailing an increased demand. Prices rise, inferior land is brought into cultivation, and rents rise.

(*b*) Increased pressure in centres of population on dwelling and business sites.

(*c*) Wars and other disturbances, which increase prices and therefore rents.

In practice, the one set of influences tends to counteract

the other, but, on the whole, the tendencies to a general rise in rents would seem to be the stronger.

Section 2.   Applications of the Doctrine of Rent

Surplus Elements in Interest, Profits and Personal Incomes

Modern economic analysis has considerably widened the rent doctrine. *Rent can be shown to be the payment for any factor of production whose productivity does not depend on the amount of income it receives, but whose reward depends upon its superiority in productive powers over that part which receives no reward.*

The following examples illustrate the presence of an element of economic rent in gross interest, profits and wages—

(i) **As Applied to Interest.** Suppose there is a sudden boom in foreign trade, and a great demand for shipping. Freights rise and large profits are made by the shipping companies. Ships take a long time to build, and a considerable period may elapse before competition from new boats forces the charges down. The extra earnings of the ships during the period of fixed supply are likened to a rent. They are similar to the rent on land, in that owing to a limited supply and consequent high charges, the owners receive a surplus beyond the normal return. Inferior vessels may be pressed into service; they become marginal, and the receipts from the superior ships rise. When further supplies of shipping are available and freights fall, it no longer pays to employ these inferior vessels, the margin rises, and the receipts from the superior ships fall.

In a short period, therefore, part of the return from fixed capital may be regarded as a kind of rent. The additional payment for those agents of production, the supply of which, though alterable in a long period, is

fixed in a short period, is technically known as a
quasi-rent.

(ii) **As Applied to Profits.** Suppose there are two firms
of similar size and situation, equally equipped and employing the same amount and quality of labour, but that
one of them, owing to some special advantage, can produce
a given article at a lower cost than the other. If the
superior firm can sell all its output at the relatively high
price that is necessary to cover the costs of the inferior
firm, it will do so. The profits it makes over and above
those of the inferior firm are of the same nature as an
economic rent.

The price of the product tends to equal the marginal costs. The "surplus" profits, like rent, do not
determine, but are determined by, the price that is
charged.

It is the differential gains, of course, that have no
place in the price of the article, not what have been
termed the normal profits. The latter must be considered
a constituent element in marginal costs, and therefore in
the supply price. Marginal land is still cultivated, though
it pays no rent. But the strictly marginal firm must make
a profit; otherwise it would go out of existence. In
partly meeting this difficulty Marshall's conception of
the "representative firm" is found helpful. This firm is
not marginal in the sense that a slight fall in the price of
the product or slight rise in costs would cause it to go out
of existence. It is "one which has had a fairly long life,
and fair success, which is managed with normal ability,
and which has normal access to the economies, external
and internal, which belong to that aggregate volume of
production." Prices tend to adjust themselves to the
cost of production, not of the strictly marginal firm, but
of the representative firm. A concern which produces
more economically than this firm, but can dispose of its

products at the price which the latter finds necessary, makes a surplus profit akin to a rent.

(iii) **As Applied to Personal Incomes.** An element of rent can often be found in personal incomes, though its extent cannot as a rule be defined with any precision. An obvious example is to be found in the large incomes of successful lawyers or surgeons who, because of their peculiar abilities, enjoy a position resembling monopoly. Their services would be no less useful if the reward were more modest, but, taking advantage of their special position, they are enabled without greater effort to charge considerable fees. Similar considerations apply, though not usually in the same degree, to the payment of wages. A workman whose personal qualities are superior to those of another may on that account receive a greater remuneration. The additional income in such cases is commonly termed a *rent of ability*.

It may be urged by way of qualification that the extra receipts, whether of the professional or the manual worker, are largely an interest on the capital originally expended on training, and that they should not therefore be classified as "unearned." In so far as a capital outlay is incurred, an appropriate deduction from gross receipts for interest is legitimate, but it is usually found that the superiority in incomes is out of all proportion to, and may be several times the size of, the normal return to investment. It could be equally maintained that the power of the recipient in his early years to lay out a capital sum, or to have it laid out for him, was in itself a major cause of the differential income, quite independently of the greater productivity that might accrue.[1]

---

[1] The *Consumer's Surplus* noted in Chapter VI, Sect. 2, may be also likened to a rent. In the same way as a producer above the margin would be willing if necessary to sell his product for less than the prevailing price, some consumers would be willing to pay more than the market price rather than go without the article. The one is a producer's rent; the other a consumer's rent.

General Conclusion on Rent

Rent has been shown to be a payment not peculiar to the natural factor of production. It frequently forms a part of the gross return to capitalists, entrepreneurs, and those who render personal services. **The main difference between rent of land and the payment for the other factors is that, while no alteration in rent can affect the supply and productivity of land, a change in interest, profits and wages does up to a point affect the supply of capital, enterprise, and labour. To that extent, interest, profits and wages are price-determining; rent is price-determined.**

The theory of rent thus throws a new light on distribution in general, and its implications are far-reaching. Some of these will be examined at a later stage in connection with taxation and social policy.

PART IV
THE MECHANISM OF EXCHANGE

CHAPTER XII

THE FUNCTIONS OF MONEY

Section 1. The Nature and Functions of Money

ALTHOUGH it is convenient to study the organization of production and the mechanism of exchange in separate sections, it cannot be over-emphasized that they are closely interlocked, and that exchange is in fact only a part of the general scheme of production. Goods are not finally produced until they have passed into the hands of the consumers, and the system of exchange has developed merely to facilitate this passage.

The Inconvenience of Barter

It is helpful, before embarking upon a study of the present-day mechanism of exchange, to consider the earlier system of barter, which, in a modified form, still persists in certain parts of the world. Barter is found to suffer from the following defects—

(i) **Want of Coincidence.** Barter requires a double coincidence of things required and offered. If A and B are going to trade their goods, A must have what B wants, and of the right amount, while B must have what A wants, also in the right amount. Further, they must both require each other's goods at the same time. If A wants bread and offers cloth, B wants cloth but can only offer boots, a way out of the difficulty may be to discover a third person C, who wants boots and offers bread, and thus complete the "triangle of exchange."

But it is obvious that, as division of labour develops,

and wants grow in number and variety, this way of adjusting one's supplies and wants becomes increasingly difficult. It is only possible, and then in a rough way, among very small communities.

Modern exchange, though outwardly complex in its mechanism, is really very much simpler in its nature than barter. The need for a double coincidence is eliminated. Nowadays, a man sells his commodity to another in return for a recognized medium, with which he can purchase from a third person, or a number of persons, at various times if need be, the goods that he requires for his own consumption. The recognized medium we call *money*.

(ii) **Want of Measure of Value.** Another drawback of barter is that, while A may offer what B wants, and B may offer what A wants, there is no satisfactory means of measuring the values of the respective commodities. A may have a large quantity of his stock, B only a small amount of his. Obviously the stocks as such will not be exchanged. What, then, is to be the measure of value?

Here, again, the need for a monetary medium is made clear. Money measures the values of goods, which may, if necessary, be directly exchanged without the actual passing of money. Barter, therefore, is of two kinds, the second more developed than the first:

(*a*) Where goods are exchanged for goods, without any system of evaluation.

(*b*) Where some third commodity (i.e. money) is used to measure the values, before the direct exchange can take place.

(iii) **Want of Means of Subdivision.** Some things are easier to split up into parts than others. Further, certain things lose in value when subdivided.

Suppose that a person's wealth takes the form of cattle or precious stones, neither of which can be subdivided without loss. If he wished to purchase anything of small value by direct exchange, he would almost certainly lose by the transaction. By the use of money, however, the difficulty is solved. A cow or precious stone is sold for a sum of money, which can be subdivided into a number of units of small denomination. The expenditure of these can, if necessary, be spread over a long period, thus demonstrating another advantage over barter.

Nature of Money

Money is a commodity chosen by common consent to serve as a means of exchange and of full discharge of obligations. It has been defined as "that which passes freely from hand to hand in full payment for goods, in final discharge of indebtedness, being accepted equally without reference to the character or credit of the person tendering it and without the intention on the part of the person receiving it himself to consume or enjoy or otherwise use it than by passing it on sooner or later in exchange." (Walker.)

It should be realized that money is, in effect, a commodity like any other. Though a metallic coin is often regarded as different from other commodities, it is not so in its real nature. To say that a sovereign buys a pair of boots means simply that the value attached to the gold in the sovereign is the same as that attached to the pair of boots; it would be just as true to say that a pair of boots buys a sovereign. The value of gold is governed in the same way as that of boots or anything else, and in the long run approximates to its cost of production.

The Functions of Money

The functions of money, which were indicated indirectly in considering the drawbacks of barter, may now be stated more positively—

(i) **Means of Payment.** Direct barter of goods for goods

to any appreciable extent is impossible in modern communities. Goods are therefore exchanged for an intermediate selected commodity, which, in turn, is exchanged for other goods, probably in another place, at a different time, and in smaller or greater amount. This commodity, or money, thus fulfils the function of a medium of exchange. Since money is used in such one-sided transactions as tax-payments or gifts, when there is no exchange in the ordinary sense, the broader definition of the function as a means of payment is perhaps preferable.

(ii) **Measure of Value.** Money serves as a basis for the comparison of values in exchange; it is, as it were, the common denominator of value. Even in barter, as has been noted, money may be used indirectly, if the goods to be exchanged are first measured in terms of money. It will be shown below that, so far as standard money is concerned, the function of a measure has come to be more important than that of an actual medium. Thus, commodities still have their values expressed normally in terms of gold, though the use of coins consisting of this precious metal is becoming increasingly rare, especially for domestic payments.

(iii) **Standard for Deferred Payments.** Closely bound up with the service of money as a measure of value is the function as a standard for future payments, or, expressed another way, as a basis for credit transactions. When payment is to be made at a future period, the parties to the contract require a medium which will have, as far as possible, the same exchange power in the future as at present. If one of the parties stands to lose by the transaction, trade is naturally impeded.

"Money is a form in which capital is held *in suspense* without loss. . . . Money is not second-hand; it will always fetch itself, and it loses nothing by keeping. . . . Cattle are good enough for present bargains, but not for the forward- and backward-looking calculations of profit and loss." (Bagehot.)

(iv) **Store of Value.** A man who wishes to conserve his wealth in some convenient form, always realizable as occasion requires, finds the money medium most suitable for his purpose. Though this function has lost much of its former importance, hoarding of precious coin is by no means unknown.

Forms of Money

Anything which fulfils these functions may for practical purposes be deemed to be money. Thus, bank notes, cheques, bills of exchange and similar instruments are covered by the term.

Currency is said to be *legal tender* when a creditor is obliged to accept payment of the debt in that form of money, if offered.

The principal forms of money passing in this country are tabulated on page 179. It will be noted that legal tender is but a part of the entire monetary system.

Section 2. Coinage and the Gold Standard

Qualities of Good Money Material

Many things have served as money at different stages of our history. Slaves, cattle, skins, furs, and shells, were employed before the metals gradually supplanted them. Silver came to be widely used as a medium, but in turn was supplanted in most countries by gold. But, while gold satisfies the conditions of a standard coinage better than any other known commodity, the ideal material has still to be discovered.

The necessary qualities of a standard coinage that actually circulates as a medium are—

(i) *Utility*. The commodity must have a utility independent of the power to serve as money, in order that it will be *generally acceptable*. Cattle, skins, gold, etc., are desirable for the satisfaction they offer in themselves.

THE BRITISH MONETARY SYSTEM

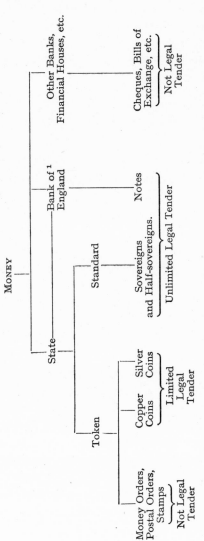

Money

State — Bank of [1] England — Other Banks, Financial Houses, etc.

Token — Standard

Money Orders, Postal Orders, Stamps
Not Legal Tender

Copper Coins — Silver Coins
Limited Legal Tender

Sovereigns and Half-sovereigns
Unlimited Legal Tender

Notes
Unlimited Legal Tender

Cheques, Bills of Exchange, etc.
Not Legal Tender

The Bank of England, which issues notes of 10s. and £1 upwards, acts in close co-operation with the Treasury, and is virtually, for this purpose, a State Department. These notes have practically replaced gold coinage for currency purposes.

(ii) *Stability of Value.* The material selected still remains a commodity whose value is influenced by changes in supply and demand. Since the value of the monetary material measures the value of all other things, any alteration automatically affects the values of everything else. Unstable prices are bad for everybody. Consequently it is essential that the material chosen should be as constant in its value as possible.

(iii) *Portability and Compactness.* This includes *transportability* without depreciation. Since money has to be moved about, it is necessary to concentrate the value into a convenient form. Iron would not be as satisfactory in this respect as the precious metals.

(iv) *Durability.* The money material should not deteriorate with keep and use. Also it should not require special attention. Cattle and corn were found unsuitable in this respect. Even among the metals there are some kinds less destructible than others. A metal that corrodes through exposure to the elements is not satisfactory.

(v) *Cognizability.* The material should be easily recognizable. A metallic medium should have a distinctive colouring; thus, nickel and silver coins circulating together would cause confusion. Gold is the most recognizable of the precious metals.

(vi) *Homogeneity.* The material should be of the same quality throughout and capable of standardization. Metals are obviously the best for this purpose.

(vii) *Divisibility.* The material should be capable of being divided without losing value. Again, metals show to advantage; after division, they can be reunited. Some of the older forms of money tended to lose heavily in value when broken up.

(viii) *Malleability.* A material which permits of moulding and stamping is essential so long as the standard currency has to pass from hand to hand.

Advantages and Limitations of Gold

It is clear that metals, in the matter of divisibility, homogeneity, durability, and malleability, are much superior to such early forms of money as cattle and skins. Among the metals, gold stands out as best fitted for use as money. It has many alternative uses, and, when necessity arises, can be reclaimed from ornamental use and converted into bullion or coin. It is compact and cognizable, does not tarnish, and can be stored without loss.

Though the stability of the value of gold leaves much to be desired, no other single metal or other commodity has been discovered that serves the purpose as well. An advantage of gold in this respect is that the world's stock is very large, in comparison with the annual output.[1] In normal times the demand for gold proceeds at about the same pace as the supply, and serious discrepancies are infrequent. During recent years, however, the demand for gold has greatly exceeded the supply, while the situation has been rendered even more difficult by a maldistribution among the countries of the world. The value of gold has thus proved to be less stable than ought to be expected of a standard medium.

With regard to portability, while gold has the highest specific value of all the coin-metals except platinum, it is too heavy and inconvenient for the huge transactions that now occur daily. Further, the transport of gold involves a certain cost. A system of accounting has developed, and paper money and other credit documents tend increasingly to take the place of gold—or rather, since the commodity value of gold is ordinarily in the

[1] The annual world production of gold is about a hundred million pounds sterling. (Of this over a half goes into coinage.) The total value of the world's coin and bullion is reckoned at over two thousand millions. The annual addition to the stock, therefore, is about 5 per cent. Thus, even if the world's annual output were doubled or trebled, the effect on its exchange-value, though appreciable, would not be as great as if the gold were literally used up as quickly as it was produced.

background, to represent gold—in modern transactions of any amount. Where the gold standard is in operation, therefore, the metal tends increasingly to serve as a basis of calculation rather than a material medium of exchange.

A limit to the wide use of gold is its heavy cost of production, and many are coming to question whether it is really necessary that the standard medium should be so expensive. In less advanced communities, in which the law of legal tender must rest on commodity value for its effectiveness, it is desirable that the value of a coin as commodity should equal its value as money. But this condition need not be observed under modern conditions, especially for home trade. Management of money supplies in accordance with the country's needs is already practised up to a point, and, it is contended, could be carried further with a considerable economy in the use of gold. Even in international trade it has been found possible to effect exchanges satisfactorily without the use of gold, and with further developments in international banking the dependence on gold may become progressively smaller.

To the extent, therefore, that paper currency and credit instruments are functioning as money instead of standard coinage, many of the attributes mentioned above are no longer of primary importance. It is not so essential now that the standard money material should be durable, homogeneous, cognizable, divisible, and so on. A high value in small bulk, and a steady level of value, are considered by most to be the chief requisites. Yet, as has been shown, the former attribute is claimed by many to be an unnecessary extravagance, while the latter, which is universally admitted to be essential, seems to be possessed by gold to an inadequate degree.

Development of the Gold Standard in England

Gold has not always been the single standard metal in the British coinage. It began to be coined regularly in 1344, but before then silver had been the standard basis. (The pound was originally equivalent to 1 lb. of silver.)

From that date until 1816 silver and gold were in circulation together, and variations in their proportionate values to each other were a constant source of anxiety to the Mint officials.

Following the recoinage of silver in 1696, when full-weight coins were issued in place of the light and base coins, the gold coinage became over-rated (i.e. its bullion value was less than its face value), with the result that people preferred to use it in the place of the silver currency, which tended to go out of circulation.[1] In 1717, the value of the guinea as measured in silver was reduced from 21s. 6d. to 21s., and gold and silver coins were supposed to circulate together at a fixed ratio. But the silver currency was still under-rated and again tended to disappear.

In 1816 the whole system was reorganized, and gold was made the single standard. The sovereign took the place of the guinea, and its weight was fixed at 123·27447 grains of standard gold, $\frac{11}{12}$ths or 22 carats fine; silver coins were reduced to the rank of tokens.[2] Other countries, too, came to adopt gold as the single standard.

Until recently the Mint accepted gold for coinage at £3 17s. 10½d. per ounce, but in practice a person took it to the Bank of England, which was legally compelled to give cash for all gold at £3 17s. 9d. per ounce. (The difference of 1½d. was not a charge for coining, but rather

---

[1] This was in accordance with Gresham's Law, which is considered, together with its wider implications, below (pp. 188–9).

[2] Token coinage has only a limited legal tender, silver up to £2 and copper up to 1s.

a compensation for loss of interest between the time of paying out coin and the minting of the bullion.)[1]

Before the Great War coins to the value of 5s. 6d. were made from an ounce of silver, $\frac{37}{40}$ths fine. As the price of silver was in those years much below 3s. per ounce, the Mint made an appreciable profit on silver coins, even after paying the costs of minting and loss through wear.

By 1918 the price of silver had risen to over 5s. 6d. per ounce. This meant that the face value of silver coins was now below their bullion value. As expected, the coins began to go out of circulation. To restore the position, the State in 1920 introduced a silver-nickel currency, which was cheaper to produce. Since then, silver has fallen again in price; but, as the silver currency is in any case only a token coinage, there seems to be no adequate reason why the older and more expensive form should be restored.

The gold standard was maintained unimpaired until the war, when its abandonment by most of the belligerent countries proved inevitable. Subsequently, a return was made to gold, usually under qualified conditions, but, owing to difficult world conditions that culminated in the crises of 1931, it was found necessary in most countries once more to resort to suspension.

Gold Standard Systems

There are three systems by which the price of gold may be fixed, within narrow limits, in terms of a country's currency.

---

[1] Gold coinage is "free" in the sense that bullion is taken in exchange for coinage up to any amount; "gratuitous" in that no charge is made for minting.

Where a charge is made by a State to cover the cost of minting, it is known as a "Mintage" or "Brassage."

Any toll that is exacted over and above the brassage is described as a "Seignorage."

(*a*) **Gold Specie Standard.** This standard operates when a government issues gold coins of a certain weight. It must be willing at any time to convert a fixed weight of gold into a definite number of coins of fixed value; also any person must be free to melt down these coins or to export them. This was the system prevailing in the United Kingdom before 1914.

(*b*) **Gold Bullion Standard.** Under this system the price of gold in terms of a country's currency is fixed without the use of gold coins. For example, from 1925 to 1931 the price of gold in this country in terms of pounds was fixed, but gold coinage had long disappeared from circulation. Gold bullion could be obtained at the Bank of England in exchange for pound notes, provided that not less than 400 oz. of fine gold was purchased. This minimum virtually ensured that the gold would be available for foreign, but not for domestic, payments.

(*c*) **Gold Exchange Standard.** This system is more complex than the other two. A country determines the value of its money in terms of gold by fixing the rate of exchange between its own currency and that of another country employing a gold basis. Thus there may not be any gold in a country, but if its Central Bank holds a reserve of notes (or equivalent credits) of another country, which is on the gold specie or bullion standard, it can fix the price of gold in terms of its own currency.

Section 3. Paper Money

Paper Tokens

A coin may be regarded as an order on a person to supply a certain quantity of goods, and is acceptable because its function is continuous and carries on this order from person to person. Gold, silver, and copper coins are orders on goods, subject to the varying conditions of legal tender. Equally effective as an order, and therefore as

money, may be a piece of paper, issued and controlled
by authority. A pound note and a half-crown have this
in common that neither contains full value in itself, but
is simply a token, though in different degree, serving in
the place of standard money.

Provided that there is no abuse in the conditions of
issue, paper notes may perform the functions of money
as well as gold and, in some cases, even better. Coins
gradually lose in metal content by constant wear and tear,
and have periodically to be replaced at public cost.
Further, if a gold coin were to be lost, not only would
the late owner be the sufferer, but the community as a
whole would be so much the poorer. The destruction of
a paper note, on the other hand, while it would involve a
reduction in the wealth of the former possessor, would
cancel a claim on the issuing authority, and thereby
inflict no loss on the nation in general.

Forms of Paper Money

(i) **Representative Paper Money.** This form of money represents an equivalent value in coin or bullion earmarked
and deposited in a bank vault or State treasury, and is
convertible into coin as and when the holder requires.

(ii) **Fiduciary Paper Money—Convertible or Inconvertible.** This is a promise to pay, not directly backed by
specie, but rather by the faith that the promissor can
inspire. If a State's credit is good, the people will accept
the fiduciary paper without demur. Though a very large
part of the Bank of England's note issue is fiduciary,
nobody questions the Bank's credit or note issue on that
account.

The British Currency note issue, that was introduced
in 1914, was mainly of a fiduciary kind. The extent of
the convertibility of Currency notes into gold was responsible for some confusion. Until 1925 the notes were, on

demand, convertible into gold coins at the Bank of England. These coins, however, could not legally be melted down, nor could they be exported without permission. Since a sovereign had no more legal exchange power than a pound note, the inducement to demand gold coins was not very strong. The notes, therefore, were virtually inconvertible into bullion.

In 1925 the Government decided to permit the export of gold, but to make the Currency note inconvertible for amounts of smaller value than 400 ounces of gold. Thus, a limited convertibility was introduced. Three years later the Currency note issue became amalgamated with the Bank of England note issue, the conditions of convertibility remaining unchanged. In 1931, however, it was found necessary once more to suspend gold payments.[1]

(iii) **Inconvertible or Conventional Paper Money.** This represents and promises nothing definite. The circulation is legally enforced, but there is no convertibility into coin on demand. It is a means sometimes adopted by governments, whose resources are low, to meet their obligations; and, though there may be some kind of promise of eventual redemption, the date may be vague, and the prospects vaguer. During the years following the war certain Continental paper currencies, with careful control and limitation, served more or less satisfactorily inside their own countries, but that did not prevent depreciation in terms of foreign currencies. The internal purchasing power of a country's currency depends largely on the trust shown in its government and on the effectiveness of the laws of legal tender. As a rule, depreciation shows itself more quickly in international than in internal exchange, since these laws do not extend beyond the national boundaries, and the foreigner will not usually accept an inconvertible currency except at a discount.

[1] See pp. 265–6.

Economy of Paper Money

A perfectly regulated paper money would have an advantage over a gold currency in that it would substitute a cheap for an expensive material, and save the heavy costs of minting. The gold so saved could be diverted to use in the arts. This does not necessarily mean that gold would cease to be the standard of value. A currency might be almost entirely paper, yet convertible on demand into gold. Provided that people freely accepted this paper currency (and they would if they had complete faith in their government), there is every reason to believe that the paper money would, in ordinary exchange, take the place of gold. It has been said, however, and with some truth, that gold has for so long been the basis of international settlements because people cannot trust governments to keep their paper issues under proper control. Before paper could take the place of gold in effecting settlements (even though gold still remained the standard of value) some scheme of international agreement would have to be evolved.

Gresham's Law

We have already had occasion to refer to the tendency for over-rated to drive under-rated money out of circulation. This tendency is in accordance with "Gresham's Law,"[1] which, in simple terms, states that, *where good and bad money are circulating together as legal tender, the bad money tends to drive out the good.*

When the law was first formulated, it referred to debased coinage only; but it can be shown to apply equally to

---

[1] This law is incorrectly attributed to Sir Thomas Gresham, who was the founder of the Royal Exchange and financial counsellor to Queen Elizabeth. It had been propounded by earlier thinkers, notably Nicholas Oresme, minister to the French King, Charles V, in the fourteenth century. (See Appendix.)

depreciated coinage not necessarily debased, and also to depreciated paper currencies.[1]

(i) *When good and bad coins of the same metal circulate together as legal tender*, the full-weight coins tend to be kept back from circulation, and may be hoarded or melted down. Further, since the laws of legal tender do not apply outside the home country, foreigners will accept coins only at their bullion value, and there is naturally a tendency to export the good coinage that commands a higher value abroad than at home.

(ii) *When coins of two different metals circulate in a bimetallic system, and the market ratio is different from the Mint ratio*, and since both kinds of coins are legal tender up to any amount, the tendency will be for the coins with a smaller market value as bullion to drive out of circulation those coins with a higher bullion value.

(iii) *When an inconvertible paper currency is circulating together with full-value coinage*, and they are both un-limited legal tender, the coinage tends to disappear, and the resultant shortage of currency may induce the State to issue still further quantities of paper.

In the long run, however, the inferior currency may bring about such unwelcome results that good money has to be re-introduced to drive out the bad. This has hap-pened on several occasions during the past decade—e.g. the substitution of the German renten-mark for the earlier heavily depreciated paper. Hence, over a long period, Gresham's Law does not necessarily operate, and, in favourable circumstances, the reverse of it is nearer the truth.

---

[1] By *debasement* is meant the interference with the weight or quality of the metal in a coin, so as to misrepresent its real value. *Depreciation* refers to the diminished purchasing value of money, and may be the result of debasement of coinage or inconvertibility of notes, or to changes in the supply of money generally. *Appreciation*, on the contrary, denotes an increase in the purchasing value of money.

Signs of Over-issue of Notes

An over-issue of paper money is usually indicated by some, if not all, of the following signs—

(i) *Premium on gold*. One of the immediate consequences of an over-issue of notes is the rise in the value of gold. This is largely due to the demands of foreigners, who are unwilling to accept the paper currency, unless at a discount. In the home country as well there may be a marked preference for gold over paper. Hence there may be a

(ii) *Disappearance of gold*. In accordance with Gresham's Law, the gold tends to be driven out of circulation by hoarding, melting, and exporting.

(iii) *Rise in prices*. In accordance with the Quantity Theory of money and prices, which will be explained in the next chapter, a rise in the general price level tends to follow an increase in the amount of effective money in circulation.

(iv) *Duplication of prices*. Where gold and paper circulate together, there may be the peculiar phenomenon of two sets of prices (i.e. relatively low gold prices and high paper prices) for the same things, though such a condition can obtain only where the legal tender laws are ineffective.

(v) *Adverse foreign exchange*. The bearing of the conditions of note issue on the rate of exchange is discussed in Chapter XVI, Sect. 2.

CHAPTER XIII

MONEY AND PRICES

The Value of Money

THE value of money is the power that money has in exchange for other commodities, i.e. its purchasing power.[1] A rise in prices, therefore, means a fall in the value of money, and a fall in prices means a rise in the value of money. Changes in the value of money are measured by changes in the general level of prices; in other words, the value of money and the level of prices are different expressions for the same condition.

It was observed in the chapters on Value, that an increase or decrease in the supply of anything tended respectively to lower or raise its value, and that an increase or decrease in the demand for anything tended respectively to raise or lower its value. The value of money, taken as a whole, is determined in no exceptional manner.

It may be stated that—

(i) *An increase in the quantity of money, unaccompanied by a corresponding increase in the quantity of goods, tends to lower the value of money (i.e. to raise prices).*

(ii) *A decrease in the quantity of money, unaccompanied by a corresponding decrease in the quantity of goods, tends to raise the value of money (i.e. to lower prices).*

---

[1] The *value of money* must be distinguished from the *price of money*. The latter is the money market term for the charge that is made for the use of money for a certain period, and is equivalent to the rate of interest or discount. It is also necessary to distinguish between the value of money and the value of gold as a commodity.

(iii) *An increase in the quantity of goods, unaccompanied by a corresponding increase in the quantity of money, tends to raise the value of money (i.e. to lower prices).*

(iv) *A decrease in the quantity of goods, unaccompanied by a corresponding decrease in the quantity of money, tends to lower the value of money (i.e. to raise prices).*

The Quantity Theory of Money and Prices

The above tendencies form the basis of the Quantity Theory of money and prices. As originally conceived, the theory stated that general prices are directly proportionate to the quantity of currency in circulation, i.e. an increase of (say) 100 per cent in the amount of money automatically results in an equal rise in the general price level. The argument in a very simple form was on the following lines: Imagine an isolated country with a given number of units of currency and an equal number of commodities offered for sale, all of equal value. If each commodity exchanged once, the price would be 1 unit of money. Suppose that the supply of money for some reason doubled in quantity, the amount of goods remaining the same. Each commodity would now exchange for two units of money; i.e. the general level of prices would be doubled. Suppose, on the contrary, that the amount of currency were halved, or, what comes to the same thing, that the number of commodities offered for sale were doubled. In such circumstances each unit of money would now be equivalent in exchange to two commodities. It would, in a sense, have twice as much work to perform as before, and the general price level would be halved.

In practice it is found, however, that price movements do not correspond to changes in money supplies in the exact ratio that the theory in its original and over-simplified form suggested. Several qualifications have to be made before the theory can be reconciled with actual conditions.

Modifications of the Quantity Theory

(i) *Notes and credit instruments*. Anything that does the work of money naturally affects the ratio between purchasing medium and the quantity of goods. Thus, an increase in the amount of paper currency or in the issues of credit tends to send up the demand for goods, with a consequent rise in general prices. When note and credit issues are contracted prices tend to fall.

(ii) *Rapidity of circulation*. It needs little demonstration to show that hoarding, by reducing the quantity of effective money, has the same restrictive tendency on prices as a physical reduction in the total quantity of money. Conversely, the repeated use of the same money has an effect similar to that of an increase in actual quantity. Thus, a pound note, which, in a given period, circulates five times, does as much work and exercises the same effect on prices as a five-pound note which changes hands only once.

(iii) *Volume of trade*. On the other hand, an increase in the volume of trade tends to lower prices, for it means that the money available has more work to do. It entails an increased demand for money, which thereby rises in value as a purchasing medium.

The volume of transactions is influenced by—

(*a*) Total amount of goods produced;

(*b*) Efficiency and organization of production;

(*c*) Number of times the goods change hands before final consumption.

To sum up the above general conclusions, one may say that **the level of general prices tends to vary directly with the quantity of money of all kinds and the rapidity of circulation (together equivalent to the supply of effective** money), and inversely with the volume of trade (equivalent to the demand for money).[1]

A caution is necessary in applying the quantity theory, which, like other economic laws, is a statement of tendency rather than a rigid formula. Various schemes for the reform of the currency have been devised, resting largely on the assumption of an automatic reaction of the quantity of money on the level of prices.[2] But the currents and counter-currents in modern exchange are too numerous and diverse to permit of instant and certain regulation by manipulation of the quantity of money. In a short period the amount of money may be reduced and prices still continue to rise, while an increased money supply may be accompanied by a fall in prices. Also, an expansion or contraction of money supplies may set up a train of circumstances, psychological as well as economic, that increase or diminish prices in a relatively greater degree. Thus, for example, an increase in the volume of trade may bring about a more than proportionate addition to the supplies of credit, and prices may rise in consequence. Or a sudden restriction in credit facilities may result in traders throwing their stocks upon the market to such a degree that prices are brought below the level justified by monetary conditions alone.

Measurement of the Price Level : Index Numbers

Changes in the prices of single commodities are of little assistance in computing the value of money, especially as these particular prices may be rising while the general

[1] This "equation of exchange," in its simplest form, may be expressed by the formula—

$$P \propto \frac{M \times R}{V}$$

Where P = Level of prices,
M = Amount of money of all kinds in circulation,
R = Rapidity of circulation, and
V = Volume of trade.

[2] See pp. 198-9.

price level is falling. But if a large number of representative articles and services are taken, and their general average trend is observed, movements in the value of money can then be satisfactorily deduced.

In the calculation of an index number of prices, a certain year is taken as a basis of comparison, the index for that year being regarded as 100. If the general level of prices rises by 15 per cent, the new index number is 115. If it falls by 15 per cent, the index number is 85.[1]

There are various methods adopted of arriving at an index number (e.g. the *Economist*, the *Statist*, the Sauerbeck systems, and those followed by the Board of Trade, which publishes an index of wholesale prices, and by the Ministry of Labour, which issues a cost of living or retail

WHOLESALE PRICES [2]

Date	Index Number (16th Sept, 1931 = 100)				
	U.K.	U.S.A.	France	Italy	Germany
Average 1913	115·8	101·1	111·1	112·0	91·9
1925	177·9	152·3	154·1	148·9	130·2
1929	150·9	139·4	141·3	146·0	126·1
1930	129·3	125·1	124·3	125·0	103·8
1931	107·7	103·5	105·5	103·5	101·9
1932	103·5	89·3	92·0	93·1	88·7
1933	103·5	93·7	87·7	86·6	85·7
1934	106·4	111·1	83·1	84·2	90·4
1935	108·1	120·3	78·4	97·2	93·5
1936	116·2	121·4	90·6	112·5	95·6
1937 (June 30) . .	136·6	134·6	121·4	—	97·4

RETAIL PRICES (Cost of Living)
Percentage increase above July, 1914 = 100.

Date	Food	Rent (including Rates)	Clothing	Fuel and Light	Other Items Included	All Items Included
End of 1925 . .	71	48	125	80–85	80	75
1929 . .	57	52	115	75	80	66
1930 . .	38	54	105	75	75	53
1931 . .	31	54	90	75	75	47
1932 . .	23	55	85	70–75	70–75	42
1933 . .	24	56	85	70–75	70–75	42
1934 . .	25	56	85–90	70–75	70–75	43
1935 . .	31	58	85	75	70	47
1936 . .	36	59	90–95	75–80	70	51

[1] A fall of 10 "points" is not necessarily the same as 10 per cent. When the index number is reduced from 200 to 190, the fall is one of 10 points, but only 5 per cent.
[2] Lloyds Bank Monthly Review.

index number), but the same general principles of calculation are more or less common to all.

Construction of Index Number

(i) A large number of commodities should be taken. A comprehensive index number should include the cost of services as well as that of material commodities.

(ii) These should be representative of as many different types of product as possible. A preponderance of foodstuffs or manufactured articles in the selection would give an unbalanced and misleading result.

(iii) Some commodities enter more into consumption than others, *cf.* bread and silk. If a simple average were taken, a rise in the price of bread might appear to be cancelled by a fall in the price of silk, thus leaving the index number unaffected, despite the fact that much greater quantities of bread are consumed than of silk. Accordingly, the device of *weighting* is adopted. Each price is multiplied by a number calculated to represent the relative quantitative importance of the commodity in question, and the resultant index number gives, therefore, a more correct statement of the change in the value of money.[1]

---

[1] Suppose, for example, that a loaf of bread costs 4d., and that a yard of silk cloth costs £1, and that subsequently the price of bread rises to 6d. and that of the silk length falls to 10s.

If a simple average were taken,

First period.		Second period.	
Bread	= 100	Bread	= 150
Silk	= 100	Silk	= 50
Average Index No.	= 100	Average Index No.	= 100

Such a calculation would suggest that in the second period there is no depreciation of the value of money. By the system of weighting, however, the index number for the second period turns out to be nearer the truth. Suppose bread and silk are consumed in the proportions of 7 to 1.

Then—

First period.		Second period.	
Bread (7 units)	= 700	Bread (7 units)	= 1050
Silk	= 100	Silk	= 50
Average of 8 units	= 100	Average of 8 units	= 137½

I.e. the Weighted Index Number for bread and silk = 137½.

PRICE MOVEMENTS IN BRITAIN
IN THE LAST HUNDRED YEARS

Years	Price Movements	Monetary and Industrial Conditions
1802–1809	Rise	Napoleonic Wars. Bank-note inflation.
1809–1849	Fall	Increase in volume of production. Relative shortage of money. Tariff reductions.
1849–1874	Rise	Gold supplies from California and Australia. Development of banking and credit system.
1874–1896	Fall	Increased demand for gold for currency. (Germany adopted gold standard in 1871, and Italy in 1873.) Expansion of industry and therefore of demand for gold and credit.
1896–1914	Rise	Gold supplies from South Africa and extension of banking and credit facilities.
1914–1920	Rise	The Great War. Inflation of currencies and credit. Restriction of normal production.
1920–1922	Fall	Reaction following abnormal war years. Increased production. Deflationist policy.
1922–1925	Rise	Temporary check.
1925–1931	Fall	Deflationist movement continued. Improvement to 1929 followed by world depression.
1931–1937	Rise	General recovery.

Falling and Rising Prices

The effects of falling prices may be briefly summarized—

(i) People whose incomes are fixed either by contract or by statute (such as fixed-interest receivers or pensioners) enjoy an increase in their real income as prices fall. On the assumption that the total real income of the nation remains the same, the receivers of fixed money incomes derive a greater proportion for themselves, leaving a smaller amount for the "residual" forms of income (such as profits), which may be inadequate to maintain the supply of enterprise and effort.

(ii) Manufacturers and other employers may find that their selling prices fall more rapidly than certain of their costs, notably wages, rentals, and other fixed charges, and tend to restrict their output in consequence. In anticipation of a continued drop in prices, sellers may throw their stocks upon the market to an excessive degree, thus intensifying the price decline.

(iii) Wholesale prices fall more quickly than retail prices, partly because the market in raw materials is keener, and partly because of the long-period conditions governing the prices of many retail products. In so far as wages are determined by the retail price level there is in consequence a certain time-lag in wage adjustments.

(iv) Falling prices and profits tend to discourage new investment, and thus retard industrial development.

(v) The revenue of the State from taxation is liable to fall, since realized profits and therefore income tax yield are less, estates subject to death duties are valued at a correspondingly low figure, *ad valorem* duties provide less as the commodities become cheaper, and so on. Furthermore, as the greater part of public expenditure is of a fixed contractual character (payments on National Debt, pensions, etc.), the real burden to the taxpayer is apt to be greater, and expenditure on unemployment to increase.

The effects of rising prices are roughly the opposite of those just enumerated. They are beneficial to manufacturers and others whose products rise in price faster than the expenses of production. They may also have a useful psychological effect in stimulating economic undertakings, provided they do not lead to injurious speculations. On the other hand, they are harmful to those whose incomes do not rise at the same rate.

On the whole, steady prices are the most advantageous to traders and industrialists in general, especially over a long period. They enable forecasts to be made with greater accuracy, and thus facilitate long-period contracts. Consequently production and employment are rendered more continuous, and the incomes of all classes more regular.[1]

---

[1] *Money and Relative Prices.* In the account so far reference has been made only to the causal relationship between the *total* quantity of money, the *general* level of prices, and the *total* volume of production. The theorizing in its present state can be criticized on the ground that it is not these aggregates that count in everyday life so much as individual variations. It is considered insufficient to regard relative prices merely as "frictional" manifestations, arising from disturbances in the total supplies of money and the general price level.

Recent developments in this theory are closely bound up with the study of trade fluctuations (see Chapter XVII). Prof. Hayek, for example (*Prices and Production*), maintains that any change in the total quantity of money must influence relative prices, and since it is relative prices that directly influence the character and direction of production, changes in total volume of money supplies must have an effect on production. He criticizes the theory that if the general price level remains constant, economic equilibrium is not disturbed by monetary changes. Such criticisms, which it is impracticable to deal with adequately in an elementary work, would, if accepted, lead to the abandonment of a theory of a direct relationship between money and the general price level and substitute a theory that attempts to trace the connection between money and relative prices, and the effects of the latter on production.

CHAPTER XIV

CREDIT AND BANKING

Section 1. The Growth of Banking and Credit

Evolution of Credit and Banking

THE beginnings of modern banking may be traced to the early goldsmiths, with whom wealth used to be deposited for safe custody, and who made a charge for the service. A depositor who wanted to pay a debt would at first withdraw his money and pay it to the creditor, who might redeposit it with the same goldsmith. This method proving cumbersome, a more convenient and economical system arose, under which the goldsmith, who was well known and trusted, gave a receipt for the money to the depositor, drawn up in such a way that it entitled *any* holder to claim the specified amount of money from the goldsmith. The depositor would now pay over this receipt to the creditor, who would take the claim to the goldsmith. The first man would have his account debited, and the second would either receive the cash or have his account credited with the sum. Thus, claims for large amounts of money could be settled without necessarily handling coin.

But the sum deposited might be so large that the receipt for the total amount proved inconvenient for paying debts. Hence a depositor might prefer to be given several receipts of smaller denominations. These were, in effect, the early form of bank notes. At a later stage cheques became more commonly used.

The goldsmiths or bankers soon discovered that, although some money was continuously being withdrawn, the amount demanded at any time was always less than the total sum in hand. A surplus could be put away, as it were, in a special safe which need rarely be opened. At the same time they found that they were being asked for loans on good security. Naturally they would think of the money lying idle, and of the possibility of substituting securities for it. Obviously, therefore, the next step in banking practice would be to lend out some of the surplus. So long as safety was assured, the depositor would raise no serious objection for besides the remission of the former charge for the "safe deposit" service, he now received an interest on his money.

Growth of the Banking System

The evolution of the banking system may be made clearer by a few illustrations.

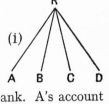

(i) Suppose R to be the only bank in a small town, and that A, B, C, D, etc., are townsmen who keep their accounts only with R. Then if A wishes to pay C some money, he draws a cheque on R and hands it to C, who pays it into the bank. A's account is debited, and C's account is credited, with the amount.

(ii) Suppose another bank, S, commences business in the town and receives the custom of E, F, G, H.

If A wishes to pay G a sum of money, he draws a

cheque on R, and hands it to G, who deposits it with S. In the same way, cheques drawn on S are deposited with R. At the end of a day or other agreed period, representatives of R and S meet and present each other with a claim equal to the total of all cheques received on behalf of the other bank. The difference at this stage may be paid in cash.

(iii) The need to pay even the differences in cash is obviated when the several banks set up a Clearing House, at which representatives of R, S, etc., periodically gather together, balance their mutual indebtedness, and pay the

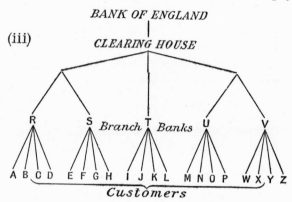

differences by drafts on the deposits that each bank keeps at the central bank, in this country the Bank of England.

The Clearing House System

The Clearing House is an essential feature in modern banking organization. Instead of each bank presenting a claim on every other bank on account of cheques accepted, and receiving cash in return, arrangements are made for representatives of the banks to meet at frequent periods and balance up the mutual indebtedness. The differences are paid not by cash, but by drafts on the Bank of England, at which the other banks keep deposits. By transfers of debits and credits in the books of the Bank of England, enormous transactions can take place without recourse to cash.

The London Clearing House is the most important, though there are local clearing houses in certain important centres such as Birmingham, Liverpool, Leeds, etc. At the local clearings cheques on local banks only are dealt with, those outside the prescribed areas being cleared through London.

The London Clearing House, to which each of the ten chief banks sends representatives four times a day, is divided into three sections—

(i) THE TOWN CLEARING—for all banks in the City area of London.

(ii) THE METROPOLITAN CLEARING—for banks and branches outside the Town Clearing area, but within the London Postal District.

(iii) THE COUNTRY CLEARING—for branches and correspondents outside the range of the Metropolitan and Town Clearings.

Functions of Banks

The general function of a banker has been defined as *the exchange of money for credit, and credit for money.* His particular functions are—

(i) **Receipt of Deposits.**

(*a*) *On Current Account,* whereby the banker is liable to pay legal tender to the depositor on demand. Usually the banks allow no interest on such accounts, and may charge a commission for the service rendered.

(*b*) *On Deposit Account,* whereby the banker is given notice of intended withdrawal, and allows interest according to the length of notice given.

(ii) **Granting Loans.** The bank lends money against security at certain rates of interest. As will be shown below, the borrower's account is credited with the agreed amount up to which cheques may be drawn.

(iii) **Discounting Bills of Exchange.** A holder of a bill payable at a future date may discount it at a bank, for which he receives its "present worth," calculated at the current market rate. Bills are a handy asset for a bank to hold, as they can be resold at any time, and automatically turn into cash on maturity.

(iv) **Balancing of Payments.** This is the collection and payment of cheques by the Clearing House System, already described.

(v) **Acting as Agent.** A banker serves in various ways as agent for customers and other banks.

(*a*) Collection and payment of interest and dividend on stocks and shares.

(*b*) Purchase and sale of stocks and shares.

(*c*) Transactions in foreign exchanges.

(*d*) Service as trustee, executor, etc.

(*e*) Provision of safe custody of valuables.

(*f*) Service as clearing agent, correspondent, etc., for other banks.

(vi) **Issue of Bank Notes.** In England, this privilege is now restricted to the Bank of England. The issue of notes used to be a more important function of banks than it is to-day. Before 1844 there were several note-issuing banks in this country, but, as will be shown later, the Bank Charter Act of that year strictly limited the issues, making provision for the ultimate abolition of all bank notes other than those of the Bank of England.

Analysis of Joint-stock Bank Statement

In view of the importance of the joint-stock banks and their power in the economic system, it is instructive to examine their balance sheets, which do not differ substantially in their mode of presentation.

Liabilities

(*a*) *Capital.* This represents the money subscribed by the shareholders for the establishment and conduct of the bank.

(b) *Surplus*. This is the undistributed profit of the bank, owing to the shareholders.

(c) *Deposits*. This is by far the largest item. It represents the money deposited with the bank by the customers.

Assets

(a) *Cash*. This comprises both ordinary cash (notes and coin) or "till money," and also the deposits of the bank with the Bank of England which it can convert into cash on demand. For reasons given below, a joint-stock bank holds cash to the extent of about 10 per cent of its total deposit liabilities.

(b) *Loans*. The remainder of the assets is normally lent out at interest. Such loans may take the form either of ordinary advances, or of the purchase of bills.

Bank Loans

Bank loans are rarely made in cash. A trader who borrows from a bank usually has the amount of the loan credited to his account. Suppose he borrows £1,000. The bank normally demands securities for that amount, plus a certain proportion to allow for possible depreciation. The account books of the bank now show an increase in liabilities and assets. Crediting the trader with £1,000 increases in effect the deposits (i.e. the bank's liabilities); the securities, on the other hand, swell the assets of the bank. An expansion of bank loans is almost always accompanied by an expansion of bank deposits.

It follows, therefore, that an increase in deposits does not necessarily denote a gain in aggregate wealth. Indeed, trade may be so sluggish that few attractive openings present themselves to would-be investors, who, until opportunity occurs, prefer to leave their money on deposit with the bank.

Two questions relating to bank loans call for consideration:

(i)   *How is it possible for the bank to lend other people's money, perhaps for a long period, yet pay the claims made upon it on demand or at short notice?*

It is found from experience that, as a general rule, only a certain proportion (about 10 per cent in this country) of the money deposited with the bank is required in cash at any one time. Many people use the bank simply to store their wealth and do not continuously withdraw it for business or other purposes. The banker works on a principle akin to the one governing insurance, i.e. that individual uncertainties and peculiarities are levelled out in the aggregate. Banking is conducted on the assumption that at any time there will be a certain surplus of cash deposited over cash required, and that this surplus can be loaned out at a profit.

(ii)   *How much may the bank lend?*

The answer to this question is suggested by that to the first. In theory, the banker need leave himself only just sufficient to pay the anticipated cash demands. In practice, of course, it is impossible to calculate with any precision what this amount should be, and the banker must necessarily allow a certain margin for safety. The liquid assets of the bank are so distributed that, in the event of unusual or even panic demands for cash, these assets can be quickly mobilized. Some bank loans carry a very low rate of interest on the express condition that they are repayable at call or at very short notice.

Amalgamation of Banks

The tendency to concentration in industry and trade generally has been very marked in the banking world during recent years. In the first three decades of this century the number of banks fell from 106 to 28, though the number of branches increased from less than 4,000 to over 11,000. The "Big Five"[1] are now predominant in British banking. The trend towards combination raised such apprehensions as to the danger of a banking monopoly that in 1918 the Government set up a Committee which, after inquiry, recommended that, before further amalgamation could take place, the Treasury must make an investigation and give its sanction. Though the proposed law was not formally enacted, subsequent schemes for amalgamation have in fact been submitted first to the Treasury for its approval.

The advantages and disadvantages of amalgamation of banking firms resemble on the whole those of large-scale enterprise generally, but the following may be specially noted—

(i) Advantages.

(*a*) The organization tends to become more efficient and co-ordination is more readily secured.

(*b*) The reserves become more concentrated and better managed.

(*c*) Risks are better distributed.

(*d*) Where private banks are absorbed, the accounts are given a greater degree of publicity.

(*e*) Foreign connections and facilities for foreign trade are improved.

(ii) Disadvantages.

(*a*) The organization is liable, under certain conditions, to become too cumbersome for maximum efficiency.

(*b*) Interest in, and special knowledge of, local conditions may be reduced.

---

[1] Viz. Barclays, Lloyds, Midland, National Provincial, and Westminster Banks. The growth of Martin's Bank has led many now to speak of the "Big Six."

(c) The concentration of national resources in very few hands might tend to insecurity rather than strength.

(d) Perhaps the most prevalent objection of all, and the one mainly responsible for the opposition, is the fear of a banking monopoly, the abuse of which would have serious national effects. Treasury sanction for further amalgamations is held by some to be an inadequate safeguard, and more direct control is urged.

Section 2. The Bank of England

Note Issues and the Gold Basis

To understand the present position of the Bank of England, it is helpful to have some knowledge of policies and legislative changes during the last hundred years. Originally the right of issuing notes was possessed by a number of banks besides the Bank of England. In the years following the Napoleonic Wars, during which cash payments had been suspended, controversy arose respecting the proper method of note issue, and two conflicting schools of opinion emerged, the *Banking School* and the *Currency School*.

The Banking School. The members of this group contended that the amount of note issues should not be rigidly restricted by the gold reserve, but should be left to the discretion of the bankers. They maintained that, if the note issues were limited by the amount of gold backing, legitimate enterprise might be curtailed. It was further held that the note issues could be perfectly convertible even though the gold reserve fell short of 100 per cent.

The obvious criticism of the "Banking Theory" was that too much power and responsibility would be given to the bankers, who might not always be able to exercise sufficient prudence or make a proper judgment of financial needs.

The Currency School. The advocates of the "Currency

Theory" adhered to the principle of a full gold basis, and regarded a bank-note merely as an economical substitute for gold rather than a pure credit instrument. Accordingly they recommended that the note issue should be strictly regulated by the amount of gold in hand.

The main criticisms of such a scheme were that the note issues would be too rigid and inelastic, and that difficulty would be encountered in the event of a temporary shortage of gold.

The members of the Currency School were more successful than their opponents in gaining the support of Parliament. Most of their recommendations were embodied in the Bank Charter Act of 1844, though the views of the Banking School were not entirely ignored.

The Bank Charter Act of 1844

The following were the chief provisions of the Act—

(i) The Bank of England to have two separate departments, namely, the Issue Department and the Banking Department.

(ii) A fiduciary issue against Government Debt (£11,015,100) and other first-class securities to be permitted up to £14,000,000, all notes over this amount to be secured by an equivalent value of bullion.

(iii) Silver to be limited to one-fourth of the gold in reserve.

(iv) The Issue Department to give notes for gold at £3 17s. 9d. per ounce.

(v) No further note-issuing banks to be established, and the existing banks to lose the right of issue in the event of bankruptcy, amalgamation, opening in the London area, etc.

(vi) The future issues of the existing banks to be limited to the average circulation for a short period preceding the Act.

(vii) On a country bank ceasing to issue notes, the Bank of England, by Order in Council, could increase the fiduciary issue by two-thirds of the lapsed note issue.

(viii) A weekly return of the Issue and Banking Departments to be published.

(ix) The existing banks of issue also to forward weekly returns.

Effects of the Bank Act on the Note Issue

(a) The Act aimed at regulation and full control of the paper currency, and at publicity respecting the issues and reserves. The Bank of England has now the monopoly of the right of note issue in England and Wales. [1]

(b) The restriction of note issues tended to limit credit facilities, though the difficulty was partly overcome by the increased use of cheques, the issue of which was not limited by any statutory bullion reserve.

(c) Notwithstanding the growth of the cheque system, the method of note issue was held to be too rigid and inelastic in the light of changing economic conditions.

The Currency and Bank Notes Act of 1928

The Act of 1844 governed the entire note issue of this country until August, 1914, when, to meet the war emergency, the Treasury issued its own Currency Notes, mainly fiduciary, to which reference has already been made. The dual note issue continued in circulation until 1928, when it was decided to transfer the Currency note issue to the Bank of England, thus modifying the provisions of the Act of 1844.

The Currency and Bank Notes Act fixed the new fiduciary limit at £260,000,000. The figure was considered to correspond very closely to the prevailing combined fiduciary issues of the Treasury and the Bank of England, after

[1] The last other bank to have these rights was Messrs. Fox, Fowler & Co., which lost its privilege on amalgamation with Lloyds Bank in 1921.

allowing for the anticipated return of notes from the Irish Free State consequent upon the introduction of their own paper currency. In order to provide for the varying needs of trade, it was made possible, under the Act, for the Treasury, on application from the Bank of England, to authorize an increase or a reduction in the fiduciary issue. (During the financial crisis of 1931, permission was granted to extend the maximum fiduciary limit to £275,000,000.)

The Act also laid down that the profits arising from the Issue Department of the Bank of England should be paid to the Treasury. In order to ensure adequate supplies the Bank was given powers to compel any person owning gold coin or bullion exceeding £10,000 in value to sell the whole or any portion of his holding to the Bank. This provision, however, was not to apply to gold held for export or industrial purposes, and therefore could not interfere with the London bullion market.

The Bank of England Return

The following is a simplified version of the Bank of England Return, which is published every Thursday—

ISSUE DEPARTMENT

Liabilities	£ million	*Assets*	£ million
Notes issued—		Government and other securities held against fiduciary issue	260
In circulation	400		
Held in Banking Dept.	60	Gold coin and bullion	200
	460		460

BANKING DEPARTMENT

	£ million		£ million
Capital	15	Government securities	70
Rest	5	Other securities.	54
Public Deposits.	30	Notes	60
Bankers' ,,	100	Gold and silver coin .	1
Other ,,	35		
	185		185

I. Issue Department.

The conditions regulating the note issue have already been observed. Items in the actual Return to which attention may be drawn are the "Government Debt," which has remained unchanged since 1833, and "Other Government Securities," which represent a strong though intangible backing to the fiduciary issue.

II. Banking Department.

(i) LIABILITIES.

(a) *Capital.* The proprietors' capital has been unchanged since 1833. The stock is fully paid (different from most of the stock of the other banks), and the liability of the shareholders is limited.

(b) *Rest.* This represents the reserve fund and undivided profits, and does not fluctuate very much. It never falls below £3,000,000.

(c) *Public Deposits.* These include Exchequer, Savings Bank, National Debt Commissioners, and Dividend Accounts. The figure varies with the incoming and outgoing of taxes and dividends respectively.

(d) *Bankers' and Other Deposits.* This is the largest sum in the Banking Department's accounts. "Bankers' Deposits" represent the money lodged by other British banks, and are regarded by them as cash. "Other Accounts" comprise the deposits by foreign banks, home municipalities, and large institutions. The amount of deposits serves as an index of the money available in the market. When high, it generally means that the banks have a large surplus of unemployed funds, and usually coincides with a low price for money.

(ii) ASSETS.

(a) *Government Securities.* These are the Bank's investments in British Government stocks and bills, and include the temporary loans to the Government in the form of "Ways and Means Advances."

(b) *Other Securities*. These represent Treasury and commercial bills that have been discounted at the Bank on the initiative of the former holders, and also loans, mainly to bill-brokers; and include in addition bills and other forms of security purchased by the Bank on its own initiative.

(c) *Notes*. These are the notes issued by the Bank itself, and compose the greater part of the cash, or "Reserve," held in the Banking Department. This Department does not directly determine the amount, which is fixed simply by the difference between the total volume of notes issued from the other department and the volume in circulation.

(d) *Gold and Silver Coin*. This item represents the till-money required in the form of coin to meet the day-to-day needs, and is included in the Reserve.

Proportion of the Bank of England Reserve to Liabilities

The Reserve in the Banking Department must not be confused with the gold reserve held by the Issue Department against notes. The minimum amount of the reserve in the Issue Department is fixed by legislation. Apart from the limited fiduciary issue, all the notes issued are ordinarily secured by the corresponding amount of gold. The Reserve in the Banking Department, it may be repeated, consists of notes from the Issue Department (which are normally convertible into, and therefore as good as, gold), together with a certain amount of specie, distinct from that held by the Issue Department.

The joint-stock banks keep a part of their own reserves at the Bank of England and have the right of withdrawal on demand. On the Bank of England Reserve, therefore, rests an added responsibility, and it is all the more essential that this line of defence should be well guarded and that the proportion to the total liabilities should not fall too low.

Until recent times the policy of the Directors of the Bank of England was to maintain the Reserve at about 45-55 per cent of the aggregate liabilities. A fall below 40 per cent used to cause uneasiness. The percentage on the 22nd July, 1914, was 52. During the war this fell considerably, and at the end of 1919 was below 10 per cent. Gradually the position improved, and ten years later the ratio had reached the accustomed level. In 1931 it declined again, but the subsequent improvement in economic conditions generally brought with it a rise in the ratio, though it was not considered necessary to adhere to the high percentage as in former years.

Drains on the Bank of England Reserve

The Bank of England Reserve is liable to a *regular and periodic drain* at certain times of the year when extra amounts of cash are required; e.g. holiday and harvest times, quarter days, dates for tax payments, etc. (Similarly, there are certain periods of the year when there is an inflow of money to swell the Reserve.)

In addition, the Reserve is liable to an *irregular and spasmodic drain*, on such occasions as foreign loans, commercial crises, or outbreak of war.

When there is a drain on the Reserve, the following are possible courses of action

(i) *To offer a high price for gold.* This method might serve to swell the Reserve, but would be very expensive. It would also make the value of gold more unstable than it is.

(ii) *To raise the Bank Rate.* This is the method that is adopted in ordinary times. As well as trying to prevent gold from leaving the Reserve, the Bank aims at inducing more gold to come into it. Movements in the Bank Rate in relation to the Money Market are considered in the next section.

(iii) *To suspend gold payments*. Only under exceptional conditions is this policy adopted. The emergency of the war and post-war years necessitated such action, in circumstances that are described later.

Section 3. The Money Market

The Money Market

Conditions in the market for money are more competitive than in the market for most other commodities, owing largely to the quickness of modern communication and to the ease of transferring credits from one place to another. The cost of this transfer, even where gold has to be sent, is comparatively small. The money market, though apparently localized in the commercial centres of the principal countries, is really world-wide in extent, and conditions in one centre quickly respond to changes in another.

The sphere of operations of the money market in this country is found in the vicinity of the Bank of England and Lombard Street. Besides the Bank of England and other banking institutions, together with the various discounting and accepting houses,[1] it includes brokers and jobbers inside and outside the Stock Exchange, dealers in foreign bills, underwriters, etc. All of these are concerned with the lending or borrowing of money, the lenders being chiefly the bankers, the borrowers mainly

---

[1] *Discount Houses* are those institutions that specialize in the discounting of bills. They are of service to dealers who are not prepared to wait until the bills mature, but require ready cash.

Accepting Houses accept responsibility for bills on behalf of traders, whose names alone are not sufficient to obtain the desired credit. They are necessary in international trade particularly, in that a creditor, who is unacquainted with a customer in another country, will unhesitatingly receive a bill which has been accepted on the debtor's behalf by an accepting house of international repute.

Though a few firms confine their activities mainly to discounting or accepting, most of this business is now done by the banks.

the bill brokers and Stock Exchange dealers. The Treasury, too, is an important factor in the money market, and in recent years especially has taken a leading part on account of its large borrowings and the disbursements of dividends.

Price of Money

While the *value* of money refers to its purchasing power, the *price* of money in the City means the rate that is charged for its use. Like the price of anything else, it is determined by conditions of supply and demand. When money is plentiful the rate of interest or discount is low; when money is scarce the rate is high.

Interest is the price that is paid for the use of money, and varies with supply and demand, with the nature of the loan, and also with the length of the period for which the loan is required.[1]

Discount is the price that is paid in order to obtain immediate realization of a bill or other claim for value which is not yet due for payment by the original acceptor.

The two rates are interdependent, and there cannot be, over a period, any appreciable difference between them. Suppose, for example, that the average rate of interest is 5 per cent, and that the rate of discount is 3 per cent, and that all other things are equal. It will seem, then, more remunerative to put money into interest-bearing investments than into the bill-discounting market. Therefore there will tend to be a transfer of money to ordinary investment, causing a drop in the interest offered, while the reduction in money supplies for the discount market will tend to bring about a rise in the discount rate.

The **Bank of England Rate** is a discount rate. It is, as a rule, slightly above the rate charged by the other banks, i.e. the **Market Rate**. A rise in the Bank rate is usually

---

[1] "Interest" in the money market sense has, of course, a wider significance than in strictly economic usage. See Ch. X, Sec. 1.

followed by an increase in the Market Rate; a fall in the Bank rate is always followed by a reduction in the market rate. Since the Bank of England, however, engages in ordinary banking business, it has, in practice, to charge its customers the ordinary market or "street" rate. Were it to insist upon the higher official rate, its customers would seek accommodation from those bankers who charge a lower price for their services.

The period of a loan is naturally taken into account in determining the rate of interest. For reasons of safety a bank has to keep a fairly large proportion of its assets as "liquid" as possible, to meet any unusual demand for cash; for it to have too much of its resources in a "frozen" form is liable to be dangerous. On the other hand, it wishes to keep the amount of idle money to the minimum. The bank, therefore, lends out a certain part of its funds to brokers and others, which can be reclaimed "at call or short notice." The "Call Rate" charged for such loans is necessarily lower than the ordinary rate.

Effects of Raising the Bank Rate

The Bank Rate is a potent factor in the money market, and exercises its influence in many directions. The events following an increase in the rate are outlined below.

(i) Usually following a rise in the Bank rate is an increase in the rate of discount of the joint-stock banks and financial houses. Would-be borrowers from the Bank of England try to get cheaper accommodation from the other banks, who, partly to secure their own reserves, partly to make a profit, raise their charges, though not necessarily to the same extent.

If, however, the market conditions are such that the market rate does not automatically rise with the Bank rate, the Bank of England may make its rate effective by selling Consols and similar stock, and also by borrowing in the open market. By such means the balances at the joint-stock banks are reduced, and the market rate is raised in proportion to the Bank rate.

(ii) In consequence, dealers and bill holders may be less willing to borrow money or to discount bills.

(iii) Since money commands a high rate in the discount market, foreigners may be induced to transfer credits to this country; an inflow of gold may result. They may also be willing to extend the credit facilities they have already given.

(iv) For the same reason, stocks and shares may be sold in order to transfer the proceeds to the more profitable discount market. The prices of securities in the investment market thus tend to fall.

(v) Traders who find it too expensive to borrow money at the high rate may prefer to dispose of their stocks at reduced prices.

(vi) Since a rise in the discount rate is usually followed by a rise in the deposit rate of interest, more money may be saved, thereby reducing the immediate demand for commodities, and thus accentuating the tendency for prices to fall.

(vii) A fall in prices, if not accompanied by a similar drop in other countries, may lead to increased exports and to diminished imports. Our foreign indebtedness may thus be lightened and the drain on the Reserve lightened. Also, for reasons discussed in a later chapter, it may cause the foreign exchanges to move in our favour.

(viii) *The general result, therefore, of raising the Bank rate is to diminish the demand for money at home, and to increase the effective supply*; this may be instrumental in bringing about a fall in the Bank rate, and a return to normal conditions.

(The events following a reduction in the Bank rate may be deduced by reversing the above.)

Qualifying Conditions

The above effects are not always completely realized, and circumstances may arise in which one or more of the several tendencies are counteracted.

(*a*) Raising the Bank rate is followed by a rise in the market rate only if the demand for money is keen. If money is not in great demand, the other banks, despite the special devices of the Bank of England for influencing the market, will not necessarily raise their rates, as customers and therefore profits may be lost in consequence. In practice, of course, the Bank rate is raised only when money is scarce, and the above contingency seldom arises. A fall in the Bank rate, on the contrary, must inevitably be followed by a fall in the market rate, if the banks wish to retain their custom.

(*b*) The influence of the Bank of England over the money market is not now so strong as formerly. The joint-stock banks have increased in size and power in recent years, and do not follow the lead of the Bank so automatically as they did in the past.

(*c*) Another factor helping to reduce the power of the Bank rate in governing market conditions is the rate of interest paid on Treasury Bills, though in practice the Treasury and the Bank work closely together.

In view of such qualifications, it may be generalized that the Bank rate should be regarded as an *index*, rather than a primary cause, of financial conditions.

The Capital Market

The market for capital naturally divides itself into two principal parts—

(i) **The Market for New Capital Seeking Investment.** Here the principal agencies are a comparatively small number of issuing houses and finance companies. On the

THE BANK RATE

The following table summarizes the normal trend of events leading to and following a change in the Bank rate. The causes and results interact and react, while the various tendencies may be offset by countervailing forces.

	Events preceding	Events following
A Rise in the Bank Rate.	1. Scarcity of money. 2. Great demand for money caused by active trade. 3. Drain of gold for periodical payments at home. 4. Drain of gold from abroad caused by unfavourable balance of trade. 5. Adverse rate of exchange.	1. Rise in market rate (usually). 2. Higher deposit rate. 3. Discouragement of borrowing. 4. Money transferred from investment market to discount market. 5. Fall in prices of stocks and shares. 6. Fall in prices of commodities, due to less spending and to unloading of stocks. 7. Transference of foreign money to London, and extension of existing credits. 8. Increased exports. 9. Improvement in foreign exchange. 10. All these events may culminate in a plentiful supply of money.
A Fall in the Bank Rate.	1. Plentiful supply of money. 2. Little demand for money caused by inactive trade. 3. Large supplies of gold, through periodical repayments. 4. Inflow of gold from abroad, if balance of trade is favourable. 5. Improved rate of exchange.	1. Fall in market rate (always). 2. Lower deposit rate. 3. Increased borrowing. 4. Flow of money back to investment market. 5. Rise in prices of stocks and shares. 6. Rise in prices of commodities. 7. Withdrawal of foreign credits in London if better rates obtainable elsewhere. 8. Contraction in exports if prices rise too much. 9. Less favourable foreign exchange. 10. All of which may culminate in conditions akin to those leading up to a rise in the Bank rate, thus completing the cycle.

Continent and in America the banks are largely instrumental in introducing fresh capital into industry, but in this country it is not the practice of the banks to lock up their capital in permanent or long term investments in industrial undertakings, but rather to lend on short term conditions.

(ii) **The Market for Capital Already Invested.** This function is performed by the Stock Exchange, where the invested capital, in the form of stocks and shares, is bought and sold on the basis, not of their original value, but of their actual value determined by present and prospective earnings. The Stock Exchange is not a market for new capital, but it is obvious that, but for the existence of such an organization where holdings may if necessary be disposed of, the supplies of liquid capital in the first place would be seriously restricted. [1]

[1] The members of the Stock Exchange consist of stock-brokers and stock-jobbers.

Brokers do not usually act as principals, but serve rather as agents between the jobbers and the public. They make their profit on the commission, and rarely carry any appreciable amount of stock on their own account.

Jobbers are usually specialists in particular branches of the stock and share market, and deal on their own account. They make their profits, therefore, not from commission, but from the difference between their buying and selling prices. The jobbers do most of the speculation in the Stock Exchange, often "selling forward" (i.e. promising to deliver certain shares at an agreed price at a future date), and similarly contracting to purchase them.

In addition, there are numerous outside brokers who effect their dealings through inside members.

The jobber on being asked for a quotation by a broker, acting on behalf of a client, states two prices, the lower one at which he is prepared to buy, the higher at which he is willing to sell. The difference is known as the "Jobbers' turn."

Contango brokers are those who lend to other brokers who need money for settlement of accounts. Instead of advancing a loan in the ordinary way, they act as pawnbrokers for shares. For a consideration, they "carry over" the shares in question until the next settlement day.

Backwardation is the opposite of "contango." If a broker has guaranteed delivery of certain shares, but cannot obtain them for the time specified, he may borrow those shares from somebody who happens to have them, depositing an equivalent sum of money as security, to be returned when the shares are paid back. The commission for this service is known as "backwardation."

Classes of Investors

Dealings on the Stock Exchange may be classified according to whether they are purely speculative in character or for purposes of investment.

The market for securities is divided into certain sections, such as those dealing in Government Stocks, Industrials, etc. This division enables dealers to specialize in particular branches of the market, and thus promote the efficiency of the organization as a whole.

The stocks and shares themselves are differentiated over a wide range,[1] catering for all types of investors—

(*a*) Those who primarily aim at a definite and constant income from investments; who are indisposed to take risks and do not wish to use their holdings as a means of controlling industry.

(*b*) Those who have no wish to remain in permanent possession of the shares, but buy only in order to sell again at a higher price.

This category is by no means rigid, and demarcation between investment and speculation is not always practicable.

(*c*) Those, such as would-be monopolists, who buy up

---

[1] The following are the principal types of capital holdings, and are enumerated in the order of their claim upon the profits of a company, or upon the assets in the event of winding up—

(*a*) *Mortgage Bonds.* ⎫ These are loans rather than shares in the
(*b*) *Debentures.* ⎬ business, and receive a fixed interest.

(*c*) *Preferred Shares.* Of the shares proper these have first claim, and receive a definite interest, with the possibility of some additional return if "participating," and of a retrospective balance of interest if "cumulative."

(*d*) *Ordinary Shares.* These involve more risk than the previous classes, and in times of good business receive higher dividends.

(*e*) *Deferred Shares.* Dividend on these shares, where they exist, is not paid until the previous classes have received their minimum return. They are naturally the most speculative, but where the earnings of the company are very large the dividend distributed on the deferred shares may be extremely high.

As mentioned in the analysis of gross interest, the proportion of pure interest in the return (i.e. the payment for the use of capital apart from the reward for risk) diminishes as one proceeds from mortgage bonds at the one extreme to deferred shares at the other.

large blocks of shares in order to acquire control of an undertaking.

Speculation

In everyday language the term "speculation" ranges from investment in anything below gilt-edged securities to sheer gambling, while even in economic terminology it is open to wide interpretation.

Ordinary Business Enterprise and Risk. People produce nowadays mainly on an estimate of what is likely to be demanded. One of the most important duties of the entrepreneur is to initiate production and to adjust it, in terms of both quantity and quality, to anticipated demand. In this, the commonest form of enterprise, an element of legitimate speculation is almost inevitable.

Legitimate Speculation. A dealer may foresee a shortage in the supply of a particular commodity and, expecting prices to rise in consequence, decide to buy in the hope of selling later at a profit. Increased demand may lead to higher prices *now*, with a resultant falling-off in consumption and an increase in production. Hence, present stocks may not be exhausted so quickly, thus rendering the total future supplies more plentiful than the dealer had anticipated. The new price, therefore, may not be as high as if some of the old stock had not been conserved, and if production had not been stimulated.

Similarly, a dealer, foreseeing a glut in supply and a consequent fall in prices, may sell now, at the higher price level, in the hope of buying back later when prices are lower. Thus there may be a fall in prices *now*, with a resultant increase in consumption and a contraction in production. When the plentiful supplies arrive, the old stocks may be so exhausted that there is a larger demand for the new supplies than had been anticipated. The price, therefore, may not fall to the level expected. Here, again, speculation may serve to regulate production and consumption, and thus to smooth out price fluctuations.

Dealings in "futures" are a common feature in the cotton and wheat markets. Speculation in the stock and share market, however, does not necessarily have the same beneficial results as legitimate speculation in the produce markets, for, although there may still be a similar tendency to level the net yields from different investments, there is not the same direct bearing on, and readjustment of, the volume of production and consumption.

Illegitimate Speculation. This is very akin to gambling, and the big profits that are sometimes made carry with them no corresponding economic service to the community. Speculating on insufficient capital, or blind dealings by outsiders who are ignorant of the market, are forms of illegitimate speculation; but unquestionably the worst kind is the deliberate manipulation of market conditions with a view to profit. The method may take the form of spreading untrue reports, or of "bull" and "bear" operations. Such methods are practised both in the stock and share and in the produce markets.

In a "bull" operation the manipulators begin by buying in such quantities as both to force the price up and to give other people the impression that they are "on a good thing" if *they* buy. When a suitable stage is reached, the "bulls" gradually begin to unload their stocks, at figures considerably higher than the original purchase price, and, if they succeed in their calculations, emerge from the operation with a handsome profit.

In a "bear" operation, on the other hand, the operators begin by selling in order to depress prices, and follow this up by buying back at figures below those at which they sold.

These operations are made still more of a gamble when the principals in a "bull" operation have not the cash to pay now, or even the certainty of it at a later date, but promise future payment presumably out of the expected receipts of the transactions; and, similarly, when the "bear" operators contract to deliver something which they have not yet in hand or even promised, but hope that out of the receipts they will be able to purchase and deliver it by settling-day.[1]

Advantages and Abuses of Credit

In view of the above considerations the advantages and abuses of credit may be summed up—

(i) **Advantages.**

(*a*) Economizes in the use of an expensive gold currency, which is altogether insufficient in quantity to meet modern requirements.

(*b*) Makes large-scale enterprise possible.

(*c*) Stimulates and finances production in anticipation of demand.

(*d*) Permits wealth to be transferred to quarters where more economic use can be made of it.

(*e*) Enables payments to be made at convenient times, and so tides over periods of difficulty.

(*f*) If its issue is properly regulated, tends to stabilize trade and reduce fluctuations in prices.

(ii) **Possible Dangers.**

(*a*) An over-issue of credit may promote unwise production and expansion, precarious speculation, with danger of "over-production" and serious fluctuations in prices and trade.

(*b*) Too easy credit may encourage extravagance.

(*c*) Where a firm is really insolvent, the granting of credit only postpones and may intensify the ultimate failure. The temporary concealment of its weaknesses may involve creditors and others in loss.

---

[1] Those speculators are known as "stags" who, when new stock and share issues are being offered at a comparatively low price, acquire large quantities with the object of selling them later when the price rises.

CHAPTER XV

Section i. The Theory of International Trade

Differences Between Home and International Trade

THOUGH the fundamental principles governing international and home trade are similar, there are certain practical distinctions to be noted. These differences are not, however, as might at first be supposed, due principally to greater expenses of transport. The cost of carriage between Dover and Calais, for instance, is much less than that between Dover and Dundee, but the presence of the national boundaries is sufficient to create peculiar problems and a special machinery of exchange that do not arise in internal trade.

An important difference between home and foreign trade is to be found in the immobility of labour and, to a smaller extent, of capital. The "flow" of labour at home is relatively free compared with that between two countries. Despite the possibility of economic gain if he goes abroad, a man ordinarily prefers to stay at home, by reason of family ties, patriotism, or simply inertia. Language difficulties and differences in the monetary systems also tend to retard international mobility.

While capital is not subject to the same personal preferences as labour and is therefore not so immobile, it tends as a rule to be invested at home rather than abroad, unless the net earnings expected on foreign investments are appreciably greater than those to be obtained in the home country.

Exports Pay for Imports

In the early days of foreign trade, imports were paid for very often in gold and silver. Such a method to-day would be very uneconomical, because—

(a) The world's stocks of specie, even if they were available as money, would be insufficient to cope with the aggregate volume of business;

(b) Transport of specie entails expense and risk;

(c) The precious metals would be diverted from internal use in the arts, and, if the country still used them as circulating money, from the currency system as well.

It is in the general interest, therefore, to reduce the payments in specie to the minimum, and, by an indirect process, all the exports of a country are, in effect, set against all the imports. Only the difference in the aggregate values need be paid in coin or bullion. By means of the modern credit system, trade to the value of thousands of millions sterling takes place annually with very little recourse to the transmission of gold.

Barter is at the basis of all exchange, but shows itself more prominently in international trade. Imports of food and raw materials and exports of manufactured goods are reckoned in terms of money, but, as will be explained in the next chapter, the transactions, taken as a whole, are largely effected by mutual cancellation of debts. When the credit system breaks down resort may be made to barter. A reversion of this kind was experienced in the years immediately following the Great War, in the exchange of goods for goods between British and Russian merchants, and again, a decade later, during the world crisis of 1931–32, in the direct barter of coffee from Brazil for wheat from the United States.

The Balance of Trade and Balance of Payments

By a country's *Balance of Trade* is meant the difference between the value of its exports over a period and the value of its imports. Reckoned in the exports and imports are the "invisible" items such as shipping, insurance, and financial services. The balance is said to be positive or "favourable" (a relic of mercantilist terminology[1]) if there is an excess of exports, negative or "unfavourable" if there is an excess of imports. Thus a country's Balance of Trade need not, and rarely does, balance in the ordinary sense of the term. An excess of goods either way has of course to be paid for by the dispatch of gold or credits.

The official statistics of the foreign trade of the United Kingdom indicate a positive Balance of Trade in the years preceding 1931. In that year the balance swung to the other side, though since then much of the lost ground has been regained.

The *Balance of Payments*, since it includes payment for any excess or deficit, must balance. On the one side of the account is the value of a country's commodity exports, gold exports, shipping, insurance and financial services, expenditure in a country by foreign tourists, gifts from abroad, etc. On the other side of the statement is the value of a country's visible and invisible imports, interest payments to other countries, gifts to other countries, expenditure by tourists abroad, etc.

The Law of Comparative Costs

Foreign trade involves an international division of function. Each country tends to specialize in the production of those commodities for which it is best fitted. It will not necessarily specialize, however, in those commodities which it can produce at a lower *absolute* cost than elsewhere; rather it will tend to supply those things in the production of which it has a *relative* advantage over another country. This tendency is usually known as the Law of Comparative Costs, which, as applied

[1] See p. 232 and pp. 315–6.

to international trade, states that a country tends to specialize in those commodities in the production of which it has the greatest comparative advantage.

The law of comparative costs may be explained by a couple of typical examples. For simplicity the expenses of transport are not considered, though in practice, of course, they are an important item in the total cost of production. Perfect freedom of trade is also assumed.

(i) Suppose there are only two countries, A and B:

A	B
Can produce wheat at £1 per bushel and cloth at 10s. per yard	Can produce wheat at £2 per bushel and cloth at £1 per yard

Under such conditions, A, being the cheaper country for both commodities, will export wheat and cloth to B, which will send money in return. Therefore, in accordance with the Quantity Theory, prices will tend to rise in A and fall in B until the respective costs of production are equal in A and B—say 30s. for wheat and 15s. for cloth. No advantage will now accrue to exchange, which will cease on this point being reached.

In both countries the relative costs are in the ratio of 2 to 1. Neither country has a permanent advantage in relative costs, and, therefore, permanent exchange is impossible.

(ii) Suppose, now, that A and B have different *relative* costs of production:

A	B
Can produce wheat at £1 per bushel and cloth at 10s. per yard	Can produce wheat at £3 per bushel and cloth at £1 per yard

Again, A has an advantage in both commodities, and will export wheat and cloth to B until, for the monetary reasons stated above, costs rise in A and fall in B. The time may arrive when wheat costs 30s. in A and £2 5s. in B, while cloth costs 16s. in both countries. A point of indifference respecting cloth is reached, but wheat will still be exported from, and money flow into, A, until the cost of cloth may conceivably be 17s. in A and 15s. in B. Permanent trade, therefore, is possible, A specializing in wheat and B in cloth.

Another way of regarding the same position, and showing the advantage of international trade, is to examine the total costs of production for the two countries together, before and after specialization. A simple calculation would demonstrate that the aggregate costs for the two countries are appreciably greater in the absence of territorial specialization and exchange. The illustration may also be adapted to any number of countries with the same general result.

From the doctrine of relative costs it follows that *it may be advantageous to a country to import something from another, even though she can produce it herself more cheaply*, provided that her resources are being applied to the production of other commodities for which she is relatively better suited. To produce all the goods herself may result in a less economical disposition of her resources than would accrue if she concentrated on those articles for the production of which she was best fitted, even if that meant her importing goods that could be produced at home at apparently less cost.

It should be observed that, while the law of comparative costs has special reference here to international trade, it applies no less to all forms of economic activity, and is indeed but a special application of the principle of division of labour. Though a business man might be able to do clerical work better than a hired clerk, it is to the general advantage that he should not do this relatively less productive work, but devote his full energies to the higher functions of business which render greater returns.

Similarly, a stores manager might be a better salesman than a man at the counter, but it is preferable that he should give his whole time to work of the higher order.

The **advantages of foreign trade** are no different in principle from those accruing to internal exchange, but, on account of the larger territory usually covered, certain of the benefits are more pronounced—

(i) Each country under free market conditions tends to produce those commodities for which it is naturally adapted. In consequence the world's productivity is increased, permitting of a reduction in prices.

(ii) Where supply and demand are spread over a large area, prices tend to be stabilized.

(iii) The variety of products available for consumers in general is considerably widened.

(iv) Local shortages do not cause as much inconvenience if supplies can be obtained from elsewhere.

(v) Since in time of war the above advantages are lost, the mutuality of trade relations and the recognition of economic interdependence should be powerful forces making for international peace.

Section 2. *Protection and Free Trade*

Early Views on Foreign Trade

International trade was hindered between the fourteenth and sixteenth centuries by the prevalent objection to importing goods of other nations. As exports, however, must be paid for by imports of some kind, the early *Bullionists* stipulated that, as far as possible, only gold and silver should enter the country, these being regarded as the staple forms of wealth. In accordance with this view, various measures were adopted to encourage the export of goods and the import of specie, while the export of specie and the import of goods were looked upon with disfavour.

When it became recognized, about the time of the Tudors, that there were certain foreign goods, apart from specie, that a country must import, the bullionist doctrine was modified by the *Mercantilists* so as to allow of the importation of these wares, provided that the total value of imports was less than that of exports, with a consequent inflow of gold and silver to pay for the difference. To ensure a "favourable balance of trade," however, measures were adopted to restrict the importation of such goods as could be produced at home. Protective duties, bounties, and other forms of preferential treatment were all part of the mercantilist plan.

One result of the continual inflow of gold and silver was that prices ever tended to rise. A country, however, whose prices are high is a good one to sell to and a bad one to buy from. Hence, exports came to be discouraged and imports encouraged, which was a situation not in keeping with mercantilist principles.

In the eighteenth and nineteenth centuries the dependence on foreign materials and foodstuffs increased, and the demand for the removal of restrictive duties gradually became insistent. The policy of free trade found favour among manufacturers and economists in this country, though rival nations, who were less dependent on international trade, were not so readily attracted to the doctrine.

In 1846 the tax on imported corn was repealed, and in subsequent years the majority of the duties on raw materials and manufactured goods were also abolished. By the end of the century less than a score of goods were liable to import duties, the object of which was revenue rather than protection.

The Revival of Protectionism

The passing years witnessed a change in Britain's relative position in production and trade. Countries that had formerly bought her goods were now producing them within their own territories, often behind the shelter of a tariff wall. Manufactures were coming into this country in increasing amounts, produced under conditions of cost with which British factories could not always effectively compete. Thus, a demand for protection gradually revived, though it was not until the war and post-war years that any change took place in our fiscal policy. The "McKenna" and "Safeguarding" Acts were the heralds of the new protectionism, the scope of which was considerably extended by the legislation of 1931 and 1932.

Though tariffs are the means most commonly employed to afford protection, other methods of attaining a similar end, possibly with fewer disadvantages according to the advocates, should not be overlooked. Some protectionists favour the practice of *Bounties* to industries which it is desired to encourage. It is held that bounties are more direct and more certain in their effects; that they encourage exports; and that they do not restrict international trade in the same way as import duties. On the other hand, of course, they do not furnish any revenue, which, though liable to diminish as the protection increases, is none the less acceptable to the Chancellor.

Another method of giving protection without tariffs is provided by *Import Boards*, which buy and dispose of the entire imported supply, permitting of no imports to pass through private agencies. Such machinery, which is favoured by many Socialistic writers, would probably be suitable only for standardized goods such as corn, wool, and the like. For goods that are not bought in bulk or are not capable of standardization, a system of licences, leading if necessary to complete prohibition, is often advocated.

Finally may be mentioned the *Quota System*, under which a minimum quantity or proportion of a given class of goods must be of home production. This system operates, for instance, in such divergent industries as agriculture and cinema film production.

Protectionist Arguments and Criticisms

The chief arguments in favour of Protection and the respective criticisms may be tabulated.

Arguments for Protection	Criticism
(i) *That essential industries need protection.* In these are commonly included agriculture, and also those industries supplying military and naval needs. Entire dependence on foreigners for these commodities might cause serious difficulty in time of war.	(i) It is sometimes difficult to decide whether, and to what extent, one industry is more essential than another. And protection of such industries might prove to be detrimental to the consumers of their products.
(ii) *That "infant" industries need protection.* It is claimed that a new industry, if protected during its infancy, will grow strong enough eventually to dispense with the need for protection.	(ii) In the same way, it is not always simple to define what is an "infant" industry. It has been remarked that a protected "infant" industry is unwilling ever to admit itself "grown up," for fear that the protection be removed.
(iii) *That protected industries benefit from increased output and diminished costs.* A popular argument, in some ways allied to (ii), is that the greater market assured to the protected industries permits of a larger production, and a reduction rather than an increase in prices.	(iii) Protection may increase the total *volume* of production in an industry, but need not increase the *scale* of production. The tariff may, in fact, cause the number of small firms to increase, and the average size of the undertakings to diminish. It may, further, subsidize the comparatively inefficient, which, but for the duty, would be driven out. The unit costs for the industry as a whole, therefore, may not be lower under protection than under free trade.
(iv) *That costs of production should be equalized.* Some tariff advocates urge that duties should be imposed of such dimensions as to offset the	(iv) The argument for equalizing costs can readily be shown to be unsound. All the advantages of international specialization would disappear,

Arguments for Protection	Criticism
lower production costs of foreign competitors.	and so, therefore, would also foreign trade. Furthermore, if the principle were logically applied, the duties would have to be differentiated according to varying costs in the several countries, not to mention the difficulty of determining what should be the basis of comparison.
(v) *That protection means high wages.* It is argued that an industry which is not undercut by foreign rivals can pay its workers better wages.	(v) Even if the workers in a protected industry were to receive higher money wages, their real income would probably be discounted to some extent by the increase in prices. And any benefit to them might entail a net loss to the workers in non-protected industries.
(vi) *That protection is necessary to guard against "dumping."* A firm abroad that enjoys monopolistic or other advantage may charge comparatively high prices in its own country, but, wishing to secure the advantages of large-scale production, may produce more than is absorbed by the home market. The surplus may be "dumped" in other countries at lower prices than in the country of origin, and appreciably below the costs in the importing countries.	(vi) Where a foreign producer deliberately sells under cost in another country in order to crush competition, with the intention of raising the price as soon as his rivals have disappeared, little objection can be raised to the adoption of preventive measures. But the importance of this kind of "dumping" should not be exaggerated. An increase in price at a later stage is liable to revive competition. Further, "dumping" is often temporary and spasmodic in nature, and satisfactory counter-measures are difficult to conceive. "Dumping" has been compared with "spring sales," it being contended that the people in the country where the goods are sold cheaply are really getting bargains. This is true, of course, only where there is no insidious motive behind the low prices.
(vii) *That unemployment is reduced.* It is maintained that	(vii) Unemployment may be reduced in the industry di-

Arguments for Protection	Criticism
the diversion of demand to home-produced goods must necessarily reduce the percentage of unemployment. Further, to the extent that the foreigner opens factories in the countries imposing the tariff, in order to avoid paying the duty, more employment is provided for the home population.	rectly protected, but, as with the higher wages argument, one must regard the effects on industry as a whole. If imports are cut down, exports are liable to follow suit —with consequent unemployment in the export trades. And it is in the export trades that unemployment has in recent years been the most acute.
(viii) *That there should be a great diversity of industries.* Under free trade, the protectionist argues, a country may specialize in very few staple industries, the failure of which would involve the country in ruin. Where there is a great variety of industries, the danger is not so great.	(viii) It is not true that a country under free trade concentrates on very few industries. The variety among the industries of the United Kingdom under free trade, for example, left little to be desired.
(ix) *That the balance of trade is improved.* Imports are discouraged by protective duties, with a corresponding improvement in the ratio of exports.	(ix) The decline in the favourable balance of trade in recent years has been due, not so much to the increase in the amount of visible imports, as to the falling-off in exports, particularly those of the invisible kind, such as the services of shipping and foreign investments.
(x) *That the foreigner may pay the duty.*	(x) It is not true that the foreigner can be made to pay the duty, except in a few isolated instances.[1] If he did pay the tax and sold his goods as before, there would not be much protection afforded to the industry. If he added the cost to the price, the consumer would suffer. It would seem, therefore, that if the home producer benefits at all, it must be at the expense, not of the foreigner, but of the home consumer.

[1] See below, pp. 285–6, note on the incidence of Customs duties.

The Case for Free Trade

The case for free trade has to some extent been presented indirectly in the criticism of protection, but it may now be restated more positively.

(i) The resources of a country, both human and material, should be allowed to flow freely into those channels where they can be most economically employed, i.e. into those industries that offer the greatest relative advantage. If a country is permitted to specialize in the production of those commodities for which it is by nature and situation best fitted, the national dividend is likely to be greater than under an artificially regulated system.

(ii) Free trade has the merit that it stimulates home producers, who are subject to foreign rivalry, to put forth their best efforts and thus increase the national efficiency, whereas protection is apt to bolster up the less enterprising firms at the expense of the consuming public.

(iii) From the point of view of the consumer, free trade is preferable, not only because it usually means lower prices, but also because it affords a wider range of choice, and does not interfere with his liberty to buy such commodities as he chooses.

(iv) Free trade is immune from such abuses as "wire-pulling" in political quarters and the creation of vested interests which are liable to arise in a protectionist system.

(v) The above arguments for free trade are generally applicable to most countries, but their relevance to the peculiar conditions of the United Kingdom is especially strong. This country is largely dependent on foreign supplies of foodstuffs and materials which cannot be produced economically, if at all, within its boundaries. Furthermore, protective duties are liable to react detrimentally, though indirectly, upon our export industries, which take up such a large share of our economic activities.

CHAPTER XVI

THE FOREIGN EXCHANGES

Section 1. The Method of Foreign Exchange

The Importance of Credit in Foreign Trade

In its early days foreign trade was carried out either by direct barter or by payment in the precious metals. The former method was very clumsy, and suffered from the drawbacks common to all forms of barter. The latter, though an improvement, was still highly inconvenient and wasteful. The risk of loss, too, was considerable. In the same way as credit largely supplanted cash payments in internal trade, it gradually became adopted in international transactions. To-day, nearly the whole of foreign trade is effected on a credit basis. By this means, *debits and credits near together are made to settle obligations far apart.*

The following simple examples illustrate this operation—

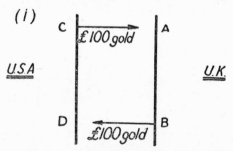

(i) Suppose B in the United Kingdom owes D in the United States £100, and that C in the United States owes A in the United Kingdom an equal sum. The debts *might* be settled by direct payment in gold, C to A and B to D. This method would be cumbersome, expensive, and risky.

(ii) Suppose now that an arrangement is reached by which the debit and credit on each side of the Atlantic are made to settle each other. Thus, B goes to A, and pays him a sum in exchange for the latter's claim on C; B then sends this claim in settlement of his own account to D, who finally presents it to C and receives the money.

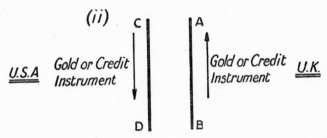

Even if this method involves the payment of gold, it is still superior to the other, in that the costs and risk of transport are reduced.

(iii) But if the system is still more developed, and the payments are effected by credit instruments, the gains are even more considerable. Under ordinary conditions the amount of bullion employed in international trade is a very small proportion of the total volume of business.

The Bill of Exchange

Though the nature and functions of the bill of exchange may best be considered in connection with foreign payments, its place in domestic trade should not be disregarded. Indeed, the principal form of credit instrument in home dealings, namely, the cheque, is nothing more than a particular type of bill that is drawn upon a banker and is payable on demand.

The bill of exchange is generally defined as "an unconditional order in writing given by one person to another, signed by the person giving it, requiring the person to whom it is addressed to pay on demand, or at a fixed or determinable future time, a sum certain in money to, or to the order of, a specified person or to bearer."[1]

A bill of exchange is known as a "trade" bill when it is based on a transaction in actual goods. It is known as a "finance" bill when it is drawn against the credit of the acceptor rather than against some specific or tangible form of wealth. The finance bill need not be any less attractive than the trade bill, and, when issued or backed by an organization of high standing, it may attain to the rank of a first-class security.

Functions of the Bill of Exchange

The bill of exchange fulfils the following main functions:

(i) *A means of obtaining ready cash.* A seller of goods may be unable to wait for some weeks or months until the buyer is in a position to pay. By drawing a bill, which is "accepted"[2] by or on behalf of the buyer, and then discounting it with a bank or other agency, the seller is able to obtain ready money, equal in amount to the face value of the bill less the appropriate deduction for discount.

---

[1] The following is a simple form of Foreign Bill:

£1,000	*London,*
Stamp 10s.	15*th September,* 19..

       Three months after sight pay this First of Exchange (second and third of even tenor and date unpaid) to *P Q* or order the sum of *One Thousand Pounds* for value received.

                                                  T V & Co.

To *R S*,
    New York.

T V & Co. are the creditors in London who draw the bill on R S in New York, making it payable to P Q or order. The bill is accepted by R S writing his signature across the face of it, or an accepting house doing it on his behalf.

[2] See p. 215, note.

(ii) *A means of investment.* Bankers and others find in high-class bills of exchange a useful form of investment, whether they keep them until the date of maturity or sell them before that date. The fact that they are self-liquidating makes them specially attractive to bankers, who do not wish to tie up their resources for lengthy periods, and who so arrange their purchases of bills as to provide a fairly regular supply of liquid money.

(iii) *A form of currency.* A bill of exchange, particularly in international dealings, may change hands several times, and thus facilitate exchange hardly less effectively than standard currency.

The Bill Broker

At any particular time there are large quantities of bills in the market seeking buyers or sellers. Traders who possess bills due to mature at a future date may need money immediately and wish to find buyers on the most advantageous terms. Banks and investors, on the other hand, are prepared to purchase suitable bills at favourable prices, while there are also debtors who are seeking bills to transmit them to their creditors abroad.

Buyers and sellers are commonly brought together, in effect, by bill brokers, of whom there is more than one kind. The smallest class comprises the "running brokers" who serve as intermediaries, and go from bank to bank ascertaining what bills are for sale and what are in demand. They work principally on commission, and require, therefore, comparatively little capital. Secondly, there are the brokers who act as principals, and depend for much of their working capital on bank loans which are granted for short periods at specially low rates. Thirdly, there are the discount houses, already mentioned, which are responsible for much of the bill-broking business in the City.

Work of a Bill of Exchange

The following diagram illustrates in simplified terms the general mechanism of international payments rather than an actual transaction. The journey of an imaginary bill begins with *A*. In practice, a bill rarely goes the whole round. The banks on both sides act as clearing agents, and arrange remittances.

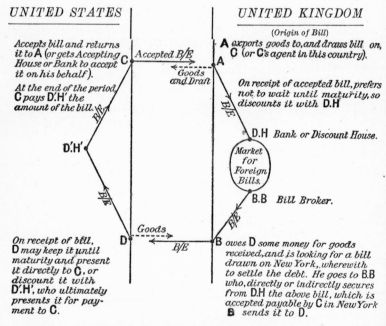

UNITED STATES | *UNITED KINGDOM*

(Origin of Bill)

Accepts bill and returns it to A (or gets Accepting House or Bank to accept it on his behalf).

At the end of the period, C pays D'.H' the amount of the bill.

A *exports goods to, and draws bill on, C (or C's agent in this country).*

On receipt of accepted bill, prefers not to wait until maturity, so discounts it with **D.H**

D.H *Bank or Discount House.*

Market for Foreign Bills.

B.B *Bill Broker.*

On receipt of bill, D may keep it until maturity and present it directly to C, or discount it with D'.H', who ultimately presents it for payment to C.

B *owes D some money for goods received, and is looking for a bill drawn on New York, wherewith to settle the debt. He goes to B.B who, directly or indirectly secures from D.H the above bill, which is accepted payable by C in New York.* **B** *sends it to D.*

Section 2. The Rate of Exchange

Exchange of Currencies

If British money were legal tender abroad or foreign money were freely accepted in this country, payments between this and other countries would be considerably simplified. It is because British debtors have to buy foreign money to meet their obligations abroad, and foreign debtors have to buy British pounds, that the complexities of the foreign exchanges arise.

There is a demand for pounds or foreign currencies, (*a*) on current account and (*b*) on capital account.

(*a*) Pounds are purchased on current account to pay for British exports, British shipping services, earnings of British investments abroad, foreign profits of British companies, foreign tourists' expenses in Britain, etc.

Conversely, foreign currencies are purchased on current account to pay for British imports, services in foreign ships, dividends on foreign capital invested in Britain, profits of foreign companies, British tourists' expenses abroad, etc.

(*b*) Pounds or foreign currencies are purchased on capital account in effecting loans, buying or selling securities, etc.

It will be shown in the following pages that, where the total demand on both accounts for a country's currency exceeds the demand by that country for foreign currency, there will usually be a premium on the home currency and the rate of exchange will move in its favour. Perhaps, too, there will be an inflow of gold to make up the balance. The opposite applies where the demand on both accounts for a country's currency is less than the demand by that country for foreign currency.

Par of Exchange

In the absence of a universal standard currency, some common measure of value has to be obtained. Where the free market for gold exists, this metal serves the purpose. During the war and post-war years the position was very vague and confusing, owing to the restrictions on gold movements and the virtual inconvertibility of many government note issues. The system may best be described, however, by reference to normal conditions.

The Mint Par of Exchange indicates the equivalence between the standard coinages of different countries as determined by a comparison of their weights and fineness. Thus a sovereign used to contain exactly the same amount of fine gold as 4·866 dollars, and the mint par therefore was £1 = $4·866.

Where one of the countries has a paper currency and a nominal gold unit, the Mint par of exchange of that unit is calculated, and then converted into terms of paper money according to the ratio-value of gold to paper.

The same procedure is adopted where one of the countries has a silver currency and a nominal gold unit.

Where a country has a silver currency only, the rate of exchange is chiefly determined by the market value of silver in terms of gold.

Variations in the Rate of Exchange

Debtors for sums in another country require bills of exchange payable in that country (or elsewhere if the acceptor is of universal standing, e.g. the London houses), while creditors for sums abroad have these bills for sale. In practice, banks and bill-brokers do most of the actual buying and selling. The price of a bill, i.e. in effect, the rate of exchange, depends upon conditions of demand and supply, which are governed by the volume of imports and exports.

A country whose imports have exceeded her exports will have accepted payment of a greater value of bills than will be payable to her.[1] The supply of bills drawn on her will be relatively great, the demand for them relatively small. Hence, the price of the bill will fall below the mint par; i.e. the exchange will be at a discount.

On the other hand, a country whose exports have exceeded her imports will be a creditor for a greater value

[1] Over a long period, of course, imports and exports must balance. When in a short period a country imports more than she exports (reckoning "invisible" as well as "visible" items), she is said to export "promises to pay" up to the difference, and, provided that her credit is good, these documents are negotiable and convertible into cash.

of bills than will be presented to her for payment. The supply of bills drawn on her will be relatively small, the demand for them relatively great. Hence, the price of the bill will rise above the mint par; i.e. the exchange will be at a premium.

During the war and post-war years, London was importing from New York more than she was exporting in return. In London, therefore, there were many people wanting bills payable in New York, while comparatively few had them for sale. Consequently, the price of a New York bill rose. Further, in New York there were many offering for sale bills payable in London, while comparatively few were wanting them. Consequently, the price of a London bill fell. Thus, the rate of exchange is favourable to a creditor nation and adverse to a debtor nation.

Where the imports have been balancing exports, and the supply of, and demand for, bills are equal, the price of a bill will tend to be equivalent to the mint par; i.e. the exchange will tend to be at par.

Currency, Prices and the Exchanges

It was observed in Chapter XIII that debasement of the coinage, or over-issue of notes, causes a rise in the general level of prices. Higher prices tend to bring about a fall in exports and an increase in imports, which between them are liable to result in an adverse exchange.

Since a par of exchange between different countries implies equivalence between their standard currencies, over-issue or abuse of one of them must necessarily be followed by a fall in the rate of exchange, unless the other currencies have suffered to the same extent.

Purchasing Power Parity

An examination of price levels in different countries, and the respective rates of exchange, suggests that there is in general a tendency to a parity of purchasing power.

This differs from gold parity in that it is not fixed, but varies with the purchasing powers of the currencies concerned. Suppose, for example, that the rate of exchange between countries A and B is 1 : 20, and that the government of B inflate the currency until the price-level is twice as high as before, but that in A currency conditions remain unchanged. The rate of exchange, or purchasing power parity, under the new conditions tends to be 1 : 40.

In this connection it is instructive to note the expansion of money supplies in different countries, the corresponding rises in the respective price levels, and the similar changes in the rates of exchange.

The table shown below is based on official statistics,[1] and shows, for some of the principal countries, the approximate equivalence between the proportion of the wholesale price level of May, 1920, to that of 1913 on the one hand, and the proportion of the rate of exchange in 1920 to that of 1913 on the other. For purposes of comparison, the proportion which the United States price level for May, 1920, bore to that of 1913 is reckoned as 100. In the second column, the figures indicate the pro-

PURCHASING POWER PARITY

Country	Price Level	Exchange
United States . . .	100	100
United Kingdom . . .	112·5	124
France	203	247
Italy	242	325
Germany	572	903
Sweden	133	125
Norway	147	146
Netherlands	95	110
Canada	97	112
Japan	100	97

[1] Brussels Conference Memorandum and Supreme Council Bulletin, quoted in *Money*, by D. H. Robertson.

portion of foreign money that American money bought in 1920 compared with that in 1913.

Though the figures are open to criticism (e.g. insufficient allowance for the varied systems of index numbers), they would seem to indicate a general correspondence between the price level and the foreign exchanges.

Limits to Fluctuations : Gold Points

A debtor buys a bill of exchange for the purpose of settling a debt only so long as it is cheaper than, or at least as cheap as, sending bullion. A creditor accepts a bill of exchange in settlement of a debt only so long as it is not more advantageous to have bullion remitted instead.

Specie or Gold Point is the term applied to that point above or below the par of exchange at which it is cheaper to export or import gold than acquire a bill of exchange.

In ordinary times, when there is an almost universal free market for gold, there are limits to the rise or fall of the exchange rates above or below par. If the price of a bill to a debtor rises so much that it is cheaper for him to send gold, the higher limit to the price of the bill is reached. If the value of a bill to a creditor falls so much that it pays him to import gold, the lower limit is reached. The former limit is termed the *export gold point*, the latter the *import gold point*.

From the point of view of the foreigner, our export point is his import point, and our import point his export point.

For example, the cost of transmitting a sovereign to New York (freight, insurance, etc.) is about 0·03 dollar. The mint par being 4·866 dollars per £ (i.e. when the gold standard was in general operation and the specie points effective), the sovereign buys in New York 4·866 *less* 0·03 dollars, i.e. 4·836 dollars. So long as a bill can be obtained at a rate which yields more than that figure in New York, gold will not be sent. But, if it yields less, gold export will be more advantageous. Thus, from our point of view, 4·836 dollars is, under these conditions, the export point for gold. On the other hand, to import 4·866 dollars from New York to London costs 4·866 *plus* 0·03 dollars, i.e. 4·896 dollars. So long as a bill yields more than that figure in London, gold will not be imported. But, if it yields less, gold import will be more advantageous. Thus, 4·896 dollars will be the import point for gold.

Automatic Correction of an Adverse Exchange

In the long run, where the free gold standard is functioning, an adverse exchange rate tends automatically to correct itself. A country which has been importing in excess of her exports has the exchange turned against her. Owing to bullion payments in settlement of the balance, the stock of gold, together with the credit based upon it, diminishes in the debtor country and increases in those countries to which the gold is remitted. In accordance with the Quantity Theory, prices tend to fall in the first country and to rise in the others. This may lead to an increase in the exports and a decrease in the imports of the country in question, until the exchange rate ultimately rights itself.

The above is the tendency in theory over a long period. In practice, it may be concealed or even offset by external and counteracting circumstances.

The Bank Rate and the Exchanges

A movement of the exchanges against this country indicates that the export gold point is being approached if not yet passed. To prevent undue depletion of the gold reserve, the Bank Rate may be raised. For reasons previously explained, the outflow of gold is checked and the inflow is encouraged. If the discount rate is higher in London than in New York, Americans will tend to transfer money to London, where it commands a higher price. This is effected by purchasing British bills, which are equivalent to so much money in London. Also, the London branches or agents of American houses may draw bills on New York and sell them in London. The result of an increased demand for London bills and an increased supply of American bills is a rise in the price of London bills and a fall in that of New York bills—i.e. an improvement in the British exchange.

In recent years movements in the Bank Rate have not always been effective in regulating the exchanges, the fluctuations in which have had deeper causes and have entailed more radical measures. Political uncertainty and currency conditions may easily negative the tendencies set up by Bank Rate changes. And when, as has commonly happened of late, exportation of gold is expressly forbidden, the effectiveness of the Bank Rate is still further impaired.

Effects of Foreign Loans on the Exchanges

When one country raises a loan in another, it may take the proceeds directly in money, or it may use the funds to purchase goods in the lending country. A loan that is virtually taken in goods has not so marked an effect upon the exchanges as one taken in money.

The *immediate effect* of a loan, by increasing the demand for bills on the borrowing country (for this is the principal means whereby the money is transmitted to the borrower), and reducing in proportion the demand on the lending country, is to make the latter's exchange rates less favourable, while improving the rates of the former.

The *ultimate effect* is just the opposite. The interest paid to the lending country involves a demand for her bills, while there is a fall in the demand for bills on the borrowing country. The exchange moves in favour of the lending country. Further, to consider more fundamental reasons, the available money is for the time depleted in the lending country and increased in the borrowing country (unless the loan has been taken altogether in goods). Therefore prices will tend to fall in the lending country and rise in the borrowing country. Hence there may be an expansion in the exports and a reduction in the imports of the former country; and the opposite tendency in the latter.

The Bank for International Settlements

During the last few years a number of important developments have taken place and exchange controls established to which reference is made in the following chapter. Mention may be made here, however, of an important innovation in international finance which promises, as it evolves from its present elementary stage, to bring a greater unity into the world's financial operations.

In 1929 the Bank for International Settlements was formed, with headquarters at Basle, originally for the purpose of conducting transfers in connection with war reparation payments (now defunct), but eventually, as its statutes show, for promoting a greater co-operation between the several central banks. The B.I.S. may keep gold deposits on account of such banks and may rediscount bills for them. Alternatively, it may deposit gold with them and have its own bills rediscounted by them. In these and many other ways provision is made for reciprocal relations between trading nations.

There seems no reason in principle why the B.I.S. should not serve, in effect, as an international clearing house. While there are safeguards against interference with individual central banks and national policies, provision is made for balances, due to and from the central banks, to be set off against each other, and thus not only simplify the world's banking system but also economize in the use of specie.

Some look to the B.I.S. as the organization best adapted for regulating exchange rates, and even world prices. These possibilities, however, are for the future. The International Bank, as it is at present constituted, has not the powers for this degree of control, and there is no certainty that, if ever the countries of the world decide on such a policy, they will administer it through this particular agency.

CHAPTER XVII

Section I. *Trade and Credit Cycles*

Characteristics of the Trade Cycle

PERIODS of good and bad trade appear from the published records to have taken place with a certain regularity during the past hundred years. An examination of the figures of unemployment or of trade returns, so far as they are available, reveals a periodicity in trade movements that suggests a cyclical trend. Thus, for example, the unemployment percentage, based on trade union returns, moved up and down during the second half of the nineteenth century, the ordinary maximum being in the neighbourhood of 7 per cent (in abnormal years, such as 1879, it rose to over 11 per cent), declining in the good years to less than 1 per cent. Though there was no uniformity in the actual rates of increase or decrease, nor an exact parallel in economic conditions during the periods, there was a sufficient similarity between the general movements to warrant the belief in rhythmical movements in trade, which were international as well as national in their scope. The statistics suggested a period of seven or eight years for the cycle to complete itself, though here again there was no uniformity. Now and again some external occurrence, such as a war, would set counter or intensifying forces in motion, with the result that the duration of the period appeared to be shorter or longer than the normal.

On the other hand, there are certain critics who question the reality of the trade cycle. They maintain that the length of the period varies so much, and that the rates of increase and decrease of trade as evidenced by the statistics are so uneven, that the facts do not bear the construction placed upon them.

Theories of the Trade Cycle

Although most economists now accept the fact of cyclical fluctuations, there is no agreed explanation as to the cause. The following are the chief attempts at elucidation—

(i) **The Excess-credit and Over-production Theory.** This theory may be illustrated by a short narrative of events in the trade cycle. To begin with, suppose trade to be improving. Under such conditions there is a keen demand for money to assist in further production, and credit facilities are extended. Prices rise because of the greater amount of effective money in circulation, and thus may encourage still further production. New firms, attracted by the profits, enter the field, and for a time there is general prosperity. Speculation may go beyond legitimate bounds. In the absence of any co-ordination, or satisfactory index of the exact amount of goods that can be economically produced, there is the risk of false optimism causing too much to be produced for the existing demand. The result is a fall in prices. This leads to a restriction in production, firms near the margin disappear, banks raise their interest rate and call in their credits, prices fall further, and for a time there is a general depression. After a while it is found that too little is being produced to meet the demand. The shortage of goods sends prices up again; production revives; and so, with the improvement in trade, a new cycle begins again.

(ii) **The Psychological Theory.** The psychological factor has already been remarked in the statement of the over-production theory, but there are certain authorities who would place it more in the foreground of determining conditions. When trade is good, people are optimistic; they buy more and prices rise; production is stimulated. Conversely, when trade is bad, people are pessimistic; they stop buying, prices fall, and production is checked.

The psychological theory, of which this is but a bare statement, undoubtedly contains much truth, which no explanation can afford to ignore. It does not, however, wholly account for the alternation of economic circumstances, and by itself must be regarded as inadequate.

(iii) **The Over-investment Theory.** In this theory emphasis is laid on the disproportionate expenditure by the community on production (capital) and consumption (final) goods. In a simple form the theory maintains that there are periodical bursts of activity due to discovery of new resources, accompanied by heavy investment in production goods. As the demand for these is not continuous a slump occurs in the capital industries and indirectly in the dependent industries. The theory in this form, while accounting for some depressions, does not explain the *cyclical* and *general* character of economic fluctuations.

A developed form of the theory maintains that the disproportionate expenditure on capital goods springs from the unequal distribution of the national income, and is made at the expense of expenditure on consumption goods. The well-to-do divert a large proportion of their income (larger than would be the case if the total income were more evenly shared out) into the making of production goods, which in turn are capable of turning out a vast quantity of consumption goods. The demand for the latter, however, is inadequate because of the restricted portion of the total income left in the people's pockets for "final" expenditure. Thus the industrial system tends to become congested with unsold products. This brings about a reduced demand for labour and capital, a period of low production, and a fall in the social income. The amount of the "surplus" naturally falls, too, and for a time there is a more balanced ratio of saving to spending. But, as the aggregate income rises again, the proportion of savings increases at a greater rate, and eventually, in Mr. J. A. Hobson's words, the "chronic impulse due to surplus income again becomes fully operative, preparing a new period of depression."

Critics of this theory deny that the trade cycle is essentially due to the ill-distribution of income. They maintain that cyclical fluctuations would still take place if the social product were more equitably distributed, and that one has therefore to search for deeper-lying causes.

The over-savings theory, however, has a wider significance. Though it may not offer a complete explanation of the causes of the trade cycle, it brings out the close and physical relationship between distribution and production, and focuses attention on the frequent lack of adjustment between expenditures on capital goods and consumption goods and on the consequent dislocation pending the restoration of the balance.

These are but a few of the attempted explanations of the trade cycle. While there is no unanimity as to the primary cause of fluctuations—and it is doubtful whether there is any single cause—it is generally agreed that the use, or misuse, of the credit system has an important bearing on industrial conditions. Even if it would not prevent periodical depressions, careful regulation of the credit system might lessen their severity.

Schemes for Dealing with the Trade Cycle

Various schemes have been put forward for "ironing-out" the trade cycle, but, as there is as yet no agreement as to the nature and causes of the fluctuations, no comprehensive scheme has yet been attempted with any success.

Briefly the schemes are as follows—

(*a*) **Palliative Measures.** The authors of these schemes, while not pretending to know *why* fluctuations occur, know that they *will* occur, and propose a redistribution of expenditure, mainly public, in such a way that large orders are, where possible, held over in years of good trade for times of depression. In consequence of these and similar measures the peak of the boom may not be so high, but the subsequent depression is unlikely to be so low.

(*b*) **Preventive Measures.** The nature of the more radical treatment naturally varies with the diagnosis of the disease. Those who see the cause in the present system of distribution of income urge simply a change of system. Those who find fault with the monetary mechanism advocate some form of co-ordination and control. Many believe that the rate of interest presents the best immediate means of exercising this control. Ordinarily, following the peak of the boom, interest rates tend to rise, and in consequence the tendency to a decline is intensified. It is proposed that the State and the Central Bank should take steps to prevent such a rise, and even make borrowing easier at such a time. Conversely, they should endeavour to keep the rate from falling too low at other times, and so discourage unwise capital expenditure.

(*c*) **Currency Management Schemes.** Apart from such major measures for smoothing out fluctuations, various other proposals have been made with a view to reducing price movements.

(i) *Regulation of Gold Supply.* According to one proposal, made at a time when gold was more available, all coins as well as paper in actual circulation should be converted into tokens that would be freely exchangeable against the standard. The government or central bank should be under the obligation to give, on demand, gold for token money, and token money for gold. Instead of the exchange-rate of gold being fixed, it should vary with the general index number in such a way that as prices tended to rise the rate of exchange of gold for tokens would fall below the market price; while as they tended to fall it would rise above the market price. Consequently, when prices were rising gold could be obtained cheaply; people would find it profitable to purchase it for direct use or export; the amount would thus be restricted, and therefore prices would fall. On the other hand, when prices were falling a good price would be offered for gold; people would find it profitable to sell their gold to the government or central bank, while gold imports would increase, leading eventually to a rise in prices.

In another scheme of this type it is proposed that the amount of precious metal in the standard coin (or bar) should vary according to the index level of prices. The standard coin need not actually circulate if there were an efficient paper currency. A rise in prices would be checked by adding to the metal value of the coin; a fall, by deducting from it.[1]

[1] The following is a summary of Prof. Irving Fisher's plan for reducing price fluctuations (*Stabilizing the Dollar*, 1920).

(1) To abolish gold coins and to convert the present gold certificates [U.S.A.] into "gold bullion dollar certificates," entitling the holder, on any date, to dollars of *gold bullion* of such weight as may be officially declared to substitute a dollar for that date.

(2) To retain the "free coinage," i.e. to be more exact, the unrestricted *deposit* of gold, and to retain also the unrestricted *redemption* of gold bullion dollar certificates.

(3) To designate an ideal composite or "goods dollar," consisting of a representative assortment of commodities, worth, at the outset, a gold dollar of the present weight, and to establish an "Index number" for recording, at stated times, the market price of this ideal goods dollar in terms of the gold bullion dollar.

(4) To adjust the weight of the dollar (i.e. the gold bullion dollar) at stated intervals, each adjustment to be proportioned to the recorded deviation of the index number from par.

(5) To impose a small "brassage" fee for the deposit of gold bullion and provide that no one change in the bullion dollar's weight shall exceed that fee.

(ii) *Management of Currency and Credit Supplies*. The schemes so far outlined depend entirely on the regulation of the supply of the standard metal, and were put forward at a time when the efficacy of gold was more widely accepted than it is at the present time. Those who advocate management of the monetary system to cope with the existing situation put forward more comprehensive schemes which are not so tied to gold, and which aim at a regulation of credit as well as of publicly issued currency.

The Macmillan Committee, in its Report issued in June, 1931 (i.e. some months before the financial crisis of that year), recommended a managed system of currency for this country, with the Bank of England as the regulating authority. Recognizing, however, the interdependence of the domestic and the international price level, the Committee expressed its belief also in some form of international currency management, to be carried into effect by the central banks of the leading creditor nations.

In detail, the Macmillan Committee proposed—

(*a*) That the monetary system of this country should be a Managed System. It was urged that such important objectives as the maintenance of the parity of the foreign exchanges and the stability of the price level could not be attained under a system of *laissez-faire* in which there was supposed to be automatic adjustment to changing conditions, but that they could be secured only through deliberate regulation exercised by persons of knowledge and authority.

(*b*) That the managing authority should be the Bank of England. It was not considered necessary, in view of the established position of the Bank of England, to create any new authority.

(*c*) That stability of production and employment should

be promoted by influencing the regular flow of investment at home and abroad. But, as the banks were concerned chiefly with short-term investment, their influence over long-term investment would be mainly indirect.

As, however, this country acting alone could exercise only a limited influence on economic conditions in general, and the price level in particular, the Committee held that some international regulatory policy was desirable. Thus, it was further proposed—

(*d*) That the international price level should, by concerted action of the principal countries, be raised; i.e. the value of gold in terms of commodities should be lowered.

(*e*) That, after prices have been raised sufficiently, their maintenance at the new level should be preserved.

As neither of these objectives could be fulfilled without international co-operation, means were proposed for bringing about the desired collaboration among governments and central banks.

Bank of England and the Note Issue

The Macmillan Committee considered that the rigid conditions imposed on the fiduciary issue by the Act of 1844, even as modified by the Act of 1928, were not justified. "If it is thought unnecessary to fetter the discretion of the Bank of England in regard to the volume of its deposits, which in a modern system is the significant and operative factor, there can be no good reason for fettering very narrowly its power to issue notes." Hence, recommendations were made for giving greater latitude to the Bank in the proportion made up of gold. With a view to improving the machinery of the Bank, it was proposed that the division between the Issue and the Banking Departments should be abolished—the arrangement having outlived the necessity—and that the weekly statements of the two Departments should be amalgamated in a single return. This return, it was suggested, should take such a form as to dispel the false suggestion that the required note circulation is necessarily related in some fixed ratio to the amount of gold in the possession of the Bank. Throughout the Report it was emphasized that, in the opinion of the Committee, the proper use of gold reserves was not to back note issues, but to meet temporary deficiencies in the balance of international payments. If gold could thus be released from this comparatively sterile function, both in this country and abroad, the shortage in its supply for the legitimate purposes would be largely remedied.

Section 2. *"The Great Depression"*

The Decline in Trade from 1929

In 1929 trade began to decline over the world as a whole, leading up to what was described as "the Great Depression." While the ordinary cyclical tendencies were doubtless at work, there were other factors to be taken into account.

(a) *Change in the distribution of world production.* With the economic development of foreign countries the position of Great Britain in the world economy was to some extent weakened. Her export trades especially were adversely affected.

(b) *Change in the general character of production.* With the increase in world income and standards of life, a larger proportion of labour and resources than before was devoted to the production of luxury and semi-luxury articles and services. The demand for such products was especially liable to fluctuation, both as regards their character and quantity, and was not therefore so stable or predictable as that for the major necessaries of life.

(c) *Incomplete rationalization.* As competitive production on a comparatively small scale was giving way to
industrial association and combination, it was more possible to avoid overlapping and waste and to co-ordinate with
greater success related economic activities. In certain
large industries, however, the rationalization was not
carried far enough to ensure adequate control over output
and prices in times of depression, and when, for some
reason, a weak link in the chain of firms broke down, the
resultant breakdown was all the more serious and
widespread.

(d) *Over-supply of primary products.* During these
years there was a marked improvement in the methods
of producing foodstuffs and raw materials, due largely
to mechanization and to scientific research. The world's
effective demand for these products, however, did not
show a corresponding increase, for the demand per head
for such articles, especially the principal foodstuffs,
was apt to be fairly inelastic, and population did not
increase fast enough to absorb all the output. For certain
primary products the world demand was definitely declining. As standards of living improved, the consumption of
bread and the like diminished, yet the world's output of
wheat was for a time greater than ever. Supplies of
certain foodstuffs and materials were on occasions so
plentiful as to make the growers resort to artificial
restriction and even destruction of stocks in order to
prevent further falls in prices.[1]

(e) *Spread of restrictive tariffs.* After the war, tariffs in
all parts of the world were raised, and the scope of these
duties considerably widened. Whatever may be the
merits of protective tariffs, so far as they affect the country

---

[1] In the cotton fields of America the boll weevil, instead of being
regarded as a pest, came to be hailed as a saviour in preventing the
crops from being too plenteous!

imposing them, there is little question that they materially contributed to reducing the world's volume of trade. Countries such as Great Britain, which depend very largely on foreign supplies and markets, were in particular adversely affected by these protective barriers.

The Financial Crisis of 1931

All the above factors played some part in bringing about the crisis of 1931. Events in this year moved quickly and, so far as they affected Great Britain in particular, may be briefly reviewed. It must be emphasized that there was no single cause of the crisis, and that, although one or two incidents appeared to precipitate it, the forces that were really responsible had been gaining in momentum over a number of years.

(a) *Decline in British exports, and adverse balance of trade.* The British export industries were especially hit by the depression, and the net balance of payments in our favour was shrinking from year to year. By 1931 it was evident that, for the first time in recent history, there was an adverse balance of payments. The rate of exchange was naturally affected, and, in the absence of precautionary measures, a drain of gold was the inevitable consequence.

The real fall in exports, however, was not so severe as the figures suggest, for prices—wholesale especially—had enormously declined, and the *volume* of exports therefore was not so much reduced as at first might be inferred. But, heavy as was the drop in the prices of our exports, the decline in the prices of our imports was even greater, particularly of wheat and of other primary products. Thus, we were able to purchase as great a quantity of foreign goods as the year before with a smaller amount of British exports.

The decline in the favourable balance of payments was

caused, not only by the falling-off in the export of goods, but also by the shrinkage in the revenue from British services usually described as "invisible" exports. In ordinary times we obtain a considerable revenue from investments abroad. Where this revenue takes the form of fixed interest receipts, such as on Government loans or railway bonds, the reduction in times of depression is not so immediate, but where it is derived from industrial and commercial undertakings, it contracts at such times much more rapidly. Similarly, the world depression severely injured the British shipping trade, the reduced earnings of which materially contributed to the decline in the net balance of payments.

(b) *The Budget deficit and the May Report.* The national accounts in 1931 were seriously affected by the depression. Tax revenue on the one hand tended to shrink, while expenditure in certain directions, notably in maintaining a growing body of unemployed, was increasing. The May Committee, which had been set up to explore the possibilities of reducing public expenditure, issued its report and drastic recommendations at a time and in a manner liable to increase foreign apprehension about Britain's financial position. Many foreign creditors feared that the Budget could not be immediately balanced by taxation, and that the Government would resort to the issue of uncovered notes, thus starting an inflationary movement the end of which could not be predicted. The pessimistic tone of the May Report, whatever may have been the salutary effects in other directions, must have accentuated this foreign nervousness.

As subsequent events proved, this apprehension abroad was not justified. By a supplementary Budget in the autumn of 1931 means were adopted to make good the deficit. Taxation was increased and reductions in certain forms of expenditure were announced. But, though the

Budget was eventually balanced, the uncertainty in the middle months of the year had much to do with the spreading of suspicion abroad, which, with the many other factors, helped to bring on the crisis.

(c) *Affairs abroad.* Foreign uncertainty was by no means confined to Great Britain's position alone. Indeed, it was not until several failures and defaults had occurred in Europe and other parts of the world that the situation of Britain came to be regarded as precarious, and it was partly her own actions in endeavouring to assist the financially stricken countries that led her into difficulties. Germany and Austria particularly were in a bad way, and their position was made even worse when, following the slump of 1929, America practically ceased lending in Europe. The British banks came to the aid of Germany and Austria, though not on the same scale as the American financiers had done, and for a short time the situation was eased. Soon, however, the German position grew serious again, and, despite the Hoover moratorium of reparations and war debts for a year, collapse in Germany appeared imminent.

Following a Prime Ministers' Conference in London, the bankers who had advanced money to Germany agreed in 1931 to renew their loans until the end of February, 1932. Thus, a large part of their resources became "frozen" for a considerable period. In the months that followed, the bankers were criticized in many quarters for advancing so much money on long-term conditions, especially as it was thought that they were largely influenced by the high rate of interest, for it soon became evident that Great Britain was short of "liquid" money to meet day-to-day demands. While there was no question that the assets vastly exceeded the liabilities, an unduly large proportion of the former was, unfortunately, in the form of long-term advances, and was therefore not quickly realizable. Having lent Germany so much of what normally would have been liquid money, British bankers found themselves in difficulties when, partly arising from all the above circumstances and partly from their own needs, foreign financiers, especially in France and America, began to withdraw funds that had been invested on a short-term basis.

Suspension of the Gold Standard, 1931

It is difficult to assess motives and disentangle causes and effects. France and America doubtless required funds for their own internal needs, and would probably have withdrawn large sums from London even if Britain's financial position had been beyond question. But, once the run had started, and it was feared that there was an insufficiency of liquid funds to meet all demands, the demands of foreign creditors for repayment became accentuated. The stocks of gold in London fell to an extremely low level. Credits were obtained from the central banks of France and the United States, but they proved inadequate to stem the rush, and in September, 1931, Great Britain was compelled once more to suspend gold payments.

The decision meant that the central bank was relieved of its obligation to deliver gold against legal tender. Gold exports, therefore, ceased and the foreign exchange rate promptly fell. The decline in the rate of exchange penalized importers, who now had to pay more English money for foreign goods, but gave a certain relief and even impetus to exporters, who could obtain better prices in home currency for their wares sold abroad, and who could therefore now compete on better terms with foreign rivals who hitherto had persistently undercut them.

The adverse exchange was in a sense tantamount to a protective tariff, and thus British manufacturers, who had been suffering from foreign competition in the home market, also gained from the suspension for the time being. Further, in so far as the imports of foreign goods were curtailed, there was a useful rectifying influence on the balance of payments.

These benefits, however, could continue only so long as foreign nations remained on gold. With the exception of the United States [1] and France, most of the important foreign countries soon followed Great Britain's lead, and therefore some of the benefit to our home manufacturers and exporters disappeared. The reasons for the suspension of gold payments in one country after another are obvious. So long as Great Britain was practically alone, her exporters enjoyed an advantage in selling abroad which was naturally resented by their competitors, and foreign governments were enjoined to adopt a like course not so much as a measure of retaliation as one of self-protection. Furthermore, the foreign central banks had held a considerable part of their reserves (*devisen*) in the form of sterling, and, when the pound depreciated in terms of gold they naturally suffered heavy losses, and in some countries had to be aided from public funds. To avoid further possible losses these central banks abandoned the gold exchange standard, and, where practicable, converted their *devisen* into gold.

Control of the Exchanges

After some months of uncertainty and adjustment to new conditions, the exchange rate of the pound settled down in the region of $3·70, and the British Government decided to stabilize the exchange for the time being at about this figure. This was deemed to be necessary, especially as the crisis in America was tending to depre-

---

[1] The United States suspended gold payments in 1933, but resumed them in the following year with a depreciated dollar equivalent to 60 per cent of the original amount of gold.

ciate the dollar and cause a flight back to the pound.
Our Treasury and bankers were reluctant not only to give
up such advantages as remained to our manufacturers
and exporters but also to be driven back to the old parity
before adequate safeguards against a repetition of the
catastrophe had been prepared.

To "peg" the dollar exchange, however, required
enormous funds. Money had to be available to purchase
dollars whenever the rate was too high, while stocks of
dollars had to be in hand ready for sale if the rate was too
low. Similarly, large funds were essential for stabilizing
the rates of exchange with other foreign currencies. The
resources of the Bank of England were not sufficient to
bear this strain, and, even if they had been, it is questionable whether the risk was one that should be borne by any
private institution.

Exchange Equalization Fund

In the Budget speech of 1932 it was announced that
the Government had decided to establish an Exchange
Equalization Fund for the purpose "of strengthening the
currency and checking undue fluctuations in the exchange
value of sterling."

The principal object of this Fund was to minimize
fluctuations in the gold exchange value of sterling. The
possible size of the operations was regarded as a powerful
safeguard against speculation, though it was not expected
that, in the uncertain world conditions, absolute stability
or freedom from loss could be guaranteed. The Fund was
also to be employed for adjusting certain accounts in the
Issue Department of the Bank of England. Part of the
assets against the note issue consisted of foreign currencies
that were liable to fluctuation in terms of sterling, and under
the new arrangement re-valuations were to be effected

each week, and any deficiencies were to be made good by transfers from the Fund, while any surpluses were to be handed over to it. These functions, however, were of minor importance compared with the primary object of exchange control.

PART V

PUBLIC POLICY AND FINANCE

CHAPTER XVIII

PUBLIC SERVICES AND EXPENDITURE

Section 1. Public Intervention and Services

IN modern times the State has assumed an ever-increasing part in economic affairs, and politico-economic problems of the first order have arisen which cannot be dealt with in the present book. The remaining chapters will be mainly concerned with the economic aspects of public expenditure and revenue, taking the politics lying behind public action largely for granted.

Public Intervention in Industry

Some general observations, however, on the conditions, forms and stages of public intervention in economic affairs may be of some help in the subsequent analysis.

Public intervention in economic affairs may be examined under two main heads—

(i) In the field of industry, where the primary object has been to secure greater efficiency and output;

(ii) In the field of income and social standards, where the chief aim has been to safeguard the citizen and mitigate the effects of the unequal distribution of income.

Government or local intervention in industry may come about—

(*a*) Where private enterprise fails to supply an essential service or commodity in adequate quantity (e.g. afforestation, bridges, etc.);

(*b*) Where private enterprise supplies a service or commodity of inferior quality;

(*c*) Where for reasons of economy and efficiency a public monopoly is desirable (e.g. gas and water supplies, postal service, etc.);

(*d*) Where the supply is in the hands of a monopolist concern which is taking unfair advantage of its position.

Stages of Intervention in Industry

The main stages of central and local interference in industry may be roughly classified. The divisions are not, of course, rigid or exclusive, and a particular public service may be found to belong to two or more of them.

(i) **Public Facilities.** These would include such State and municipal functions as the provision of currency, standard weights and measures, fairs, markets and exhibitions, etc.

(ii) **Public Encouragement.** In some ways similar to (i), this goes further and provides a stimulus to economic activity by means of research departments, information bureaux, protective duties, bounties, etc.

(iii) **Public Regulation and Control.** A more advanced stage is reached when the State or local body sets out to regulate and control an industrial or commercial concern. Such intervention may range from a simple regulatory action, without any actual participation, to a full control of the undertaking. Though the ownership of the business may still be in private hands, the direction may rest more or less with the public body. For example, gas companies and other public utility services are given monopoly rights on condition that they conform to certain conditions affecting the price and quality of their products.

(iv) **Public Ownership.** The final stage is reached when the public authority, not content with powers of regulation and control, acquires the ownership of the undertaking.

The policy may now take either of two forms—

(a) To continue the service on a more or less commercial basis, and to make a profit or at any rate avoid a loss—e.g. the Post Office, and the railways in a number of countries;

(b) To provide the service without charge, making good the cost out of general revenue—e.g. the freeing of bridges and roads for which tolls to private owners had formerly to be paid.

Public Intervention in the Social Field

There is, of course, no marked division between the social and industrial activities of the public authority. Any one of the above instances of intervention in the industrial field could be shown to have immense social significance. Similarly there are certain forms of public activity which so belong to both fields that to classify them in either would be misleading. For example, a public authority may embark upon a scheme partly for economic purposes and partly for providing work for unemployed men and bringing relief to distressed areas.

Subject to such qualifications public intervention in the social field may be said to be mainly concerned with safeguarding the individual against certain evils which are liable to arise in modern society, and against which the citizen by himself has little protection. Thus, safeguarding is undertaken in a number of ways—

(a) By general protective legislation benefiting the community as a whole, e.g. smoke nuisance abatement schemes;

(b) By legislation benefiting the consumer, e.g. Food and Drug Acts, weights and measures precautions, etc.

(c) By legislation giving protection against unsatisfactory working conditions, e.g. Factory and Shop Acts.

(d) By legislation protecting workers in certain

industries against under-payment, e.g. the Trade Boards Acts and Agricultural Wages Act.

The different forms of intervention in the social field mentioned so far do not involve much direct action by the public authority or cost to the taxpayer. They are for the most part restraints rather than positive intervention. It is when the State becomes concerned with ensuring a minimum standard of income, entailing, if necessary, some revision of the system of income distribution, that intervention becomes marked and the cost to the taxpayers assumes large dimensions. The wages legislation mentioned under (d) is, in a sense, an intermediate stage, in that employers of labour, or the buyers of their products, may be taxed, in effect, in order that the workers shall get a decent wage (that is, of course, if there is no corresponding increase in efficiency to bear the extra wages bill). A further stage is thus reached—

(e) By the provision of social services, paid for to a large extent out of taxation, which serve up to a point to bring about a redistribution of the national income. In recent years there has been a tremendous increase in the volume and cost of these services, the chief of which are unemployment and health insurance, old age, widows' and orphans' pensions, education facilities, health and housing schemes. The transference of income that is effected by the social services is substantially less than their gross amount, partly because the beneficiaries of the social insurance schemes in particular have to make contributions to the fund, and partly because the taxation to meet the bill comes, in varying degree, from all classes. The cash equivalent of the social services in the workers' incomes nevertheless shows a marked increase in recent years. Fifty years ago it amounted to less than a shilling in the

pound of wage income. The proportion has steadily
grown, especially since the Great War, and now
stands at three to four times as high, while commodity
taxation, which falls especially on the classes benefiting
from these services, has increased, over the whole
period, at a lower rate.

Section 2. *The Cost of the Public Services*

Public and Private Finance Compared

Although fundamentally all forms of finance must
be governed by the same economic principles, there are
certain considerations which distinguish the practice of
public and private finance.

(i) **The Relationship of Expenditure to Income.** In
private finance the amount that can be spent is naturally
limited by the amount of income. In public finance
the authority first determines what expenditure must be
incurred, and adjusts the taxes accordingly, so as to bring
in the necessary revenue. Essentially and in the long run
the same criterion will apply as in private finance.

(ii) **Difference in Motive and Function.** In private
finance the prospect of a surplus of revenue over expenditure is ordinarily the determining factor. This is not
true of public finance, except in the case of revenue-
bearing services (e.g. the Post Office, gas undertakings)
where a profit may be deliberately aimed at.

(iii) **Long-period Investment.** Reference has already
been made to the function of the public authority in
providing a service (e.g. afforestation) which is essential
yet not normally attractive or profitable in the ordinary
commercial sense. The long-period factor is especially important in such services as road and harbour construction.

Public Expenditure

The expenditure of the State has grown enormously
in recent times, even after allowing for changes in the

price level. It is natural that the cost of providing the public services should increase, especially when the growth of population and, normally, of the national income is taken into account, but the rate of expansion of State expenditure has been far greater than that of the population or the national income. Prominent among the causes of this expansion was the Great War, which, apart from the considerable expenditure from revenue during the years 1914-18, left behind an unprecedented National Debt, representing an annual charge of over £300 millions. The expenditure on the Social Services has also been an important factor in the growth of State expenditure. Whereas before the war the ratio of public expenditure (State and local) to the national income was about one-eighth, the proportion during the last few years has been between one-quarter and one-third.

Several attempts have been made to classify public expenditure, but none of them has been very satisfactory.

(*a*) J. S. Mill attempted a division between "necessary" and "optional" expenditure, but where one ends and the other begins it is not always possible to say.

(*b*) J. S. Nicholson classified expenditure according to whether it resulted in no financial return to the Treasury (e.g. poor relief); indirect benefit to the revenue (e.g. education, causing an improvement in production and income); partial return (e.g. education for which fees are received); full return or even a profit (e.g. the post office). The limitations of this classification, however, are readily seen, for financial return to the Treasury is by no means the only or even the principal criterion of public expenditure.[1]

(*c*) Several writers distinguish simply between "productive" and "unproductive" expenditure. The dis-

---

[1] Professor Plehn (*Introduction to Public Finance*) adopts a classification according to common and special benefit.

tinction is useful up to a point, though care has to be taken not to measure the "productiveness" (where it can be measured at all) in terms of profit, for obviously there are many invaluable public services, such as education and sanitation, which are distinctly productive in their effects, though their specific additions to the national income cannot be assessed.

(*d*) Expenditure can be viewed according to whether it is "exhaustive" in character or simply entails an internal transference of income. Belonging to the former category are the outlays on roads, armaments, etc., which may be productive or otherwise as judged from the previous point of view. Chief in the second class come the payments of interest on the National Debt, representing about one-third of the Government expenditure.

CHAPTER XIX

Section 1. *The Canons of Taxation*

State Revenue

IT is only in abnormal times, as in war, that the State depends for a large part of its revenue on loans, or on currency inflation which, through its effects on prices, is but a veiled form of indirect taxation. Apart from such means, the revenue of the State is obtained as follows—

(i) Revenue from State ownership—

(*a*) Of land and buildings. British Crown lands have yielded only about a million pounds in recent years;

(*b*) Of industries and services. In this country the Post Office is the outstanding public service of this type.

(ii) Revenue from miscellaneous sources, casual and irregular in nature, such as fines, gifts, etc.

(iii) Revenue from taxation—representing over 90 per cent of the total revenue in this country.

The Nature of Taxation

A tax may be defined as *a compulsory contribution to the public authority to meet the expenses of government and the provision of general benefits.* It must be distinguished from a fee, which is a payment for a special benefit enjoyed by the payer. Of the nature of taxation in general several theories have at different times been put forward.

(i) **The " Benefit " Theory.** In the earliest days of taxation there was a certain connection between the contribution made and the benefit derived. A man might commute his manorial or other dues to his overlord by a money payment, while a lord might commute his obligations to supply military aid to the king by paying an equivalent annual sum. But these were not taxes in the modern sense. Nowadays, if the benefit theory were generally applied, it would mean that those who derived most help from the services provided by the State would have to pay most in taxation—a position which would be impossible as well as unjust. This theory is no longer maintained as applying to national finance, but a trace of it still lingers in local taxation, where, on account of the smaller area and population, it is more possible to connect payment made and value received.

(ii) **The " Financial " Theory.** A tax is sometimes regarded simply as a means of enabling the State to carry on. The exponents of this view are not concerned with the equity or inequity of the distribution of the social product, but aim simply at methods of obtaining the necessary revenue as expediently and cheaply as possible.

Related to this theory is the "cynical" view held by those who attempt to secure the needed revenue in such a way as to encounter the minimum vexation and least opposition. The supporters of this method maintain that any tax is good which yields a large income with comparatively little protest. The policy of "plucking the goose with as little squawking as possible" may not be advocated in such terms, but it has doubtless been acted upon by many a finance minister who prefers to follow the line of least resistance.

(iii) **The Socio-political Theory.** According to this view a tax is regarded as an economic or social instrument, as well as a source of revenue, to be employed as a means of reducing the inequality of incomes. While the "financial" advocates would levy taxation in such a way as to leave the people in the same relative positions as before the tax was imposed, others would deliberately use the fiscal machine to reduce the gap between high and low incomes. Others, again, protectionists for example, would employ duties more with a view to some industrial end than to raising revenue.

(iv) **The Sumptuary Theory.** Certain commodity taxes serve to restrict the consumption of luxuries or of noxious articles. But, while there may be such a purpose in these taxes, the finance minister does not despise the revenue derived, which is frequently of such dimensions as to throw doubt on the sumptuary effect achieved. In any case there are more satisfactory and direct ways available of reducing undesirable consumption.

Taxable Capacity

The extent to which a nation or an individual can be taxed without inflicting damage on the power and will to produce is known as the limit of taxable capacity. This limit, however, is a relative, not an absolute quantity. In times of emergency, such as war, the citizens are willing to make greater sacrifices than in ordinary times, and the capacity to pay is accordingly greater. In wartime, too, it may be necessary to encroach on capital resources, whereas in peace time a system of taxation that falls on capital is open to severe criticism.

The chief factors determining taxable capacity are—

(i) *The character of the taxation.* Certain taxes are more scientifically devised than others, arouse less resentment, and are thus more likely to bring forth a greater yield.

(ii) *The distribution of the national income.* As one's income increases, the proportion devoted to necessary consumption diminishes and the "surplus" available for taxation increases. The more equal the distribution of the social income, the smaller the aggregate surplus, and the less therefore the taxable capacity. The more unequal the distribution the greater, up to a point, the taxable capacity. (If distribution were so unequal that production suffered, the total income and the taxable capacity might be reduced.) A decline in taxable capacity, that resulted directly from a more equal division of income, would not necessarily be a cause for apprehension, for presumably the need for public expenditure on the maintenance of the poor would also on the same account be reduced.

(iii) *The size of the population.* Where the national income is increasing faster than the population, the taxable capacity tends to increase; and *vice versa.*

(iv) *The nature of the public expenditure.* Where expenditure takes the form of an internal transference (such as interest on the National Debt), the limits of taxation are wider than where the expenditure involves a physical consumption of resources. Also, the taxable capacity is likely to be greater where the revenue is applied to reproductive as compared with unproductive purposes.

(v) *Political and psychological factors.* As suggested above, circumstances may arise, not economic in themselves, which lessen the resistance of the taxpayer, and which indirectly may increase the capacity as well as the will to pay.

The Canons of Taxation

The four canons laid down by Adam Smith are still the starting-point of sound public finance—

(i) "The subjects of every State ought to contribute towards the support of the Government, as nearly as possible in proportion to their respective abilities; that is in proportion to the revenue which they respectively enjoy under the protection of the State. . . .

(ii) "The tax which each individual is bound to pay ought to be certain, and not arbitrary. The time of payment, the manner of payment, the quantity to be paid, ought all to be clear and plain. . . .

(iii) "Every tax ought to be levied at the time, or in the manner, in which it is most likely to be convenient for the contributor to pay it. . . .

(iv) "Every tax ought to be so contrived as both to take out and to keep out of the pockets of the people as little as possible over and above what it brings into the public treasury of the State." [1]

These maxims, which are usually summarized under the headings of *Equality*, *Certainty*, *Convenience*, and *Economy*, may be examined in greater detail.

Equity and Progressive Taxation

Justice in taxation is a phrase which bears of more than one interpretation. It may mean, on the one hand, levying upon the people in proportion to their individual ability to pay; on the other hand, it may be taken to imply a scheme of taxation intended to modify the distribution of income. But, whatever the view taken, one method of securing a fair apportionment is that of a *progressive* levy, i.e. one which increases in percentage as the income increases. As was noted in Chap. VI, a *proportionate* impost causes more sacrifice to a poor than to a rich man, and is therefore to be criticized on grounds of equity. Progressive rates are more possible in direct than in indirect taxation, though, in judging the equity or otherwise of a scheme of taxation, regard should be paid to the system of apportionment as a whole.

Taxation is said to be *regressive* when the proportion of income taken in taxation diminishes as the income increases. While regression is, as a general rule, to be deprecated, it is sometimes unavoidable if the maximum revenue has to be obtained.

[1] *Wealth of Nations*, Book V, Chapter II, Part II.

Economy, Certainty and Convenience in Taxation

While the first canon laid down by Adam Smith, viz. equality of sacrifice, may be regarded as an ethical precept, the others—certainty, convenience, and economy —are largely administrative rules. To a great extent, the maxim of economy covers the three; and one writer[1] at least has gone so far as to include in it *all* the canons of taxation, equity included, for, it is contended, what is equitable must eventually be in the true economic interests of the community.

The canon of *certainty*, in its broadest sense, requires, on the one hand, that the taxpayer shall know exactly what he has to pay, enabling him to make the necessary adjustments in his income; on the other hand, that the State shall know as far as possible the amount of revenue likely to be derived. Vacillation tends to instability, and should be avoided. Hence the dictum that "an old tax is a good tax, and a new tax is a bad tax."

Though the rule of *convenience* in taxation has special reference to the taxpayer, it may also be taken as applying to the Exchequer, in view of its regular periods of large out-payments, and the desirability, therefore, that corresponding amounts of revenue should be available at the appropriate times.

With regard to the canon of *economy*, in the ordinary sense of the word, it is evident that as little as possible consistent with efficiency should be spent on administration and collection. Some taxes entail less expense than others. The income tax, for instance, in relation to the total revenue raised, is much cheaper to administer than commodity taxes. On the other hand, attempts to place special taxes on luxuries have sometimes entailed an inordinately high cost of supervision and collection.

[1] Jones, *The Nature and First Principle of Taxation.*

Further Rules of Taxation

The canon of economy may be interpreted to include rules of taxation not so far specified.

(i) The tax should have a high net *productiveness*, but not so high as materially to damage the wealth-yielding sources whence it is derived. A tax may be immediately productive of a large revenue, yet under certain conditions may ultimately result in a reduction in the nation's income; i.e. it may be the reverse of productive, in the wider sense of the term.

(ii) It is better to have a *few productive taxes* than many less productive. This rule is allied to the maxim of economy, in that it is naturally cheaper to collect a few remunerative taxes than a large number of smaller amounts spread over a wide field.

(iii) The tax should permit of an *automatic growth* as the wealth and population increase. Taxes on land (as distinct from land values), for instance, are not so satisfactory in this respect as those on incomes, or on commodities in wide and growing demand.

(iv) The tax should be *elastic*; i.e. it should allow, if necessary, of an increase in the rate and the yield without a corresponding increase in the cost of administration. Factors to be borne in mind are the nature of the commodity and the demand. If the latter is very sensitive, an increase in the tax may lead to a fall in the yield.

Summary of the Canons of Taxation

The various canons of taxation may be re-classified—

(i) **From the Exchequer's Point of View.**

(*a*) *Yield*. A tax should be productive of sufficient revenue.

(*b*) *Elasticity*. In case of need, the Exchequer should be able to increase the revenue without necessarily devising new taxes.

(c) *Certainty.* The amount and the time of payment should be known as far as possible.

(d) *Convenience.* The convenience not only of the tax-payer but also of the Exchequer should be considered.

(e) *Cost of administration.* Low cost of administration and collection is essential. A tax may seem desirable on grounds of equity, but the expenses may be so high as to swallow up an undue proportion of the revenue.

(ii) **From the Economic Point of View.** The chief principle under this head is that the tax should do as little harm as possible to the economic powers and activities of a community. It is short-sighted policy to aim at the maximum revenue without regard to the effects on the capacity for production.

(iii) **From the Ethical Point of View.** The outstanding principle in this category is that of *ability to pay.* Individual taxes may be proportionate or even regressive, but the scheme of taxation *as a whole* should be on a progressive basis.

Section 2. *The Incidence and Effects of Taxation*

Factors Governing Incidence

The *incidence* of a tax is said to be on the person who finally pays it. The *impact* is said to be on the person from whom the tax is first collected. If the two persons are the same, the tax is said to be direct; if they are different, i.e. if the tax has been shifted, the tax is said to be indirect.

Incidence has also to be distinguished from *effects*, which are concerned, not with the question of who actually pays the taxes, but with the wider problem of the ultimate repercussions on economic activity, both of the individual taxpayer and of the community in general.

The principal factors determining the incidence of taxation may be summarized: [1]

[1] For a more detailed analysis see the author's *Taxation: Its Incidence and Effects* (Macmillan).

(i) **Nature of the Tax.** Much depends on whether the tax is exclusive to a particular article or whether it applies to a whole range (*cf.* tea and coffee). A tax of the former type is more difficult to shift. Also, the amount of the tax is of importance. If the tax is very small, the seller may bear it himself rather than go to the trouble of altering his prices, and thus possibly incur friction with his customers.

(ii) **Conditions Inherent in the Object Taxed.** Taxes on income are seldom, if at all, shifted. Taxes on commodities are usually intended to be passed on.[1] The extent to which shifting takes place depends partly upon the nature of the demand (subject also to the possibility of substitutes) and partly upon that of the returns to the producer.

If the demand is relatively inelastic the consumer may be compelled to pay the whole of the tax. If the demand is elastic the tax may be borne partly by the producer.

Again, if the article is produced under increasing returns (i.e. diminishing costs), and the addition of the tax to the price results in a smaller demand, a smaller output will tend to bring about a higher cost of production per unit. This may lead to a still further rise in the price, which may now include not only the amount of the tax, but also the extra costs. Thus the consumer may pay more than the amount of the tax.

If the article is produced under diminishing returns, and an addition to the price reduces the demand, a smaller output will tend to reduce the cost of production per unit. This will tend to prevent the price from rising by, and therefore the consumer from paying, the full amount of the tax.

In all these instances, free competition has for sim-

---

[1] This does not mean, however, that all commodity duties are indirect. For instance, taxes on goods brought into a country by a person for his own consumption are direct in nature, for he bears the incidence as well as the impact of the duties.

plicity been assumed. Frictional forces may for a time hinder the above tendencies, but sooner or later the money burden of the tax is likely to fall in the way described.

(iii) **Degree of Competition or Monopoly.** The force of competition sometimes prevents a tax from being passed on, particularly if it is comparatively small. If the duty is levied on the article, shifting may ordinarily be assumed. If it is laid on profits, however, competition, if present, can be relied upon to prevent it from being passed on. The presence of the marginal producer who makes no profit, or at any rate too little to become liable to income tax, is usually sufficient to prevent the more prosperous rivals from getting rid of their tax in the form of higher prices.

Incidence under monopoly is readily understood from the general reasoning in previous chapters. If the tax is on the commodity, and if it is of small amount, it may be less disadvantageous for the monopolist to bear it himself than to raise the price (which he has the power to do if he wishes), for presumably he is already charging the highest price consistent with the maximum net revenue, which is his object. If the tax is of large dimensions, however, possibly equal to, if not greater than, the profit per unit, the monopolist will be induced to increase the price, even though a marked reduction in sales results.

Where the tax is imposed, not on the products, but on the profits of monopoly, shifting is very difficult, for, since the monopolist is assumed to have been already charging the most remunerative price, any addition to this would be liable to diminish his profit.

The Incidence of Customs Duties

Though the incidence of Customs duties is subject to the same general principles, there are some special considerations mainly relating to the extent of producers' or consumers' monopoly.

If, for instance, A is the *only* market for country B's *only* product, and exports in return commodities for which B has a very inelastic demand, it may be possible for A to impose a tax on B's goods which the merchants in B have to bear. Or if country A has a monopoly of something urgently required by country C, but has a demand for C's product that is very elastic, an *export* duty on the goods so urgently required by C might be passed on to that country.

These examples, however, are of hypothetical rather than practical interest. The British import duty on Greek currants has been quoted as an approach to the first position; the export duty on nitrates and coffee from South American countries seems to go half-way in the second instance. A duty suddenly imposed may catch the foreign producers unprepared, who, rather than suffer complete loss, may for the time being bear part of the tax themselves. But to obtain from them a permanent contribution to home revenue is another matter. In the long run the tendency remains for the burden to be transmitted to the home consumer, or for the foreigner to divert his products to other markets.

Qualifying Conditions

In tracing the connection between taxation and prices, the following cautions should be borne in mind—

(*a*) The consumer may pay the tax, even though the price remains unaltered, if the quality or the size of the article is reduced to compensate for the duty.

(*b*) External factors may conceal the incidence of a duty. The price of an article may be tending to drop (e.g. on account of an increasing scale of production), and in such circumstances the continuation of the old price is tantamount to an increase. Similarly, changes in monetary conditions may cause general prices to fall or rise, thus rendering incidence more difficult to trace, and giving perhaps a false impression of the actual position.

(c) Prices may be altered following the imposition of taxation, but not necessarily as a result of straightforward shifting. A tax may set up such reactions in supply and demand as to bring about a new point of equilibrium. In such circumstances the change in price becomes a problem not of incidence but of effects.

Effects of Taxation

It is not always possible to observe where the problem of incidence passes over into that of effects, and some of the economic consequences of taxation have, in fact, already been indicated in the above account of shifting. The chief economic reactions of a tax may be classified as follows—

(i) **Effects on the Standard of Living and Efficiency.** Where taxes are levied on necessaries of life, there is the danger lest they depress the real income of those workers who are already at the minimum compatible with efficiency, and thus cause a shrinkage in the volume of production.

(ii) **Effects on the Scale of Production.** On the assumption that the demand for a taxed article is elastic, an increase in the price entails a contraction in the scale of production. If the article is being produced under conditions of diminishing returns (i.e. increasing costs), the price, as already shown, may not rise by the full amount of the tax. But if, as is more likely, the production obeys increasing returns (i.e. diminishing costs), the duty is liable to inflict some damage on the efficiency of the organization, and thus transgress the rule that taxation should be so devised as to interfere as little as possible with the economic capacities of a nation.

(iii) **Effects on Savings.** High taxation may restrict savings, and thus affect the supplies of capital for production—

(*a*) Directly, by reducing the taxpayer's surplus of income over necessary expenditure. The effect here is a physical one.

(*b*) Indirectly, by discouraging the taxpayer from investing such surplus as he may have available, especially as "unearned" incomes are liable to a somewhat higher rate of taxation. The effect here is largely psychological.

Savings in the twentieth century bear a smaller proportion to the total income than they did in the nineteenth, but the discouraging influence of taxation in this connection is apt to be exaggerated. Possible other explanations are that there is not the same need, relatively, for new capital as in the days when this country financed a large part of the world, and that, whether for good or evil, people nowadays attach more importance to advancing and maintaining their standard of living, even if the improvement is to some extent at the expense of savings.

(iv) **Effects on Enterprise.** Under this head, too, both physical and psychological effects may be observed.

(*a*) The smaller savings noted in (iii) may prevent a business from expanding, even though the will and the ability are present.

(*b*) The liability to heavy taxation may exercise a generally depressing influence, and serve to discourage business men from embarking upon new ventures.

But here, also, possible other explanations should not be overlooked. Enterprise may be held in check by general industrial conditions, by world forces, by economic uncertainty that springs from circumstances much deeper and more widespread than heavy taxation.

The Conception of Surplus as Applied to Taxation

The implications of the theory of economic rent (considered in Chapter XI, Sect. 2) have led certain writers in recent years to make a division of incomes into "costs" and "surpluses," and to advocate the principle of taxing the latter. Mr. J. A. Hobson, for instance, in his *Taxation in the New State*, states—

" (1) That all taxes must be treated as deductions from real income.

(2) That income is divisible into—

(a) Economically necessary payments for the use of factors of production, i.e. costs.

(b) Unnecessary or excessive payments, i.e. surplus.

(3) That all taxation should be directly laid upon surplus, because, if any taxation is put upon costs, the process of shifting it on to surplus first involves waste and damage to production, and is frequently made a source of extortion from customers; secondly, it deceives the public by concealing the final incidence."

Costs are taken to indicate the minimum income necessary to evoke an *increasing* supply of the agents of production, not merely the maintenance of existing amounts. The term covers a standard efficiency wage for labour, a normal profit for organization and enterprise, and a minimum interest necessary to induce saving. The surplus is the difference between income and costs. While it would be possible to impose a tax on costs for a short period, the ultimate result is bound to be harmful to production. In the long run, it is claimed, a tax on costs must rebound on to the surplus. A tax imposed directly on the surplus, however, cannot be shifted and, owing to the nature of the surplus (i.e. income not the result of specific effort), may yield a large revenue with the minimum of sacrifice.

In practice, however, it is extremely difficult, and in

certain cases quite impossible, to estimate with any precision the amount of surplus. There is the liability, too, for surpluses to become capitalized; e.g. in the purchase of a piece of land, the price may be based partly on an estimate of possible increments in value. Yet, notwithstanding these and other difficulties, the general principle of applying taxation as directly as possible to the surplus element in incomes cannot be lightly dismissed, and as a broad guiding rule still commends itself to many on grounds both of equity and economy.

CHAPTER XX

Section 1. Direct and Indirect Taxes

Income Tax

THE income tax in its modern form was first imposed during the Napoleonic Wars, but, being regarded specifically as a war tax, was repealed after Waterloo. It was re-introduced in 1842, at first for a period of three years only, but it proved so productive that, after a series of renewals, it became permanent in our system of taxation. At first there was a flat rate (it fell to 2d. in the £ in 1874), though a certain measure of progression was in effect permitted by moderate exemptions at the lower end of the scale. In the present century two important modifications were introduced. In 1907 differential rates of duty were imposed on earned and unearned incomes, and in 1910 the principle of progression was extended by the introduction of a graduated sur-tax in addition to the standard rate.

The income tax has the advantage of elasticity, though recent events have suggested that the limits are being approached. Secondly, it is very productive and is economical to administer. Thirdly, it observes more satisfactorily than indirect taxation the principle of equity, in that the tax can be graduated according to the ability of the taxpayer, and that approximate exemptions and allowances can be devised.

The equity of the income tax consists largely in the fact that it can rarely be shifted. Where it falls on dividends or on personal earnings, it is extremely difficult to move, either backwards to the source of the income or forward to the purchaser of the goods or services. Where it is levied on the profits of a business, the obstacles to passing it on are almost as great, for, as tax is not paid until there is a realized excess of revenue over expenditure, it does not directly affect the marginal firms, which would be able to undercut the more prosperous firms if the latter attempted to raise their prices. The fact, too, that the effective rate of income tax and sur-tax varies with the amount of profits makes it still more difficult for firms in competition to pass on the charge to their customers.

Death Duties

The income tax, however, is not perfect, and some of its limitations are up to a point made good by the duties payable on estates passing at death.

(a) Death duties are imposed on accumulations, some of which (e.g. increase in capital value of shares) are not liable to income tax.

(b) They are levied upon wealth that yields a "psychic" though not a money income (e.g. furniture and art treasures).

(c) They make for a more equitable apportionment of aggregate tax burden as between earned and investment income receivers. People enjoying investment incomes are not under the same obligation during their lifetime to set aside large sums against a "rainy day," or for the maintenance of their dependants in the event of early death or incapacity, and they are, therefore, free to spend a larger proportion of a given amount of income on current requirements. Duties on the wealth left behind serve to rectify this discrepancy.

Graduation of Death Duties.

Death duties may be graduated in a variety of ways—

(a) According to the value of the estate. This is the

chief method adopted in the British system, the rate of estate duty increasing from 1 to 50 per cent.

(*b*) According to the relationship of the successor. In this country the legacy and succession duties (varying from 1 per cent in the case of relatives in direct line to 10 per cent in the case of distant or non-related persons) provide about one-eighth of the yield of the estate duty.

Other methods, employed in other countries, or proposed for adoption, are—

(*c*) According to the amount of the individual inheritance.

(*d*) According to the wealth of the inheritor.

(*e*) According to the "relative age" of the estate. Usually known as the Rignano plan, this method would impose a comparatively low duty on the first time of passing, but higher rates on subsequent occasions. [1]

Taxes on Land and Land Values

The old land tax in this country is not very remunerative, yielding much less than £1,000,000 in recent years. Under Schedules A and B, however, of the income tax, income from the ownership, and from the profits of occupation, of land is liable to tax. Also, in local rating, land is an important source of revenue.

A tax on land must be distinguished from one on land values. Land value taxation was introduced in 1909 (the increment value duty, the reversion duty, the undeveloped land duty, and the mineral rights duty), but was subsequently repealed. In 1931, a similar measure was passed, but its operation was almost immediately suspended.

Where the tax is calculated according to the rent of the land, it tends ultimately to be borne by the landowner, for reasons explained in Chapter XI. Since land at the

[1] See E. Rignano, *The Social Significance of Death Duties*, edited by Sir Josiah Stamp.

margin pays no rent, and therefore no tax, the owners of superior land are unable, according to the traditional theory, to recoup themselves by passing on the duty to their tenants or to the purchasers of their products. In practice, however, as previously pointed out, there may be forces in operation that modify this theoretical tendency.

Where the tax, however, takes the form of a fixed annual charge—as in this country—the extent of its shifting is governed by the general principles of incidence already outlined. If the marginal landowner is affected as well as the others, the consumer is almost bound to pay some, if not the whole, of the duty. There is, however, a tendency for such a tax to become capitalized when the property concerned first changes hands, the buyer offering the ordinary value less the capital equivalent of the annual liability taken over with the land. Thus, in a sense, the tax is held to become "burdenless" with the passing of time.

Direct Taxation

The advantages and drawbacks of direct taxation may be briefly summarized:

(i) **Advantages.**

(*a*) The incidence of a direct tax is easier to determine than that of an indirect tax.

(*b*) Direct taxation can be made progressive, and so be in accordance with the principle of equity. This is generally impracticable in indirect taxation, except in so far as the taxation of luxuries, consumed largely by the wealthier classes, affords a limited degree of progression.

(*c*) The cost of collection is comparatively low.

(*d*) An increase in national income automatically yields an increase in tax revenue.

(*e*) Within reasonable limits, direct taxation is elastic in its yield.

(*f*) The taxpayer knows exactly how much he pays.

(*g*) Direct taxation enables the State to reach those people who make their income in one country but live for a large part of the year in another.

(ii) **Disadvantages.** The drawbacks, such as they are, occur mainly in the method of administration, and are too small to weigh seriously against the advantages.

(*a*) There is more possibility of evasion in direct than in indirect taxation. It has been alleged that the income tax is a "tax on honesty."

(*b*) The inconvenience entailed in filling up forms has been stated to be a drawback, compared with the simplicity of indirect taxation.

(*c*) Many people prefer to pay in very small instalments, finding these more convenient than large cash payments. Linked with this is the argument that some people prefer to be taxed "in the dark." It is suggested that some persons who unthinkingly pay a tax on, say, cigarettes or wines would resent having to make instead a seemingly heavy single payment to the State, though it might be appreciably less than the total amount paid in small instalments. To exploit such ignorance, however, savours of the "cynical" principle mentioned in the previous chapter.

Indirect Taxation

The merits and drawbacks of indirect taxation have to some extent been indicated or implied, but may be more positively stated as follows—

(i) **Advantages.**

(*a*) The taxpayer does not feel the burden so heavily when spread over many purchases throughout the year.

(b) Collection is comparatively easy.

(c) A tax on luxuries falls on the "surplus" element of the incomes of the relatively wealthy.

(d) Indirect taxation enables those with small incomes to be reached. A direct tax on such incomes would prove more difficult, and certainly more expensive to administer.

(e) Evasion is more difficult than in direct taxation.

(f) To a certain extent, indirect taxation is elastic, i.e. capable of yielding a higher or lower revenue according to the rate. The nature both of the article and of the demand is very important. A tax on a necessary can be moderately increased or decreased, and the expected revenue fairly accurately estimated. Such a tax would accord with the canon of certainty. On the other hand, a tax on something with a variable demand would not bear appreciable expansion. Thus an indirect tax is elastic (i.e. in the resultant revenue) when the demand for the article is inelastic; and *vice versa*.[1]

(g) Where it is desired to check the consumption of a noxious article, a tax may have the desired effect so far as comparatively poor people are concerned, but it would not materially reduce the consumption on the part of the well-to-do.

(h) Indirect taxation enables the State to exact some revenue from foreign visitors, who would be exempt from paying direct taxes.

(ii) **Disadvantages.**

(a) Indirect taxation is usually regressive in character, for, as one's income increases, the percentage taken in commodity duties perceptibly diminishes. Further, where the tax is specific, and not *ad valorem*, it is apt to be

---

[1] A high tax may bring about such a restriction of the demand that the revenue is less than when the tax is smaller. This actually happened a few years ago, when an increase in the duty on cigars yielded a smaller revenue; the subsequent reduction in the duty was followed by such an expansion of the demand that the revenue was greatly increased.

doubly regressive in that a poor person, who purchases the cheaper grades, pays a higher proportion in tax. For example, if the tax on tea were *ad valorem* it would still be regressive for the reason that the consumption of tea does not increase in proportion with one's income. But the fact that it is a specific sum per lb. irrespective of price involves a still more than proportionate burden to the purchaser of 1s. 6d. tea than to the purchaser of 5s. tea.

(*b*) The revenue is uncertain unless the demand for the article is very inelastic.

(*c*) The incidence is not always easy to determine.

(*d*) It is comparatively expensive—

1. To the State, in that the costs of collection are often heavy (though it is contended sometimes that the shopkeeper serves as a tax-collector without pay).

2. To the consumer, in that the tax may cause a rise in the price higher than that actually warranted; e.g. a fraction of a penny added to the tax on tobacco may add a full penny to the price. It may be contended, however, that the shopkeeper has to incur a larger capital outlay, thus losing the corresponding amount of interest, and that the addition to the price, over and above the tax, is really a compensation for the added cost. But this only serves to emphasize the uneconomical nature of such a tax.

(*e*) It is harmful to industry when levied on an article that is used, not for "final" consumption, but for use in further production. Because of the interest to be paid on the larger initial outlay of capital, and other additions to "overheads," the cost of production is increased and the price of the finished product may be advanced out of all proportion to the original duty. In such circumstances not only the Treasury, but the whole of the community, is the sufferer.

(*f*) Indirect taxation is also harmful to industry and

to consumers in general in so far as it disturbs the marginal
equilibrium between taxed and untaxed commodities.
Theoretically, as was indicated in an earlier chapter,
a condition of securing maximum utility of all articles
offered for sale is that they should be marketed at
prices equivalent to their marginal costs of production.
Where articles are taxed, their price is raised above
marginal cost, while untaxed articles still sell at marginal cost level.   In consequence there tends to be,
under competitive conditions, an uneconomic diversion
of the agents of production from industries making the
taxed to those making the untaxed articles.

Section 2.   Local Taxation

Local and National Taxation Compared

It is unnecessary to enter here at length into the economics of local taxation, as the general principles are the
same for local rates as for national taxes. What has been
said about the one can be applied with little qualification
to the other. Certain differences, however, in the administration of national and local finance may be noted:

(i) When money is raised within a narrow area, and
is spent in providing a local service, there is a more direct
relationship between payment made and value received
than is to be found in national undertakings. The "benefit" or *quid pro quo* element, however, is not so much
stronger in local finance as it at first appears, for there
is no necessary relationship to *individual* rate payments,
even though the service as a whole represents a local
benefit.

A certain distinction has been drawn between "onerous"
and "beneficial" services. The former, such as education and poor relief, are as much of national as of local

advantage. The latter, such as drainage and street lighting, result in special benefit to local property owners and
occupiers. Some contend that the costs of the "beneficial"
services should be locally defrayed, and those of the
"onerous" services borne by the State. Usually, however,
national and local advantages are so interwoven as to be
indistinguishable, and the proposed differentiation, therefore, even if it were otherwise sound, is not practicable.

(ii) Whereas national taxation rests on a comparatively
broad basis and is adjusted according to a number of
criteria (e.g. income, estates, consumption, etc.), local
rates are calculated entirely by reference to the value of
occupied property, whether it be houses, land, factory,
or other business premises. In national finance, property
has been found to be a very inadequate criterion of ability
to pay, and now occupies an unimportant place in im-
perial taxation as a whole. In local finance, the deficiencies of this method are also coming to be recognized, and
reliefs to certain types of occupiers have been found inevitable. By the Act of 1929, industrial premises were
"de-rated" to the extent of 75 per cent; a similar concession was granted to the transport industries on the understanding that freight charges to agriculture and the
"heavy" industries would be correspondingly reduced,
while agricultural property, already relieved to some
extent, was exempted altogether. To compensate the
local authorities for the loss of revenue, the grants-in-aid
from the central Exchequer were increased, thus transferring a part of the burden from the ratepayer to the
taxpayer.[1]

---

[1] Various schemes have been put forward for a *local income tax*. The
difficulties adduced against such schemes are, first, that people who
make their incomes in a particular locality may live outside the area
covered by its powers; secondly, that many large businesses are not
concentrated in any one area (e.g. banks, railways, multiple stores, etc.),
and that taxation on such enterprises is more effective and economical
when conducted entirely on a national basis.

Grants-in-Aid

Grants-in-aid are the contributions from the Consolidated Fund towards local expenditure. Local developments and improvements are matters of national importance, and full local responsibility for the cost is both undesirable and impracticable. While local authorities are justified in demanding financial help from the central government, the latter is equally justified in watching over and checking the outlay of such bodies, and the assistance given is almost invariably subject to the observance of certain conditions.

The case for grants may be more fully stated—

(i) They are essential when a local authority engages upon developmental work of national importance.

(ii) They are necessary where the local body is incapable financially of carrying out its proper functions.

(iii) They provide a stimulus to local authorities to undertake necessary functions.

(iv) They help to reduce the inequality of burden as between one district and another—particularly as regards the cost of alleviating poverty and distress, the causes of which are by no means localized, and the relief of which is coming to be recognized as a national responsibility.

(v) They are necessary to give weight to the suggestions, criticisms and instructions of the central authority, which is naturally more experienced than smaller authorities in anticipating and providing for public needs.

(vi) They are the means of enforcing on local authorities the "national minimum" of efficiency so necessary in the national interests.[1]

Though the case for grants-in-aid is unanswerable, the following difficulties should be noted—

(i) The difficulty of fair apportionment among various

[1] See S. & B. Webb, *Grants-in-Aid*.

localities. Latterly the central authority has been giving grants above the average to localities where trade is depressed and in need of special assistance.

(ii) The difficulty of effective parliamentary control over local expenditure.

(iii) The possibility of local extravagance, particularly where the assistance takes the form of percentage as distinct from block grants.

Incidence of Local Rates

The principles governing the incidence of local rates are essentially no different from those which determine the incidence of taxes in general and which have already been considered. In practice, however, the task of ascertaining who ultimately bears the burden is more complicated—

(*a*) Because of the number of parties involved. Though the rates are levied upon the occupier, they may be shifted backward to the building owner (and perhaps to an intermediate leaseholder) and eventually to the landowner, or, in the case of business premises, forward to customers or clients.

(*b*) Because of the slowness of production and consumption of building and property, and therefore the long delay in the adjustment of supply and demand. Meanwhile the rates may be prevented from falling on the parties intended.

(*c*) Because of long-term leases commonly entered into, and the difficulty during their period of making adjustments consequent upon a change in the rates.

(*d*) Because of the difficulties of the occupier in moving to new premises, thus strengthening the normal tendency for a tax to stick at the point of impact.

The chief factors determining the apportionment among the principal parties may be briefly indicated.

(i) **The Landowner.** As shown in Chapter XI, economic rent does not enter into price, which approximates to the cost of the production at the margin at which there is no pure rent. Thus, a tax or rate intended to fall on economic rent could not, in theory, take the form of an addition to price. In practice, however, the whole burden does not always reach the landowner, partly because the ratio of pure rent to gross rental may be so small that it is impracticable to separate the items, and partly because of the frictional conditions noted above.

(ii) **The Building Owner.** It is only because of the peculiar conditions attaching to the production of buildings that special considerations of incidence, as affecting the owner, arise. Rates may increase or diminish from year to year, but, as noted above, the owner, different from a seller of other commodities, cannot quickly adapt his supplies to changing circumstances. Within a limited period the building owner is in a similar position to the landowner, and may have to bear part of the rate burden. The same applies to leaseholders who take over responsibility for a considerable period.

(iii) **The Occupier.** Under favourable conditions the rates on the occupier may, to some extent, be shifted backward to the building owner or to the landowner. More usually, however, they move forward to the purchaser of the goods made or sold in the rated premises. It is not always possible, however, to transmit the whole of the burden, especially where the price is largely determined by firms that produce their goods in comparatively lightly-rated areas. As for private dwelling houses, it may be safely generalized that, as the opportunity of shifting the burden in a forward direction is rarely present, and as backward shifting is seldom practicable, the rates in almost all cases remain, as is the intention, a direct charge on the occupier.

Effects of Local Rates

In the same way as the general principles of incidence may be applied, with little qualification, to the special problem of local taxation, so the principles governing effects may also be applied. The outstanding qualification that has to be made is that, in local rating, property is chosen as the sole criterion and basis, and in consequence a number of peculiar problems and criticisms arise. Reference has already been made to the inadequate basis of assessment of ability and the inequitable rating as between one type of occupier and another. Local rating is essentially regressive in character. The levy is unevenly computed not only between householders with different incomes, but also between occupiers of different types of business premises. "Heavy" industries that require more space and buildings than "light" trades and vocations may be required to pay a disproportionately high rate. Similarly the ratepayers in one area, where the calls on the local exchequer are heavy because of local depression and poverty, may be called upon to make a contribution much greater than is required in another area where conditions are more prosperous and the ability of the ratepayer is higher. The uneconomic effects of the rating system have been partly remedied by the legislation of 1929 mentioned above, but the defects of a system based exclusively on property are too radical to be dealt with satisfactorily in this way.

CHAPTER XXI

Sources of Public Funds

IT is a rule of public finance that normal expenditure should be met as far as possible out of normal revenue. In ordinary times taxation is sufficient to provide the required income for the State, but in times of war and other emergency resort may be made to—

(*a*) Currency inflation.

(*b*) Sale of national property.

(*c*) Loans.

Extraordinary expenditure is usually met by borrowings, though supplementary use may be made of currency manipulation and the sale of national property.

(*a*) As shown in Chapter XIII, currency inflation leads to depreciation in the purchasing value of money. The higher prices that have to be paid for goods and services are tantamount to a forced levy on the people. If all incomes were equal, such depreciation would hit everybody alike and be little different in its effects from a general tax. But, as incomes vary considerably, the burden of inflation and higher prices falls more heavily on the poor than the rich, for the effect is similar to that of a proportionate as compared with a progressive tax. This method of raising revenue is also to be criticized on the grounds of its harmful effects on industry and trade.

(*b*) From the sale of property modern States cannot expect to raise an appreciable amount. The tendency seems to be for Governments to acquire further property rather than to dispose of it, and large sales of public lands, etc., might be considered to be a retrograde measure. Following a war, of course, there is a certain amount of surplus stock to be disposed of, which may add a useful amount to the State's income for the time being, but as a regular source of income the sale of property can be disregarded.

(c) In this category, loans are the chief source of public revenue, and the present chapter will be mainly concerned with the nature of public loans and the means adopted, or proposed, for their reduction.

General Limits to Government Borrowings

It was noted above that taxation, if carried beyond a certain point, was bound to injure the productive capacity of the nation. Similarly, there is a limit to which wealth may be borrowed without damage to economic powers.

The general limits to public borrowings may be very broadly indicated. The first limit is set by the amount that is saved over and above the sum necessary for depreciation, renewal, and the provision of new capital. The second limit is determined by the surplus that is physically possible (in time of emergency) over a country's bare needs. For a time it is possible to go beyond these limits and live on capital, but the uneconomic effects of such a policy are very soon felt.

Furthermore, the precise limit is determined largely by the nature of the expenditure for which the loan is raised. At the time it may make little difference whether the wealth is to be consumed productively, as in the purchase or development of a railway, or unproductively as in the pursuance of a war, but ultimately the economic condition of the country, and the capacity for further investment, is very much affected according to the nature of the original expenditure.

The British National Debt

The British National Debt, which amounted to £700 millions in 1913, reached ten times this amount by the end of the Great War. The capital sum owing per head increased from £15 to £175, while the annual charge rose from 10s. to £7 10s. Prices had, of course, more than doubled during the war years, thus making the real increase in Debt less than at first appears, but as prices subsequently declined the Debt, in money terms, remained constant for a number of years, thereby causing the real burden on the community to increase.

It is instructive to compare the situation with that following the Napoleonic Wars. Price level differences are obviated by comparing percentages of Debt to national wealth, and of charge to national income, at the different periods. At the end of the Napoleonic Wars the percentage of Debt to national wealth, so far as this can be computed, was a little over 30 per cent; in 1914 it had fallen to less than 5 per cent; at the end of the Great War it stood at about the same proportion as after the Napoleonic Wars. Similarly the percentage of Debt charge to national income fell from 8 per cent in 1817 to 1 per cent in 1914, and rose again to 10 per cent in 1919. It is interesting also to note that, while 63·75 per cent of the cost of the Napoleonic Wars was met out of taxation, only 28·74 per cent of the cost of the Great War was met in this way.[1]

The National Debt is almost entirely due to wars. The British Government spent more in the six years 1915-20 inclusive than in the previous two and a quarter centuries. Of the £22,000 millions spent by the Government between 1688 and 1920, no less than £14,000 millions was spent on war, and two-thirds of this sum in the last six years of the period.

[1] Harvey E. Fisk, *English Public Finance.*

Real Burden of National Debt

The real burden of a National Debt depends on a number of factors—

(i) **The Purpose of the Loan.** Where capital is borrowed for national productive purposes, there is ordinarily an economic return, which may exceed the outgoings in interest. Very little, however, of the National Debt is of this character.

(ii) **The Effect of Home and Foreign Holdings.** When the Debt stock is held by the country's own nationals, the payments involve internal transferences and so to some extent prove less burdensome than if they were made to foreign stock-holders.

(iii) **The Period of the Loan.** Long-period loans at fixed interest rates are liable to increase the burden on the taxpayers and confer a benefit on the stock-holders as prices decline, and conversely as prices rise. As, however, loans are for the most part created in times of war when prices are high, it is the rentier classes who mostly benefit. The burden is especially noticeable when wages and other charges are reduced to keep pace more or less with prices, yet the dividends on government stocks remain unchanged.

(iv) **The Distribution of Wealth and Income.** Most of the Debt stock is owned by a comparatively small proportion of the people, mainly well-to-do. Taxation, though on a progressive basis, is not so concentrated as the ownership of Government stock. Hence, an appreciable part of the Debt burden falls upon the poorer classes of the community.

Reduction of National Debt

The following are the principal means by which the National Debt is being, or can be, reduced—

(i) **Application of the surplus annual revenue.** This is perhaps the simplest method, but it cannot be very effective unless the Debt is very small. At the present time little opportunity for a reduction of the capital amount is provided from this source. The possibility of any surplus is liable to evoke a cry for a reduction in the rate of taxation, although, of course, an already realized surplus automatically goes to the reduction of the Debt.

(ii) **Extra taxation.** While taxation for the reduction of Debt ought not to be shirked, the limits to taxable capacity should not be overlooked. It is true that certain nations have not made as full use of the taxing instrument as might be reasonably expected. In this country, however, the Debt is so large and taxation already so high that there is little hope of a rapid reduction by this means.

(iii) **Redemption by purchase of stock.** When Government stock is offered on the market at a comparatively low price, public officials may purchase a certain amount of such stock and cancel it, thus substituting a smaller for a larger debt. This method is practicable, of course, only when money is available at lower rates than are being paid on Government stock. There is, however, the likelihood of a rise in the price of the stock if the State officials show themselves too eager to effect purchases for cancellation.

(iv) **Conversion.** Conversion into stock bearing a lower rate of interest is another means adopted. If the loan can be repaid after a certain time, and if new money can be obtained at a lower rate than is being paid to the fund-holders, the Government may present to these creditors the alternative of a lower rate of interest or, if they refuse, repayment of their principal. A very successful Conversion operation took place in July, 1932, when nearly the whole of the 5 per cent War Stock, amounting altogether to £2,000,000,000, was converted to a $3\frac{1}{2}$ per cent basis. Later in the year there was a conversion of other outstanding stocks, of smaller value, to 3 per cent.

(v) **Terminable annuities.** By this means permanent is converted into temporary debt. An annuity is purchased through the Post Office or from Chancery funds, and interest is paid for a definite period or a lifetime. The rate of interest is higher than the ordinary rate on the Debt (involving higher taxation during the period of the annuity), but, when the payments cease, so much Debt has been redeemed. This device, however, is not so popular as in former times, and accounts for a very small proportion of the total sum.

(vi) **Sinking funds.** The principle of a sinking fund, stated shortly, is to provide out of income a certain sum of money so calculated that, invested at compound interest, it will accumulate to the amount required by the time the loan is to be redeemed. Terminable annuities involve a form of sinking fund, but the payments on this account are very small in comparison with the annual amounts set aside for accumulation. A Chancellor of the Exchequer who is anxious to keep down the Budget expenditure may be tempted to omit or reduce the annual provision for this purpose, but as a general rule the practice of "raiding the sinking fund" is to be deprecated.

Other Proposals for Reduction

There are some who maintain that the National Debt is far too large to be paid off out of income in a reasonable number of years, and that the only practicable way of lightening the burden is to impose a special levy on accumulated wealth as distinct from current income. Such an impost should not be confused with repudiation on the one hand or a forced reduction in the rate of interest on the other.

Repudiation is opposed on both moral and economic grounds. Contracts and obligations were entered into, and, quite apart from ethical considerations, a breach of public faith would so upset the economic and credit organization that the ultimate gain would be very doubtful. Foreign creditors and resultant complications have also to be considered. Besides this, there is no reason why people who lent their money to the State should be penalized, while those who invested their money elsewhere should go scot-free. Any sacrifice necessary should be generally borne, and not confined to a particular class of investment holder.

A compulsory reduction in the rate of interest on the Debt is open to similar criticism, though not to the same degree. It seems justifiable from one point of view that the nominal rate of interest should be reduced with a fall in prices in such a manner that the real purchasing value of the income so derived remains constant. It might be contended that, in the same way as some wages vary on a sliding scale, based on the cost of living, so also should the rate of interest. But a forced reduction might seriously prejudice future public borrowings, while it would also entail an unequal distribution of the sacrifice as between those who lent to the State and those who invested in other directions. Conversion on a voluntary basis finds more general support. In any case, only the annual interest charge would be reduced, and not the capital amount of the Debt itself. To cut down the actual Debt in proportion to the decline in prices would be tantamount to a levy on capital, except that the loss would fall entirely on Government stock-holders.

The advocates of a capital levy would spread the charge over wealth-owning classes in general. One proposal was to reduce the National Debt by about one-half, which would involve a levy of roughly £3,000 millions on wealth accumulations of all kinds. In order to obtain an equality of sacrifice, the imposts would be reckoned on a progressive basis. Small amounts would be exempt, and the proportion exacted by the State would increase with the amount of wealth in one's possession.

The proposal for a capital levy is criticized on the grounds of its grave effects on industry and credit. It is urged, in the first place, that a levy, however well planned, would cause such a wholesale realization of property that values would seriously decline. Trade in general would inevitably suffer, and as a result the Government would probably fail to secure the full value of the levy originally contemplated. The effects on credit might be more serious. Government stocks are a common security against bank loans, and if a large proportion of the total value were suddenly cancelled, serious deflation might immediately follow.

It is significant that many former advocates of a capital levy have modified their opinion in view of the changed economic circumstances of the last few years. They supported it in the years immediately following the War, when credit and prices were greatly inflated. They maintain that, though it would have resulted in deflation, the effects would not have been so serious as those that followed the deliberate deflationist policy pursued since 1921. But the opportunity is admitted by them to have gone by. These one-time supporters of the capital levy, therefore, while regretting that the opportunity was not taken to apply the scheme at the peak-point of inflation, are content in a period following deflation to adopt less heroic methods of reducing the National Debt.

Local Debts

Reference, finally, may be made to the problem of local debts, which also have considerably increased in recent years. Different from the National Debt, local debts are to a large extent backed by solid assets in the form of public works, transport services, housing estates, and other possessions. Loans incurred for the maintenance of the destitute involve a net charge on the community, but the greater part of the annual outgoings in interest and principal payments is offset by income, in money or in services, from the public undertakings. Hence the existence of a large aggregate local indebtedness need not be regarded with the same apprehension as the National Debt (quite apart from the difference in the respective amounts), for practically the whole of the latter was incurred for purposes of war, which destroyed the wealth subscribed instead of putting it to productive use.

Local loans are most commonly raised by the issue of stock, which, since it is secured upon rates, revenues, and property of the local authority, finds a ready market among investors. Where the authority has not the legal powers to borrow in this way or prefers not to do so, it may issue mortgages on its property and revenue for periods of varying length. Subsidiary methods are loans from banks for temporary needs, and the issue of bills.

Local debts incurred for capital purposes are required by the Government to be redeemed within a period not exceeding the estimated life of the assets to be created. The usual way of paying off the debts is the sinking fund method described above. Other ways are fixed instalments of the principal sum with diminishing interest payments on the balance, and fixed annual payments, covering principal and interest, for the whole term of the loan.

APPENDIX

THE DEVELOPMENT OF ECONOMIC THOUGHT

ECONOMICS was stated at the beginning of this book to be but one branch of the general science of social relations. Only in modern times has a serious attempt been made to study the subject as distinct from its sister sciences. It was natural, with the great industrial and commercial changes in the eighteenth and nineteenth centuries, that people should grow more concerned with the principles underlying the economic system, and that thought should become more specialized. But long before economics achieved the dignity of a science its problems were occupying men's minds and rough generalizations, later to be reduced to more or less precise "laws," were being formulated.

The Early Period

Our survey may begin with the early Greeks, among whom, despite the predominance of a small aristocratic class in the city-states, there gradually grew up a new class consisting of traders, who introduced a certain commercial spirit, and developed the monetary and credit systems in a way hitherto unknown. This gave rise to inquiry into the nature of money and, particularly, of interest. Thought was also stimulated on the question of slavery, by which system most of the production was then carried on. It was pointed out by more than one writer of the time that slave-labour was not necessarily economical; in effect, to use modern terms, that while the expense of such labour might be low, the real cost might be high.

Prominent among the Greek socio-economic philosophers was *Plato*, who in his "Republic" drew up a scheme for an ideal society, containing some noteworthy contributions to economic knowledge. *Aristotle* also is outstanding in this respect, and his contention that money was "barren," and therefore interest unjustifiable, influenced men's ideas on this question for many centuries. Other Greek writers were *Thucydides* and *Xenophon*, who considered rather the domestic side of economic life.

The Romans did not add much on pure doctrine. A small amount was written on husbandry; but *Cicero* voiced the general opinion when he deprecated trade, maintaining it was not a fit occupation for a true Roman.

It was not until the Renaissance that any serious attention was given to economic problems, which were still overshadowed by religious and political considerations. The influence of Aristotle was still felt, and the deprecation of usury was to a large extent due to his teaching. Capital as yet had not become very important as a factor of production, and, since money borrowed was often put to a non-productive use, the medievalists could readily find reasons for denouncing the payment of interest. It was maintained, too, that a trader was not justified in charging more than a fair value for his goods. Hence developed the common practice of fixing a "just price" for articles of sale. Most of the organization was in the hands of the gilds, which, particularly at first, had a strong religious and social element. Among the medieval theorists on economic problems was *Nicholas Oresme*, who, in a work on money (1373), formulated the law relating to "good" and "bad" money, usually associated with Sir Thomas Gresham. *Copernicus*, too, wrote on monetary matters.

Until now, English writers had not been very prominent,

but the sixteenth century proved to be a period of trade activity and literary attainment. *Sir Thomas More*, in his well-known "Utopia," visualized with remarkable prescience what was then regarded as an ideal community. The writings of *Francis Bacon*, also, contain some valuable additions to economic literature.

This was the period of great commercial expansion. The manorial had given way to a national economy. English traders were laying the foundations of the Empire, and the current economic writings were full of reference to England's foreign trade and maritime policy. Gradually there emerged the doctrine of **Mercantilism**, which dominated British economic activity for over two hundred years. Mercantilism was the expression of nationalism in economic life, and showed itself in numerous forms. Exports were encouraged, and imports of many goods were subjected to heavy duties or forbidden altogether. By the Navigation Acts attempts were made to capture the shipping trade and wrest economic advantage from the foreigner. The doctrine was based to some extent on the assumption that, in every exchange, if one party gains, the other must lose—an assumption that does not stand serious examination. This intense national economic feeling was not peculiar to England alone; in the seventeenth century it was characteristic of all the European States, particularly France and Prussia.

Thomas Mun (1621) was one of the principal exponents of the Mercantilist doctrine. He was followed in this country by *Child, Temple,* and *Davenant,* who confined their attentions mainly to foreign trade. Other writers with a Mercantilist bias—though it gradually became less pronounced—were *Sir William Petty* ("Political Arithmetic," 1671), noteworthy as having employed statistical methods; *David Hume* ("Essays," c. 1752), a critic of the system in its more pronounced forms; and Sir James Steuart, "the last of the Mercantilists," whose "Inquiry into the Principles of Political Economy" was issued in 1767, only nine years before Adam Smith's "Wealth of Nations."

The decay of gild regulation of industry and commerce was accompanied by a decline in the Mercantilist policy, which was too narrow and restrictive to satisfy the new conditions of the eighteenth century. There was a reaction against Mercantilism, particularly in France, where the Physiocrats or *Economistes* promulgated the new doctrines. The new school believed in a Law of Nature, which was held to govern all man's activities and guide them to the best common advantage. The rule of free competition was supreme; any attempt at public intervention was considered harmful. The policy of "let alone," so popular in the eighteenth and early nineteenth centuries, was summed up in the famous expression: "*Laissez-faire, laissez-passer.*" What was good for the individual was good for everybody; therefore remove the impediments to the full operation of the natural law, and let private enterprise have free play.

Chief among the Physiocrats was *Quesnay*, who is noted among other things for the stress he laid on the importance of agriculture, which was claimed to be the true source of all wealth. Manufacture merely changed the form of things, and commerce distributed them. Land yielded a *produit net*, or surplus, which did not arise in industry and trade. Quesnay's conception of the surplus from land foreshadowed Ricardo's theory of rent, and led to the proposal even then of the single tax on land. *Gournay* was another leading Physiocrat, whose views, however, were not so dogmatic as those of Quesnay, but were open enough to recognize the productiveness of industry and trade. Other members of the school were *Turgot* and *Cantillon*, who were interested largely in money, capital, and public finance. Discussion on the last subject was popular with all the Physiocrats, due doubtless to the very heavy taxation in eighteenth-century France.

The Physiocrats rendered a useful service in their destructive criticism of many of the older theories. On the positive side they helped to distinguish economics from the other social sciences; they applied scientific methods, made useful contributions to the study of taxation and capital, while the emphasis they laid on the land and the derived surplus proved to be of great consequence.

The Modern Period

Modern theory is commonly said to begin with *Adam Smith*, the outstanding figure in the whole of economic literature. His "Wealth of Nations" (1776) presented the most comprehensive and constructive work that had yet appeared. In order to get a proper view of Adam Smith's teaching, it is necessary to take his other writings into account. In the "Theory of the Moral Sentiments" (1759), he dealt with social philosophy and general conduct. In the work upon which he was engaged when he died, he treated of law and politics. The "Wealth of Nations" was the intermediate work. The three together demonstrated from various aspects his belief in the "Invisible Hand" which controlled man's actions in this world. But his successors severed the practical conclusions from the larger context, and converted his broad philosophy into a doctrine of narrow individualism.

"An Inquiry into the Nature and Causes of the Wealth of Nations" not only served as a title, but as a definition of what Adam Smith considered the scope of political economy. Book I deals with "the causes of improvements in the productive powers of labour, and . . . the order according to which its produce is naturally distributed among the different ranks of the people"; it considers, in turn, the division of labour, money, prices, wages, profits, and rent. Different from the Physiocrats, Smith attributed the source of wealth not to land but to labour. Book II, embracing "the nature, accumulation, and employment of stock," discusses the nature of capital and interest. Book III surveys historically "the different progress of opulence in different nations"; and Book IV, treating "of systems of political economy," criticizes Mercantilism and shows up its limitations. Book V examines "the revenue of the sovereign or commonwealth," and the rules there laid down respecting taxation and debts are still of practical guidance.

Again the conditions of the age were reflected in the current economic writings. The Industrial Revolution was beginning, and Adam Smith fully realized the necessity of removing restrictions, particularly on foreign trade. Not that he altogether severed himself from the Mercantilists; he still supported, for example, the Navigation Laws on the ground, as he put it, that defence was more important than opulence. Nevertheless his work marks the beginning of a new period in economic thought. Some of the abuses that were committed in the name of the new freedom of action (such as the refusal at first to introduce factory legislation, and the repression of labour organizations) were due, apart from private motives, to the interpretation that his many followers put upon his writings rather than to the advocacy of Adam Smith himself.

The contemporaries and immediate successors of Smith suffer by comparison, but with the exception of Ricardo their contributions were of limited worth. *Malthus's* doctrine of population was considered in Chapter II; his outlook would probably have been less pessimistic had he been able to foresee the results of man's inventiveness. *Bentham* was a jurist rather than an economist, but had considerable influence on economic thought and practice. His attack on the restrictive usury laws was followed (though not immediately) by their repeal. The *utilitarian* school, whose object was "the greatest happiness of the greatest number," found much inspiration in his writings and leadership.

Adam Smith had combined the deductive and the inductive methods with remarkable skill. *David Ricardo* drew most of his inspiration from Smith's work, but, not possessing Smith's historical sense, concentrated on the abstract deductive method of reasoning. His "Principles of Political Economy and Taxation" (1817) showed a distinctly original line of thought. His theory of rent became generally adopted and, as shown in the present work, it has evolved into a theory which attempts to explain not merely the payment made for the use of land, but the remuneration that goes as "surplus" in greater or less degree to all the agents of production.

Following Adam Smith, Ricardo favoured a labour theory of value, but from his writings it is not clear whether he did not really mean a cost of production theory, so as to include a return to capital. Labour was held to have its cost of production like everything else. It will be noted below how the rent and value theories of Ricardo, a capitalist and millionaire, were converted by Lassalle, Marx, and others into essentially Socialist doctrines. Hence the statement that Ricardo was both "a prop and a menace to the middle classes."

Characteristic of Ricardo and his group was the cold, dogmatic method of treatment, which at times tended to become so abstract as almost to ignore the human factor. The materialist and pessimistic doctrines earned for economics the epithet of " the dismal science." Economic laws were reduced to bald statements, and *N. W. Senior* ("Political Economy," 1836) was perhaps the most deductive and abstract of the school. He condensed the whole of economic tendency to four premises: (*a*) that every man desires to obtain additional wealth with as little sacrifice as possible; (*b*) that the population of the world is limited only by moral or physical evil or by fear of a deficiency of material comforts; (*c*) that the powers of the agents of production may be definitely increased by using their products in further production; (*d*) that agriculture is subject to diminishing returns. Senior also developed the abstinence theory of interest, which for a time was generally accepted.

These writers, who comprised the **Classical School**, made a considerable advance in economic analysis. Cost was taken as the basis of value and welfare was considered to increase or decrease with the stock of goods. Their doctrines became the philosophical basis of the Manchester School, which was cosmopolitan in outlook and ardent in support of free trade between nations. The Classicists in Germany, though similar in many ways, were less abstract and more nationalist in outlook. *List* in the "National System of Political Economy" (1841) advocated a system which in some ways was akin to Mercantilism. In France, the tone was more that of an idealist and optimistic liberalism; *Say* and *Bastiat* were the chief exponents, the latter going so far as to contend ("Economic Harmonies") not only that the organization of society which was due to competition was the best possible, but that it was also the best conceivable.

It was now time for the various doctrines to be brought together and co-ordinated, which task was attempted by *J. S. Mill*, who is sometimes regarded as the main successor to Adam Smith. Mill, too, was a social philosopher, and did much to widen the scope of economics. He did not add much that was new in the way of doctrine; his theory of the wages fund, for instance, was soon found to be defective. His chief work was to give economics a new spirit; he moulded it into something more than a merely materialist and "dismal" science, finding a place for welfare besides wealth in his philosophy. Mill's later writings were not so individualist in their attitude as his earlier works, though he still clung, on the whole, to the rights of the individual. He states that "*Laissez-faire* should be the general practice; every departure from it, unless required by some great good, is a certain evil." Speaking of Government interference, he concludes his "Principles" (1848) thus: "Even in the best state which society has yet reached, it is lamentable to think how great a proportion of all the efforts and talents in the world are employed in merely neutralizing one another. It is the proper end of Government to reduce this wretched waste to the smallest possible amount, by taking such measures as shall cause the energies now spent by mankind in injuring one another, or in protecting themselves against injury, to be turned to the legitimate employment of the human faculties, that of compelling the powers of Nature to be more and more subservient to physical and moral good."

From Mill onwards, at least three lines of development in economic reasoning can be traced; these correspond to the "Historical School," the Socialist writers, and the "Neo-Classical School."

It was inevitable that there should be a stronger reaction against the abstract reasoning followed by the Classical School than was evident in Mill's writings. The **Historical School** attacked the deductive method of inquiry and tried to place the science on a historical basis, substituting inductive for deductive principles. It was contended that, without reference to the facts of life, theory tended to soar above realities; that reasoning should be more realistic and be subject to verification whenever possible. In Germany the reaction against the old methods was very marked. *Roscher*, one of the earliest of the school, maintained that political economy should be studied in close relation to the other social sciences; that in order to derive universal laws, study should be made not of one set of people, but of several, and particular attention should be paid to ancient races who, having run their full course, were peculiarly instructive. He was followed by *Knies*, *Schmoller*, and many others in Germany and elsewhere. In England, the chief exponents of the historical method were *Rogers*, *Leslie*, *Toynbee*, *Cunningham*, and *Ashley*.

Traces of **Socialist** thought can be found very early in economic writings. The works of Plato and More have been previously mentioned. *Rousseau* and *Godwin* in the eighteenth century helped to spread the doctrine; and in the first half of the nineteenth century an academic and utopian form of Socialism was advocated by *St. Simon*, *Fourier*, *Blanc* and others in France; and by *Owen* and *Thompson* in England. But Socialism did not gain much force until the second half of the century, when the new "scientific" approach was adopted. Its chief exponents were *Rodbertus* and *Marx*, with *Lassalle* as the militant organizer. The last-named is often thought of in connection with the Iron Law of Wages which was held to be the only explanation under a capitalist system.

The new Socialism was termed "scientific" in contrast to the utopian ideas of the earlier writers. Karl Marx, who was the most potent force in the movement, was, like

other German economists, historically minded; his
"Capital" (Vol. I, 1867) combines the results of acute
observation and powerful abstract analysis. Adopting
a "dialectic" method of investigation, he attempted to
show that the basis of society was economic, that the
prime motive force of every kind of activity is the production of the means of life. He maintained that in
modern communities there were two main classes, one
possessing labour power, the other the means of production. The latter class was created by the appropriation
of the "surplus value," measured by the difference between the real productivity of labour and the actual wages
paid. Being a firm believer in the evolutionary process,
he contended that capitalist organization would become
increasingly concentrated until the means of production
were held by comparatively few capitalists. Ultimately,
the State would take over and run the economic machine.

Though much of Marx's doctrine has been modified, he
still exerts, directly and indirectly, considerable influence
on Socialist thought and action.

There remain those economists whose methods resemble in some ways those of the old Classicists, and who,
for want of a better name have been termed the Neo-
Classical School. Their method is chiefly deductive, but
there is not the same tendency to over-abstraction as was
prevalent in the early part of last century. Historical research and the growing use of statistical records have
served to check imaginative flights and keep economic
science within the bounds of reality. *Cairnes* (1874)
restated the theory of value and introduced the conception
of "non-competing groups." In a sense, he was the link
between the old and the new Classicists. *W. S. Jevons*
applied statistical and mathematical methods, giving
economics a definitely scientific semblance. In his "Theory

of Political Economy" (1871) and other works, he discussed the conception of final utility, and made a useful analysis of exchange, money, and prices.

Less mathematical and more psychological were the Austrian economists, representative of whom were *Menger, Wieser*, and *Böhm-Bawerk*. They are noteworthy as having worked out the utility theory of value in opposition to the cost of production theory of the older Classical School. Böhm-Bawerk in his "Positive Theory of Capital" (1888) submitted the theory that interest was the money-equivalent of the difference between present and future satisfactions. Discussion on interest has been very common among the Austrian School, but the theory of wages has been given scant attention.

In America economic theory has been developed in important directions. Professors *Ely* and *Taussig*, among others, adopting an objective point of view, stress the cost of production side of value and favour a broad application of the Ricardian doctrine of rent to all forms of distribution. In some ways different are Professors *Clark* and *Fisher*, who lean towards the subjective and psychological method of approach, and so resemble the Austrian School. Clark's "Distribution of Wealth" (1899) has for its theme the tendency under "static" conditions for the factors of production to receive shares corresponding to, and measured by, the productivity of their marginal increments. Fisher has made fruitful inquiry into capital and interest. Like Böhm-Bawerk, he supports the *agio* or time-preference theory of interest ; like Jevons, he is prone to a mathematical mode of treatment.

Chief among British economists at the beginning of the present century was *Alfred Marshall*, whose "Principles of Economics" (1st edition, 1890) and other works ranked him in line with Adam Smith and J. S. Mill. Though Classical in outlook, he kept his reasoning in close accord with facts. He combined the deductive method with the inductive, theory with realism. He brought together the cost of production ideas of the Classicists and the utility doctrines of the Austrians, and enunciated, as a result, a balanced marginal theory of value. Besides the harmonizing of the different theories, his constructive powers resulted in many new ideas and much new light on the old. Characteristic was his belief in the principle of continuity: "There is a unity underlying all the different parts of the theories of prices, wages, and profits. The remuneration of every kind of work, the interest on capital, and the prices of commodities are determined in the long run by competition according to what is fundamentally the same law. This law of Normal Value has many varieties of detail and takes many different forms. But in every form it exhibits value as determined by certain relations of demand and supply" (*Economics of Industry*).

In the evolution of modern economic thought the pendulum swung fairly regularly between the study of production and that of distribution. Fifty years ago, production, which had formerly occupied most attention, gave place to distribution as the centre of attention. Subsequently the close interdependence of the two subjects, and the undesirability of placing greater emphasis on one than the other became generally realized, while at the same time greater recognition was given to problems of consumption, which came to be of first importance in a world that had largely solved the physical problem of increasing supplies.

Since Marshall there have been many modifications in the science, especially in the light of important economic events, but we are too close to the theories and events to permit of any assessment. The practice of some writers in discarding the traditional divisions of the science and studying it, in the main, in terms of equilibrium and variation, makes for unification, and accentuates the interdependence of all economic activity, but so far it has proved to be as much a change in methodology as in essential doctrine.

SELECT BIBLIOGRAPHY

INTRODUCTORY GENERAL WORKS

Cannan	. Wealth.
Chapman	. Outlines of Political Economy.
Clay	. Economics for the General Reader.
Dobb	. An Introduction to Economics.
Ely and Wicker	. Elementary Principles of Economics.
Gide	. Principles of Political Economy.
Henderson	. Supply and Demand.
Lehfeldt	. Descriptive Economics.
Marshall	. Economics of Industry.
Nicholson	. Elements of Political Economy.
Roll	. Elements of Economic Theory
Silverman	. The Groundwork of Economics.
Todd	. Science of Prices.

MORE ADVANCED GENERAL WORKS

Birck	. Theory of Marginal Value.
Cassel	. Theory of Social Economy.
Davenport	. Economics of Enterprise.
Hadley	. Economics.
Hobson	The Industrial System.
,,	. Wealth and Life.
Keynes	. The General Theory of Employment, Interest and Money.
Marshall	. Principles of Economics.
,,	. Industry and Trade.
Marx	. Capital.
Meade	. Economic Analysis and Policy.
Nicholson	. Principles of Political Economy.
Pierson	. Principles of Economics.
Pigou	. Economics of Welfare.
,,	. Economics of Stationary States.
Phelp Brown	. The Framework of the Pricing System.
Radford	. Patterns of Economic Activity.
Robbins	. The Nature and Significance of Economic Science.
Seager	. Principles of Economics.
Seligman	. Principles of Economics.
Silverman	. Economics of the Industrial System.
Smart	. Introduction to the Theory of Value.
Taussig	. Principles of Economics.
Veblen	. Theory of Business Enterprise.
Watson	. The Groundwork of Economic Theory.
Wicksell	. Lectures on Political Economy.
Wicksteed	. Common Sense of Political Economy.

THE NATIONAL INCOME

Statistical—

Bowley	. Division of the Product of Industry.
,,	. Changes in Distribution of the National Income, 1880–1913.
Bowley and Stamp	. The National Income, 1924.

THE NATIONAL INCOME—(contd.)

Statistical—(contd.)

Carr-Saunders and Jones	*Social Structure of England and Wales.*
Clark	*National Income and Outlay*
Stamp . . .	*British Incomes and Property.*

General Distribution—

Carver	*Distribution of Wealth.*
Clark	*Distribution of Wealth.*
Dalton . . .	*Inequality of Incomes.*
Dickinson . . .	*Institutional Revenue.*
Hobson . . .	*Economics of Distribution.*
Smart . . .	*Distribution of Income.*

Interest, Profits, and Rent—

Böhm-Bawerk . .	*Theories of Interest.*
,, . . .	*Positive Theory of Capital.*
Brown . . .	*Theory of Earned and Unearned Income.*
Cassel . . .	*The Nature and Necessity of Interest.*
Fisher . . .	*The Nature of Capital.*
,, . . .	*The Rate of Interest.*
Gonner . . .	*Interest and Saving.*
Knight . .	*Risk, Uncertainty and Profit.*

WAGES

Bowley . . .	*Wages in the United Kingdom in the Nineteenth Century.*
Burns	*Wages and the State.*
Dobb	*Wages.*
Douglas . . .	*The Theory of Wages.*
Gray . . .	*Family Endowment.*
Hicks . . .	*The Theory of Wages.*
Milnes . . .	*Economics of Wages and Labour.*
Rathbone . .	*The Disinherited Family.*
Richardson . .	*Study on the Minimum Wage.*
Robbins . . .	*Wages.*
Rowe	*Wages in Practice and Theory.*
Sells . . .	*The British Trade Board System.*
Wallis . . .	*Prices and Wages.*

LABOUR PROBLEMS AND MOVEMENTS

Beveridge . .	*Unemployment.*
Clay . . .	*The Problem of Industrial Relations.*
,, . .	*Post-War Unemployment Problem.*
Cunnison . .	*Labour Organization.*
Fay . . .	*Co-operation at Home and Abroad.*
Lloyd . . .	*Trade Unionism.*
Silverman . .	*The Economics of Social Problems.*
Strachey . .	*The Nature of Capitalist Crisis.*
Tawney . .	*The Acquisitive Society.*
Watkins . .	*Labour Problems.*
Webb . . .	*Industrial Democracy.*
,, . .	*The Consumers' Co-operative Movement.*
Williams . .	*Social Aspects of Industrial Problems.*
Woolf . . .	*Co-operation and the Future of Industry.*
Wright . .	*Population.*

Report on Profit-sharing and Labour Co-partnership, 1920.
Reports of Committee on Industry and Trade, 1927–29.

COMBINATION AND MONOPOLY

Allen	*British Industries and their Organisation.*
Brown	*Prevention and Control of Monopolies.*
Carter	*The Tendency to Industrial Combination.*
Chamberlin	*The Theory of Monopolistic Competition.*
Clark	*Control of Trusts.*
Fitzgerald	*Industrial Combination in England.*
Hilton	*Trusts and Industrial Combinations.*
Jenks	*The Trust Problem.*
Levy	*Monopolies, Cartels and Trusts in British Industry.*
Liefmann	*International Cartels, Combines, and Trusts.*
Macrosty	*The Trust Movement in British Industry.*
Marquand	*Dynamics of Industrial Combination.*
Meakin	*New Industrial Revolution.*
Rees	*Trusts in British Industry, 1914–21.*
Robinson	*The Economics of Imperfect Competition.*
Urwick	*Meaning of Rationalization*

Report on Trusts 1919.

MONEY AND PRICES

Cannan	*Money.*
Feaveryear	*The Pound Sterling.*
Fisher	*Purchasing Power of Money.*
Gregory	*The Gold Standard and its Future.*
Hawtrey	*The Gold Standard.*
Harrod	*The Trade Cycle.*
Hayek	*Prices and Production.*
Jack	*Economics of the Gold Standard.*
Jevons	*Money and the Mechanism of Exchange.*
Keynes	*Treatise on Money.*
Layton	*Introduction to the Study of Prices.*
Lehfeldt	*Money.*
Macfie	*Theories of the Trade Cycle.*
Marshall	*Money, Credit and Commerce.*
Robertson	*Money.*
,,	*Banking and Price Level.*
Roll	*About Money.*
Todd	*Mechanism of Exchange.*
Lavington	*The Trade Cycle.*
Mitchell	*Business Cycles.*

BANKING AND THE MONEY MARKET

Easton	*Money, Exchange and Banking.*
Hirst	*The Stock Exchange.*
Kisch and Elkin	*Central Banks.*
Leaf	*Banking.*
McKenna	*Post-War Banking Policy.*
Sykes	*Banking and Currency.*
Bagehot	*Lombard Street.*
Hawtrey	*Currency and Credit.*
Lavington	*The English Capital Market.*
Spalding	*The London Money Market.*
Spicer	*The Money Market.*
Withers	*The Meaning of Money.*

INTERNATIONAL TRADE AND TARIFFS

Bastable	. . .	*The Commerce of Nations.*
,,	. . .	*International Trade.*
Hobson	. . .	*International Trade.*
Taussig	. . .	*International Trade*
Ashley	. . .	*The Tariff Problem.*
Beveridge	. . .	*Tariffs: The Case Examined.*
Hirst .	. . .	*Safeguarding and Protection.*
Ramsay	. . .	*Economics of Safeguarding.*
Robertson	. . .	*The New Tariffism.*
Taussig	. . .	*Free Trade, The Tariff and Reciprocity.*
Wolfe .	. . .	*Theory and Practice of International Commerce.*

FOREIGN EXCHANGE

Cassel .	. . .	*Money and Foreign Exchange after 1914.*
Clare .	. . .	*A B C of Foreign Exchange.*
Gregory	. . .	*Foreign Exchange.*
Spalding	. . .	*Foreign Exchange and Foreign Bills.*

Report of Committee on Currency and Foreign Exchanges, 1918 and 1919; Cmd. 9182 and 464.
Report of Committee on the Currency and Bank of England Note Issues, 1925; Cmd. 2393.
Report of the (Macmillan) Committee on Finance and Industry, 1931.

ECONOMICS OF POST-WAR CONDITIONS

Bowley	. . .	*Some Economic Consequences of the Great War.*
Cassel .	. . .	*The Crisis in the World's Monetary System.*
,,	. . .	*The World's Monetary Problems.*
Cole	. . .	*Economic Tracts for the Times.*
,,	. . .	*The Next Ten Years.*
,,	. . .	*British Trade and Industry.*
,,	. . .	*The Intelligent Man's Guide Through World Chaos.*
Einzig .	. . .	*The World Economic Crisis, 1929–31.*
Hawtrey	. . .	*Trade Depression and the Way Out.*
Loveday	. . .	*Britain and World Trade.*
Salter .	. . .	*Recovery.*
Salter and Others .		*The World's Economic Crisis.*

PUBLIC FINANCE

General—

Bastable	. . .	*Public Finance.*
Burns .	. . .	*Modern Finance.*
Dalton	. . .	*Public Finance.*
Fisk .	. . .	*English Public Finance.*
Hunter	. . .	*Outlines of Public Finance.*
Pigou .	. . .	*Public Finance.*
Plehn .	. . .	*Introduction to Public Finance.*
Robinson	. . .	*Public Finance.*
Shirras	. . .	*The Science of Public Finance.*

Taxation—
Armitage-Smith . . *Principles and Methods of Taxation.*
Hobson . . . *Taxation in the New State.*
Jones . . . *The Nature and First Principle of Taxation.*
Mills and Starr . . *Readings in Public Finance and Taxation.*
Seligman . . . *Essays in Taxation.*
" . . . *The Income Tax.*
Silverman . . . *Taxation: Its Incidence and Effects.*
Stamp . . . . *Fundamental Principles of Taxation.*
" . . . *Wealth and Taxable Capacity.*

Public Debts—
Adams . . . *Public Debts.*
Hargreaves . . . *The National Debt.*
Pethick Lawrence . . *The National Debt.*
Moulton and Pasvolsky . *War Debts and World Prosperity.*
    See also general works.

Local Taxation—
Cannan . . . *History of Local Rates.*
Grice . . . . *National and Local Finance.*
Webb . . . . *Grants-in-Aid.*
    See also works on Taxation.

Administration—
Higgs . . . . *Primer of National Finance.*
" . . . *The Financial System of the United Kingdom.*
Hills and Morison . . *Finance and Government.*
Young . . . *The System of National Finance.*

    Annual Budget Statements.
    Report of (Colwyn) Committee on National Debt and Taxation, 1927.
    Report of (May) Committee on National Expenditure, 1931.
    Report of (Ray) Committee on Local Expenditure, 1932.

HISTORICAL

Economic Development—
Ashley . . . *The Economic Organization of England.*
Bücher . . . *Industrial Evolution.*
Clapham . . . *An Economic History of Modern Britain.*
Cressy . . . *Outline of Industrial History.*
Fay . . . . *Life and Labour in the Nineteenth Century.*
Hobson . . . *Evolution of Modern Capitalism.*
Knowles . . . *The Industrial and Commercial Revolutions in Great Britain.*
Macgregor . . . *The Evolution of Industry.*
Meredith . . . *Economic History of England.*
Rees . . . *Social and Industrial History of England, 1815–1918.*
Shields . . . *Evolution of Industrial Organization.*

Economic Thought—
Boucke . . . *Development of Economics.*
Gide and Rist . . *History of Economic Doctrines.*
Gray . . . *Development of Economic Thought.*
Haney . . . *History of Economic Thought.*
Ingram . . . *History of Political Economy.*
Price . . . . *History of Political Economy in England.*

INDEX

MADE IN GREAT BRITAIN AT THE PITMAN PRESS, BATH
C7—(B.1881)

PITMAN'S
ECONOMICS SERIES

GENERAL EDITOR: PROFESSOR J. H. JONES, M.A.

Professor of Economics and Head of the Commerce Department
University of Leeds

A SERIES of popular introductions to the study of Economics, specially written by eminent University and other authorities for the use of commercial students and business men. Each volume covers the fundamental principles of the important branch of economic science with which it is concerned, and lucidly discusses their application to modern business.

A PRIMER OF ECONOMIC GEOGRAPHY

By L. W. LYDE, M.A., F.R.G.S., F.R.S.G.S., *Emeritus Professor of Geography in the University of London.* **5s.** net.

TRANSPORT AND COMMUNICATIONS

By K. G. FENELON, M.A., Ph.D., *Lecturer on Economics at Edinburgh University.* **2s. 6d.** net.

BUSINESS FORECASTING

By J. H. RICHARDSON, M.A., Ph.D., *Montague Burton Professor of Industrial Relations in the University of Leeds.* **2s. 6d.** net.

FINDING CAPITAL FOR BUSINESS

By DAVID FINNIE, M.A., C.A. **2s. 6d.** net.

INTERNATIONAL TRADE

By D. T. JACK, M.A., *Lecturer in Economics, University of St. Andrews.* **2s. 6d.** net.

CURRENCY AND BANKING

By D. T. JACK, M.A. **5s.** net.

BRITISH ECONOMISTS

By FRANCIS C. HOOD, M.A., *Lecturer in Economics and History in the University of Durham.* **2s. 6d.** net.

THE ECONOMIC FUNCTIONS OF THE STATE

By ROGER H. SOLTAU, M.A., *sometime Assistant Lecturer in Political Science, London School of Economics.* **5s.** net.

PRODUCTION

By HUBERT PHILLIPS, M.A. (Oxon), *late Head of the Department of Economics in the University of Bristol.* **5s.** net.

VALUE AND DISTRIBUTION

By HUBERT PHILLIPS, M.A. (Oxon). **5s.** net.

OVERHEAD COSTS: THEIR NEW ECONOMIC SIGNIFICANCE IN INDUSTRY

By SIR HENRY N. BUNBURY, K.C.B. **2s. 6d.** net.

SOCIALISM

By ROBERT RICHARDS, *formerly Under-Secretary for India.* **2s. 6d.** net.

METHODS OF REMUNERATION

By ROBERT WILSON, M.A. B.Sc. **2s. 6d.** net.

SIR ISAAC PITMAN & SONS, LTD. PARKER STREET, KINGSWAY, W.C.2

A SELECTION FROM THE LIST OF

COMMERCIAL HANDBOOKS

PUBLISHED BY

SIR ISAAC PITMAN & SONS, LTD.

The following Catalogues will be sent post free on application : COMMERCIAL, EDUCATIONAL, TECHNICAL, LAW, SHORTHAND, FOREIGN LANGUAGES, ARTS and CRAFTS, and GENERAL

Obtainable through any Bookseller or direct from the Publishers

LONDON : PITMAN HOUSE, PARKER STREET, KINGSWAY, W.C.2
BATH : The Pitman Press. MELBOURNE : Pitman House, Little Collins Street.

Associated Companies

NEW YORK : Pitman Publishing Corporation, 2 West 45th Street.
CHICAGO : 205 West Monroe Street
TORONTO : Sir Isaac Pitman & Sons (Canada), Ltd., (Incorporating the Commercial Text Book Company) 381-383 Church Street.
INDIA : A. H. Wheeler & Co., Hornby Road, Bombay ; 11 Clive Street, Calcutta ; and 15 Elgin Road, Allahabad.

The Prices contained in this List apply only to Great Britain.

CONTENTS

ARITHMETIC, ETC.

BOOK-KEEPING AND ACCOUNTANCY

PRICE

Accountancy
By WILLIAM PICKLES, B.Com. (Vict.), F.C.A., A.S.A.A. (Hons.). **Key** 12/6 . . . . **15/-**

Accountants' Dictionary
Edited by F. W. PIXLEY, F.C.A. In Two Vols. Net **67/6**

Accounts of Executors, Administrators, and Trustees
By WILLIAM B. PHILLIPS, F.C.A., A.C.I.S. Revised by F. T. WRIGHT, A.C.A. **5/-**

Advanced Accounts
Edited by ROGER N. CARTER, M.Com., F.C.A. . . **7/6**

Key to Advanced Accounts
By R. A. GOODMAN **20/-**

Advanced Book-keeping Exercises for Commercial Schools
By A. J. FAVELL, B.Sc. (Econ.), A.C.I.S. . . . **2/6**

Audit Programmes
By E. E. SPICER, F.C.A., and E. C. PEGLER, F.C.A. Net **4/6**

Book-keeping, A Course in
By R. W. HOLLAND, O.B.E., M.A., M.Sc., LL.D. . **4/-**

Book-keeping, Advanced
By HENRY J. CLACK, F.C.R.A., F.R.S.A. . . . **4/-**

Book-keeping for Beginners
By W. E. HOOPER, A.C.I.S. **2/-**

Book-keeping for Retail Classes
By JOHN MILLER ANDERSON, F.L.A.A. . . . **5/-**

Book-keeping for Retailers
By H. W. PORRITT and W. NICKLIN, A.S.A.A. . Net **2/-**

Book-keeping, Stage I
By A. J. FAVELL, B.Sc. (Econ.), A.C.I.S. . . . **2/6**

Book-keeping, Stage II
By A. J. FAVELL, B.Sc. (Econ.), A.C.I.S. . . . **3/6**

Book-keeping, Modern Methods of
By R. H. EPPS, *Chartered Accountant* . . . **4/-**

Builders' Accounts and Costs
By ROBERT G. LEGGE . . . . . **Net 3/6**

3

Book-keeping and Accountancy—contd.

Book-keeping and Accountancy—contd.

PRICE

Elementary Graded Book-keeping Exercises
By A. J. FAVELL, B.Sc., A.C.I.S. **1/–**

Estimating. By T. H. HARGRAVE . . . Net **5/–**

Full Course in Book-keeping
By H. W. PORRITT and W. NICKLIN, A.S.A.A. . . **5/–**

Graded Book-keeping Exercises for Commercial Schools
By A. J. FAVELL, B.Sc., A.C.I.S. **2/–**

Hotel Book-keeping By M. E. PITCHER . . . **2/6**

Investigations : Accountancy and Financial
By J. H. BURTON . . . . . . Net **5/–**

Manual of Cost Accounts
By H. JULIUS LUNT, F.C.A., F.C.I.S., F.C.W.A.
and A. H. RIPLEY, F.C.W.A. **8/6**

Modern Methods of Stock Control
By N. GERARD SMITH, M.I.P.E. . . . Net **3/6**

Practical Book-keeping and Commercial Knowledge
By E. E. SPICER, F.C.A., and E. C. PEGLER, F.C.A. Net **7/6**

Principles and Interpretation of Accounts
By H. L. ELLIS, M.Com. **3/6**

Principles of Accounts
By J. STEPHENSON, M.A., M.Com., D.Sc. . Part I **3/6**
Part II **5/–**

Principles of Auditing
By F. R. M. DE PAULA, O.B.E., F.C.A. . . . **8/6**

Principles of Bank Book-keeping
By HERBERT G. HODDER, Cert. A.I.B. . . Net **5/–**

Secretarial Book-keeping and Accounts
By H. E. COLESWORTHY, A.C.A., A.S.A.A.. . Net **5/–**

Sharles's Elementary Book-keeping
By F. F. SHARLES, F.S.A.A., F.C.I.S. . . . **2/6**

Sinking Funds, Reserve Funds, and Depreciation. By J. H. BURTON . . . . Net **3/6**

Trade Union Accounting and Financial Administration
By A. E. WARD and C. R. SWEETINGHAM . . Net **3/6**

CAREERS

		PRICE
Dictionary of Careers		
By L. H. TURNER, M.R.S.T. . . . . Net		3/6
Banking as a Career		
By F. A. WILLMAN, Cert. A.I.B. . . . Net		3/6
Commercial Art as a Career		
By CECIL WADE . . . . . . Net		5/–
How to Become an Auctioneer and Estate Agent. By W. F. NOKES, F.A.I. Revised by D. McINTYRE, B.A., LL.B. . . . . Net		3/6
How to Become a Company Secretary		
By E. J. HAMMOND . . . . . Net		3/6
How to Become a Private Secretary		
By J. E. McLACHLAN, F.I.P.S. (Hons.) . . Net		2/6
How to Become a Qualified Accountant		
By R. A. WITTY, F.S.A.A. . . . . Net		3/6
How to Choose Your Career		
By W. LESLIE IVEY, M.C., M.S.M.A. . . Net		3/6
How to Secure a Good Job		
By W. LESLIE IVEY, M.C., M.S.M.A. . . Net		3/6
How to Secure Promotion		
By W. LESLIE IVEY, M.C., M.S.M.A. . . Net		2/6
Insurance as a Career. By F. H. SHERRIFF . Net		3/6
Journalism as a Career		
Edited by W. T. CRANFIELD . . . . Net		5/–

CIVIL SERVICE

	PRICE
Arithmetic for Civil Service Students	
By T. H. TEARE, B.Sc., and F. W. TEARE, B.Sc. .	4/–
Civil Service Guide By A. J. T. DAY . . Net	3/6
Civil Service Essay Writing	
By W. J. ADDIS, M.A.	2/–
Civil Service Shorthand Writers' Phrase Book	
Compiled by ALFRED MARSHALL, P.C.T. . .	2/–
Civil Service Test Papers—English : Junior	
By GORDON S. HUMPHREYS, M.A. . . .	1/9
Civil Service Test Papers—English: Senior	
By W. B. FARRER, M.A.	2/6
Civil Service Test Papers—Geography	
By R. J. FINCH, F.R.G.S.	2/6
Civil Service Test Papers—Mathematics : Clerical Class	
By JAMES READER, B.A., B.Sc. **With Answers** .	2/6
English for Civil Servants By WALTER SHAWCROSS	2/6

PRICE

Practical Branch Banking
By A. FORRESTER FERGUS . . . . Net   8/6

Principles of Currency, Credit and Exchange
By WILLIAM A. SHAW, Litt.D. . . . Net   3/6

Profits from Short-Term Investment and
How to Make Them. By COLLIN BROOKS . Net   3/6

Securities Clerk in a Branch Bank, The
By F. J. LEWCOCK, Cert. A.I.B., A.C.I.S. . . Net   7/6

Theory and Principles of Central Banking, The
By WILLIAM A. SHAW, Litt.D. . . . Net   12/6

Theory and Practice of Finance, The
By W. COLLIN BROOKS . . . . . Net   10/6

INSURANCE

Accident Risks, The Surveying of
By J. B. WELSON, F.C.I.I., and FENWICK J.WOODROOF, A.C.I.I. . . . . Net   5/–

Actuarial Science, The Elements of
By R. E. UNDERWOOD, M.B.E., F.I.A. . . Net   5/–

Average Clauses and Fire-Loss Apportion-
ments. By E. H. MINNION, F.C.I.I. . . Net   8/6

Building Construction, Plan Drawing, and
Surveying in Relation to Fire Insurance
By D. W. WOOD, M.B.E. . . . . . Net   6/–

Compound Interest, Principles of
By H. H. EDWARDS . . . . . Net   5/–

Dictionary of Accident Insurance
Edited by J. B. WELSON, LL.M., F.C.I.I., F.C.I.S. Net   60/–

Fire Insurance, Dictionary of
Edited by B. C. REMINGTON, F.C.I.I., and HERBERT G. HURREN, F.C.I.I. . . . . . . Net   30/–

Fire Insurance, Principles and Practice of
By F. GODWIN . . . . . . Net   5/–

Fire Insurance, The Law of
By SANDFORD D. COLE, *Barrister-at-Law* . Net   6/–

Fire Policy Drafting and Endorsements
By W. C. H. DARLEY . . . . . Net   7/6

Guide to Marine Insurance. By HENRY KEATE Net   3/6

How Shall I Insure ? By F. G. CULMER . Net   2/6

Industrial Assurance Organization and Routine
By R. DINNAGE, F.I.A., and T. HILLS, A.C.I.I. Net   7/6

Insurance—contd.

14

Insurance—contd.

PRICE

Principles and Practice of Accident Insurance
By G. E. BANFIELD, A.C.I.I. . . . . Net   6/-

Principles and Practice of Industrial Assurance
By R. B. WALKER, F.I.A., and D. R. WOODGATE, B.Com.,
F.I.A. . . . . Net   7/6

Successful Insurance Agent, The
By J. J. BISGOOD, B.A., F.C.I.S. Revised by JOHN B.
CUSHING, F.C.I.I. . . . . . . Net   2/6

Workmen's Compensation Insurance
By C. E. GOLDING, LL.D., F.C.I.I., F.S.S. . Net   5/-

SHIPPING

Charter Parties of the World
By C. D. MACMURRAY and MALCOLM M. CREE. With a
Foreword by R. S. DALGLIESH . . . Net   15/-

Exporter's Handbook and Glossary, The
By F. M. DUDENEY . . . . . Net   7/6

How to Export Goods. By F. M. DUDENEY . Net   2/-

How to Import Goods. By J. A. DUNNAGE . Net   2/6

Importer's Handbook, The. By J. A. DUNNAGE Net   7/6

Manual of Exporting
By J. A. DUNNAGE . . . . . . Net   7/6

Shipbroking, Introduction to
By C. D. MACMURRAY and M. M. CREE . . Net   3/6

Shipping. By A. HALL, F.I.C.S. and F. HEYWOOD,
F.C.I.S. . . . . Net   2/-

Shipping Office Organization, Management,
and Accounts. By ALFRED CALVERT . . Net   6/-

Shipping Practice. By E. F. STEVENS . . Net   6/-

INCOME TAX

Burn's Income Tax Guide
By JOHN BURNS, W.S. . . . . . Net   5/-

Income Tax Law, Practice, and Administration
By F. F. SHARLES, F.S.A.A.; R. P. CROOM-JOHNSON,
LL.B., K.C.; L. C. GRAHAM-DIXON, *of the Inner Temple,
Barrister-at-Law*, and W. J. ECCOTT, Three Volumes Net   84/-

Dictionary of Income Tax and Sur-Tax Practice
By W. E. SNELLING. . . . . . Net   25/-

Income Tax for Professional Students
By W. T. BAXTER, B.Com., C.A. . . . Net   7/6

Income Tax—contd.

SECRETARIAL WORK, ETC.

Secretarial Work, etc.—contd.

INDUSTRIAL ADMINISTRATION

18

Business Organization and Management—contd.

MUNICIPAL WORK

Municipal Work—contd.

ADVERTISING AND COMMERCIAL ART

Advertising and Commercial Art—contd.

PRICE

Law Relating to Advertising, The
By E. LING-MALLISON, B.Sc. (Lille) . . . Net 7/6

Lettering, Plain and Ornamental
By E. G. FOOKS . . . . . . Net 3/6

Modern Lettering from A to Z
By A. CECIL WADE . . . . Net 12/6

Poster Designing
By W. S. ROGERS . . . . . . Net 7/6

Poster, The Technique of the
Edited by LEONARD RICHMOND, R.B.A., R.O.I. . Net 21/-

Routine of the Advertising Department
By REGINALD H. W. COX . . . . Net 10/6

Ticket and Showcard Designing
By F. A. PEARSON . . . . Net 3/6

Training in Commercial Art
By V. L. DANVERS . . . . . Net 10/6

Types and Type Faces By C. M. TREGURTHA Net 2/6

What the Press Artist Should Know
By JOHN R. TURNER . . . . . Net 7/6

SALESMANSHIP

Building Retail Sales. By C. C. KNIGHTS . Net 5/-

Craft of Silent Salesmanship
By C. MAXWELL TREGURTHA and J. W. FRINGS Net 3/6

Direct Mail Advertising for the Retail Trader
By H. DENNETT . . . . . . Net 7/6

Modern Sales Correspondence
By D. M. WILSON . . . . . . Net 3/6

More Sales Through the Window
By C. C. KNIGHTS . . . . . Net 3/6

Outline of Sales Management, An
By C. C. KNIGHTS, *Sales Consultant* . . Net 3/6

Personal Salesmanship. By R. SIMMAT, M.A. Net 3/6

Practical Aids to Retail Selling
By A. EDWARD HAMMOND . . . . Net 3/6

Practical Commercial Travelling
By RONALD T. LEWIS . . . . . Net 3/6

Salesmanship—contd.

PRICE

Practical Salesmanship
By N. C. FOWLER, Junr. . . . . Net 7/6

Principles of Store Practice
By FRANK CHITHAM and S. A. WILLIAMS, M.A. . . 5/-

Psychology as a Sales Factor
By A. J. GREENLY . . . . Net 7/6

Retail Distribution, Principles of
By S. A. WILLIAMS, M.A. . . . . Net 5/-

Retail Management. By C. L. BOLLING . . Net 15/-

Retail Salesmanship. By C. L. BOLLING . Net 7/6

Sales Management. By C. L. BOLLING . Net 10/6

Salesmanship
By W. A. CORBION and G. E. GRIMSDALE . Net 3/6

Salesmanship. By WILLIAM MAXWELL . . Net 5/-

Salesmanship, Technique of
By C. C. KNIGHTS . . . . . . Net 5/-

Shop Fittings and Display
By A. E. HAMMOND . . . . . Net 5/-

Successful Retailing. By E. N. SIMONS . . Net 5/-

Training for More Sales
By C. C. KNIGHTS, *Sales Consultant* . . Net 5/-

Training for Travelling Salesmen
By F. W. SHRUBSALL . . . . . Net 2/6

TRANSPORT

Canals and Inland Waterways
By GEORGE CADBURY and S. P. DOBBS, B.A. . Net 5/-

Commercial Motor Road Transport
By L. M. MEYRICK-JONES . . . . Net 15/-

Elements of Transport
By R. J. EATON . . . . Net 2/6

History and Economics of Transport, The
By A. W. KIRKALDY, M.A., B.Litt., M.Com., and
A. D. EVANS . . . . . . Net 16/-

How to Make the British Railways Pay
By M. F. FARRAR . . . . . . Net 3/6

Transport—contd.

PRICE

Modern Dock Operation
By D. ROSS-JOHNSON, C.B.E., V.D., M.Inst.I. . Net 5/-
Modern Railway Operation
By D. R. LAMB, M.Inst.T. . . . . Net 5/-
Port Economics
By B. CUNNINGHAM, D.Sc., B.E., F.R.S.E. . Net 5/-
Railway Electrification and Traffic Problems
By P. BURTT, M.Inst.T. . . . . . Net 5/-
Railway Rates : Principles and Problems
By P. BURTT, M.Inst.T. . . . . . Net 5/-
Railway Statistics : Their Compilation and Use. By A. E. KIRKUS, O.B.E., M.Inst.T. . Net 5/-
Rights and Duties of Transport Undertakings
By H. B. DAVIES, M.A., and F. M. LANDAU, *Barrister-at-Law* . . . . Net 10/6
Road Making and Road Using
By T. SALKIELD, M.Inst.C.E. . . . . Net 7/6
Road Passenger Transport
By R. STUART PILCHER, F.R.S.E., M.INST.T. . Net 10/6
Road Transport Operation—Passenger
By R. STUART PILCHER, F.R.S.E., M.Inst.T. . Net 10/6
Transport Management, Practical
By ANDREW HASTIE . . . . . Net 10/6

LAW

Administration of Estates, The
By A. H. COSWAY . . . . . Net 5/-
Bankruptcy, Deeds of Arrangement, and Bills of Sale
By W. VALENTINE BALL and DONALD GEDDES Net 15/-
Business Tenant, The
By EDWARD S. COX-SINCLAIR, and T. HYNES . Net 7/6
Business Transfer Agent and Trade Valuer
By J. OTWAY CAVE . . . . Net 7/6
Pitman's Commercial Law
By J. A. SLATER, B.A., LL.B. Revised by R. H. CODE HOLLAND, B.A., *of the Middle Temple, Barrister-at-Law* 3/6
Companies and Company Law
By A. C. CONNELL, LL.B. (Lond.). Revised by W. E. WILKINSON, LL.D. 6/-
Company Law
By D. F. DE L'HOSTE RANKING, M.A., LL.D., and ERNEST EVAN SPICER, F.C.A. Edited by H. A. R. J. WILSON, F.C.A., F.S.A.A. . . . . Net 10/-
Commercial Law Cases. By ALBERT CREW Net 6/-

23

Law—contd.

24

Law—contd.

25

REFERENCE BOOKS

PRICE

How to Make a Speech
By RICHARD JOHNSON, M.A. . . . . Net 2/6

How to Run a Copying Office
By GLADYS C. MENZIES . . . . . Net 5/–

How to Speak Effectively
By Charles Seymour. . . . . . Net 7/6

Human Psychology
By JUDSON REA BUTLER and THEODORE FRANCIS
KARWOSKI . . . . Net 10/6

Markets of London. By CUTHBERT MAUGHAN . Net 6/–

Mercantile Terms and Abbreviations . Net 1/6

Money Making in Stocks and Shares
By SYDNEY A. MOSELEY . . . . Net 7/6

Normal English Pronunciation
By OSCAR BROWNE . . . . . Net 3/6

Office Desk Book, Pitman's . . . Net 2/6

Parliament
By HENRY MORRISON and WILFRID S. ABBOTT, M.A.
(Oxon). With a Foreword by Rt. Hon. SIR JOHN
SIMON, M.P. . . . . Net 2/6

Personal Psychology
By MORLEY DAINOW, B.Sc. . . . . Net 5/–

Political Parties and Policies
By E. ROYSTON PIKE . . . . . Net 2/6

Public Speaking
By ARCHIBALD CRAWFORD, K.C. . . . Net 6/–

Raw Materials of Commerce
In 2 vols. Edited by J. H. VANSTONE, F.R.G.S. Net 20/–

Speak in Public, How to
By C. F. CARR and F. E. STEVENS . . . Net 3/6

Statistics for Professional Students
By R. L. A. HOLMES, B.Com. . . . . Net 5/–

Statistics in Theory and Practice
By L. R. CONNOR, M.Sc. (Econ.), *Barrister-at-Law* Net 12/6

PITMAN'S ECONOMICS SERIES

General Editor: PROFESSOR J. H. JONES, M.A.

A Primer of Economic Geography
By L. W. LYDE, M.A., F.R.G.S., F.R.S.G.S. . Net 5/–

British Economists
By FRANCIS C. HOOD, M.A. . . . . Net 2/6

28

FOREIGN LANGUAGES

FRENCH

Progressive French Grammar
By Dr. F. A. HEDGCOCK, M.A. 5/6
Commercial French Grammar
By F. W. M. DRAPER, M.A., L.ès.L. . . . 2/6
**French-English and English-French
Commercial Dictionary**
By F. W. SMITH . . . . . . Net 7/6
Handbook to French Examinations
By E. DONALD NISBET, B.A., Hons. (Lond.) . Net 1/6

GERMAN

Commercial German Grammar, Pitman's
By J. BITHELL, M.A. 3/6
**German-English and English-German
Commercial Dictionary**
By J. BITHELL, M.A. . . . . . Net 16/-
Commercial Correspondence in German. . 3/6

SPANISH

Spanish Commercial Grammar
By C. A. TOLEDANO 4/6
**Spanish-English and English-Spanish
Commercial Dictionary**
By G. R. MACDONALD, F.I.L. . . . . Net 12/6
Manual of Spanish Commercial Correspondence
By G. R. MACDONALD, F.I.L. 4/6

ITALIAN

Italian Commercial Grammar
By LUIGI RICCI 4/-
**Italian-English and English-Italian
Commercial Dictionary**
By G. R. MACDONALD, F.I.L. . . . . Net 30/-
Mercantile Correspondence, English-Italian . 5/-

PORTUGUESE

**Portuguese-English and English-Portuguese
Commercial Dictionary**
By F. W. SMITH . . . . . . Net 16/-
**Mercantile Correspondence, English-Portu-
guese.** 3/6

PITMAN'S SHORTHAND

TYPEWRITING

Typewriting—contd.

PRICE

Shorthand-Typist's Senior Course, The
By A. C. MARSHALL, B.Com., and AGNES M. MILLS, B.A. **4/-**

Short Course in Typewriting
Being the Third Edition of "New Course in Typewriting"
By MRS. SMITH CLOUGH, F.Inc.S.T. (Hon.) . . **2/-**

Pitman's Keyboard Mastery Course
By MAXWELL CROOKS. The book is prepared for use
with Pitman's *Gramophone Course of Keyboard Instruction.* In large post 4to **1/6**

Pitman's Gramophone Course of Typewriter Keyboard Instruction
Arranged by MAXWELL CROOKS
Complete, in strong case, together with one copy of
Instruction Book. Comprising twelve 10-in. records
(six discs) . . . . Net **35/-**

COMMON COMMODITIES AND INDUSTRIES

Each book in crown 8vo, illustrated. 3s. net.

In each of the handbooks in this series a particular product or
industry is treated by an expert writer and practical man of
business. Beginning with the life history of the plant, or other
natural product, he follows its development until it becomes a
commercial commodity, and so on through the various phases
of its sale in the market and its purchase by the consumer.

Asbestos (SUMMERS)

Bookbinding Craft and Industry (HARRISON)

Books—From the MS. to the Book-seller (YOUNG)

Boot and Shoe Industry, The. (HARDING)

Brushmaker, The (KIDDIER)

Carpets (BRINTON)

Clocks and Watches (OVERTON)

Clothing Industry, The (POOLE)

Cloths and the Cloth Trade (HUNTER)

Coal (WILSON)

Coal Tar (WARNES)

Coffee—From Grower to Consumer (KEABLE). (Revised by PARHAM)

Concrete and Reinforced Concrete (TWELVETREES)

Cordage and Cordage Hemp and Fibres (WOODHOUSE and KILGOUR)

Cotton Spinning (WADE)

Engraving (LASCELLES)

Explosives, Modern (LEVY)

Furs and the Fur Trade (SACHS)

Gas and Gas Making (WEBBER)

31

Common Commodities and Industries—contd

Glass and Glass Manufacture (MARSON). Revised by L. M. ANGUS-BUTTERWORTH.

Gums and Resins (PARRY)

Ironfounding (WHITELEY)

Jute Industry, The (WOODHOUSE and KILGOUR)

Knitted Fabrics (CHAMBERLAIN and QUILTER)

Linen (MOORE)

Locks and Lock Making (BUTTER)

Match Industry, The (DIXON)

Meat Industry, The (WOOD)

Paper (MADDOX)

Photography* (GAMBLE)

Pottery (NOKE and PLANT)

Rice (DOUGLAS)

Rubber (STEVENS and STEVENS)

Silk (HOOPER)

Soap (SIMMONS)

Sponges (CRESSWELL)

Sugar (MARTINEAU). (Revised by EASTICK)

Sulphur and Sulphur Derivatives (AUDEN)

Tea (IBBETSON)

Textile Bleaching (STEVEN)

Timber (BULLOCK)

Tin and the Tin Industry (MUNDEY)

Tobacco (TANNER). (Revised by FAIRWEATHER)

Weaving (CRANKSHAW)

(Wool) (HUNTER). (Revised by KERSHAW)

Worsted Industry, The (DUMVILLE and KERSHAW)

The following Complete Catalogues will be sent, post free, on application—COMMERCIAL, EDUCATIONAL, TECHNICAL, LAW, SHORTHAND, FOREIGN LANGUAGES, ARTS AND CRAFTS, AND GENERAL.

Sir Isaac Pitman & Sons, Ltd. Parker Street, Kingsway, London, W.C.2

MADE IN GREAT BRITAIN AT THE PITMAN PRESS, BATH
(D.3603)